THIS RIVER OF COURAGE
Generations of Women's Resistance and Action

PAM McALLISTER

Second of the Barbara Deming Memorial Series:
Stories of Women and Nonviolent Action

NEW SOCIETY PUBLISHERS
Philadelphia, PA, and Gabriola Island, BC

Inquiries regarding requests to reprint all or part of *This River of Courage: Generations of Women's Resistance and Action* should be addressed to:
New Society Publishers
4527 Springfield Avenue
Philadelphia, PA 19143

ISBN USA 0-86571-197-6 Hardcover
ISBN USA 0-86571-198-4 Paperback
ISBN CAN 1-55092-140-1 Hardcover
ISBN CAN 1-55092-141-X Paperback

Printed in the United States of America on partially recycled paper by BookCrafters of Chelsea, MI.

Cover art by Betty LaDuke.
Cover design by Laurie Sandow.
Book design by Martin Kelley.

In the image on this book's cover, Jamaica: Tomorrow (Homage to Edna Manley), Betty LaDuke honors another artist, Jamaican sculptor Edna Manley. Manley's vital contributions to Jamaican life, culture and politics over seven decades include monumental wood carvings, bronze and fiberglass castings through which she became known as "the mother of Jamaican art." Her strong vision of women's role in society includes and transcends the roles of wife and mother: in her focus on older women, grandmothers, women in relationship to nature and to each other, she expresses with power and depth her belief that "One must always look forward to the future with hope."

To order directly from the publisher, add $2.50 to the price for the first copy, 75¢ each additional. Send check or money order to:
New Society Publishers
4527 Springfield Avenue
Philadelphia, PA 19143
In Canada, contact:
New Society Publishers/New Catalyst
PO Box 189
Gabriola Island, BC VOR 1XO

New Society Publishers is a project of the New Society Educational Foundation, a nonprofit, tax-exempt, public foundation. Opinions expressed in this book do not necessarily represent positions of the New Society Educational Foundation.

This River of Courage: Generations of Women's Resistance and Action is the second in the multi-volume Barbara Deming Memorial Series: Stories of Women and Nonviolent Action.

ACKNOWLEDGMENTS

I am grateful to the many family and friends who have encouraged my passion to seek, preserve, and proclaim examples from around the world of women's nonviolent actions for truth and justice. I am especially grateful to my parents, Helen and Arden McAllister, and to the others who reviewed portions of the rough draft—Rev. Constance M. Baugh, Diane Berg, Ruth Dreamdigger, and Norman Taylor. I would also like to thank my friends at New Society Publishers who worked with me along the way to make this book a reality, especially Barbara Hirshkowitz, David Albert, T. L. Hill, and Marie Bloom whose creative juices flowed just in time to propose a book title everyone liked.

This book documenting women's courage was written as I confronted the debilitating effects of agoraphobia. I give my deepest thanks to Connie who has helped me recognize my own courage in this bewildering struggle and has kept me laughing along the way.

Finally, I again express gratitude for my cat-companion Emily, the Beloved Distraction and furry wonder of my life.

—P.M.

ABOUT THE AUTHOR

Pam McAllister has written *This River of Courage* (1991) and *You Can't Kill the Spirit* (1988) and an award-winning one act play *Approaching the Apple* (1978) about women and organized religion. She has edited two anthologies, *Reweaving the Web of Life: Feminism and Nonviolence* (1982) and *The Bedside, Bathtub and Armchair Companion to Agatha Christie* published by Frederick Ungar Publishers (1979). McAllister's essays, articles and poems have been published in numerous periodicals including *Radical America, Woman of Power*, and *off our backs*. She has also lectured widely on women and nonviolence.

Currently residing in Brooklyn, Pam is the administrator of the Money for Women/ Barbara Deming Memorial Fund, Inc. which gives small grants to feminists in the arts. She is also the coordinator of a prison correspondence program at The Church of Gethsemane, a Presbyterian church which is an intentional congregation of prisoners, ex-offenders, their families and people in solidarity with the poor and the incarcerated. Finally, she is the organist and music director for two Brooklyn churches and serves on the Board of Directors of the A. J. Muste Memorial Institute.

ABOUT THE COVER ARTIST

The vibrant color, rich imagery and vigorous compositions of feminist artist and educator Betty LaDuke draw us into a luminous internal landscape, celebrate women's strength and resilience, and inspire us to struggle in defense of human rights. As Professor of Art at Southern Oregon State College, LaDuke bases her work on visits to Third World cultures in transition. She has expanded her work into two books, *Companeras: Women, Art and Social Change in Latin America* (City Lights, San Francisco, 1985), and *Africa Through the Eyes of Women Artists* (Africa World Press, Trenton NJ, 1991).

LaDuke's art brings together the experience of her extensive travels in Latin America, Asia and Africa, her interest in mythology, and her deeply felt, woman sense of human harmony with nature, with spirits and with other humans. Cross-cultural images of women convey themes which LaDuke finds common to every continent: the central place of women in creation myths and the fabric of culture; the nurturing strength and creative power of women; the sensual relationship between women and nature; and the intricate weaving together of women's lives with other beings in the human, spirit and animal worlds.

Just as *This River of Courage* helps make the actions of ordinary women the world over visible and known, so Betty LaDuke's art helps to translate the hopes and power of women from every continent into images. Laduke's particular focus on Third World women infuses her work with urgency as well as joy.

Betty LaDuke's art is available in card form from **Multicultural Images, 610 Long Way, Ashland, Oregon 97520.**

DEDICATION

For the memory of my grandmothers Mabel and Millicent and for the courageous, ornery, wise and wistful grandmothers of us all.

PUBLISHER'S NOTE

I can think of no better way to introduce *This River of Courage* than to tell the story of how I met Pam McAllister. In the spring of 1982 family business brought me from California to New York City where Taylor, one of my cousins, told me about this terrific book she was working on as part of the indexing business she had just started. It was called *Reweaving the Web of Life* and pulled together readings on feminism and nonviolence. Connecting these subjects seemed rare and wonderful to me and I arranged to receive a copy of the book as soon as it was available.

In the excitement of going to Buffalo, New York to join the World Peace March I forgot all about the book. I had been dreaming of joining this nine month pilgrimage ever since they walked through Davis, California, the town where I lived. The World Peace March began on October 24, 1981 (United Nations Day) in San Francisco with about fifteen people. They were walking across the United States speaking about the United Nations Second Special Session on Disarmament (UNSSDII) and asking everyone to work for world peace. The message woke something in me that autumn when I helped host the march in my home town. The stories that the walkers told about why they were walking and what had happened in the ten days of walking so far touched me deeply. At the same time I could see that they were ordinary people who were giving of their lives in an extraordinary way. The march planned to arrive in New York City for the opening of UNSSDII. Most walkers also planned to join in the mass rally and march scheduled for June 12th. Little did we know one million people would join us!

Since I had to come East because of my family business I took a month's leave of absence from work in order to join the march in its final month. Walking through the towns and cities of New York with people from eighteen countries, aged seven to seventy, talking about issues of disarmament and justice, was the most exhilarating and demanding experience I'd ever had. Leaving before the end of the march seemed impossible. The more I contemplated participating in my first civil disobedience action ("Ban the Bombmakers" on June 14) the more I realized that going back to work seemed more like going to jail than getting arrested and going to jail did. But, I'm getting ahead of the story.

A few days out of Buffalo the World Peace March came to Medina, New York. There I was hosted by two wonderful people, the McAllisters. We talked and laughed over dinner but the bit of information that stayed in my mind was that their daughter lived in New York City and was editing a book on feminism and nonviolence. Hmmm. Now where had I heard that before?

The McAllisters promised to meet me in New York and introduce me to their daughter. Amazingly, they found me among the throngs (I mean tens of thousands of people) in the Isaiah Peace Park across from the United Nations and introduced me to Pam. Well, I'd met about 500 people in the month or so since I'd met them so truthfully, I was too overwhelmed to appreciate the significance of this event.

Months later I received a copy of *Reweaving the Web of Life* from New Society Publishers, edited by Pam McAllister, and all the connections fell into place. The book made a profound impression on me: taking two philosophical lines and combining them in a way that has seemed logical and obvious everafter.

It wasn't too much later that I came to work for New Society Publishers, and met Pam again (and her parents too) at a party celebrating *You Can't Kill the Spirit*, the first volume in the Barbara Deming Memorial Series: Stories of Women and Nonviolent Action. Honoring the legacy of Barbara Deming, a fine writer and a committed activist for several decades until her death, by collecting the untold stories of women using courage and ingenuity in their struggles, is extremely appropriate. How I know about Barbara Deming ... but that's another story.

Pam's own story and the stories she tells in this series serve as the best inspiration for me, especially in times of despair. It's not always possible to be on a journey for peace as clearly and in as completely absorbing a way as I was on the World Peace March. Fortunately, I can always read these stories, finding nourishment and courage in the lives of countless women, named and unnamed, from every corner of the world. I hope you can too.

Now that my circle of stories is complete I am proud to present to you *This River of Courage: Generations of Women's Resistance and Action*. We here at New Society Publishers hope you will spread these stories far and wide, collect and share your own stories in the process, and eventually complete the circle by sending some new stories back our way.

Barbara Hirshkowitz

Barbara Hirshkowitz
for New Society Publishers, Philadelphia, PA, USA
April, 1991

ANNOTATED TABLE OF CONTENTS

We say everything comes back. And you cannot divert the river from the riverbed. We say every act has its consequences. That this place has been shaped by the river, and that the shape of this place tells the river where to go....

We say look how the water flows from this place and returns as rainfall, everything returns, we say, and one thing follows another ... and everything moves. We are all a part of this motion, we say, and the way of the river is sacred, and this grove of trees is sacred, and we ourselves, we tell you, are sacred.

—Susan Griffin
Woman and Nature: The Roaring Inside Her (1978)

INTRODUCTION
The Way Of The River Is Sacred

> The way of the river is sacred, and this grove of trees is sacred, and we ourselves, we tell you, are sacred.
>
> —Susan Griffin, *Woman and Nature*

On the day that my father received his World War II draft notice, he also received a letter from his parents. In it they wrote that his Uncle Harry had gone berserk.

My great uncle Harry was employed by the U.S. Postal Service as a letter carrier. Ordinarily it was a good job. He knew the families on his route; he delivered their love letters, wedding invitations, birth announcements, and get well cards. But now that a new world war had started up, his work weighed on him. First there were the draft notices he delivered to young men in house after house. Then there were the battlefield letters addressed to the worried parents who waited on the front porches as he made his way slowly up the street. On each block, young women watched impatiently, barely hiding their disappointment and anxiety when he brought no word from their homesick soldier sweethearts. And then there were the strangely hushed families for whom he had only a few days' worth of sympathy cards.

According to my grandparents' letter, Uncle Harry had awakened one night in a sweat of despair at the thought of his sons and all the other young men who would be sent off to fight in yet another war. In a wild-eyed frenzy he wondered why such insanity must once again tear families apart limb by limb. Hadn't his best buddies died in World War I, the "war to end all wars"? And if more boys were now being sent off to blood-drenched battlefields, didn't that mean his buddies had died in vain?

This particular night, Uncle Harry jumped out of bed, grabbed his bathrobe, and raced down the street to the fire bell, shouting into the cold night air until people poured out of their homes. Fire fighters

1

arrived calling, "Where's the fire?"—but the only fire was the one in Uncle Harry's heart and tormented soul. With his audience assembled, he began to plead for some explanation, for someone to make sense of a world gone mad. The driven man stood alone that night, searching for the words to change the world. I imagine that he wanted to ask questions like, "Why can't life on this once-in-a-universe-green-and-blue-planet be filled with love and joy and laughter instead of pain and death?" and "Why can't young people grow up to follow their dreams instead of battlefield commands to kill other young people they don't know?" and "Why can't we just live simply, get along with each other, take care of each other?"

With no visible fire in sight, poor Uncle Harry was soon arrested and locked up as a madman. But something of his frenzied despair, his lonely witness to the dream of a peaceful planet, was born years later in me.

When I was a child, I decided that someday I would climb on top of a gigantic box in the field behind the barn from which I would be able to see half the planet. I would call all the people from one half of the planet together. When they had assembled and I had gotten their attention, I would simply explain that everyone should, from now on, be nice to each other. I would tell them that it's okay if we are all different and have different customs and ideas and hairstyles, that in fact that's what makes this planet so exciting. We just have to stop hurting and killing each other, stop yelling and pushing. After they heard my message, I was sure that all the people would go home and be happy and kind to each other, wars would cease, the boys would stop hitting the girls. Then, I would pick up my box, go to the opposite field, climb up and call the people together from the other side of the planet and tell them the same thing. And all the earthlings would at last live in peace with each other.

Is it just coincidence that long before I heard about how my great uncle Harry rang the firebell in the middle of the night to call the world to peace, I fantasized standing on a box to address the planet? Something in me still wants it to be that simple. Something in me still wonders why it's not.

Embracing Complexity

A Japanese poet once wrote, "The world grows stronger as each story is told." But we long to ignore the stories, write history books only from the white, Eurocentric, male perspective, speak the day's story in the authoritative voice of the television newscaster, pretend that white feminists from the United States know what's best for the world's women, and gloss over the stories that embarrass us. We want the truth to be simple, but every time we insist on such simplicity, we diminish truth, deprive ourselves of its richness, and turn our own complicated lives into cartoons.

While it is easier to seek our truth in the kernel of only one story, the many-storied truth, though more elusive, is a far more wondrous and useful treasure. Storytelling makes the world stronger because the stories reveal the complexity of our truth. In telling our stories we resist diminishing our truths into vague or generalized abstractions; we maintain the urgency and intensity of the concrete. To move from telling only one story to cherishing each story is to move from the attitude of a conqueror to that of a friend. And how many stories might there be in a universe, a nation, a lifetime, a moment?

When we listen to each other's stories and tell our own, the truth takes shape like the tiny pieces of brightly colored glass inside a kaleidescope. Turn it and the pieces fall into a new pattern. Turn again, another pattern. The truth is a fluid web of connected shapes and colors within a moving whole, always changing and full of promise.

Cherishing Diversity

After college, I left my rural hometown and settled in New York City where I could feast to my heart's content on the joyous, troubling, undeniable fact of human diversity. One weekend, I was invited to Albany, New York, to celebrate with friends as a Peace Ribbon was wrapped around the state capitol building. It would later be added to the eleven-mile-long national Peace Ribbon wrapped around the Pentagon on the fortieth anniversary of the Hiroshima and Nagasaki bombings. Across the nation, over 20,000 people had embroidered yard-long panels after meditating on the theme, "What I cannot bear to think of as lost forever in a nuclear war." They had thought about the possibility of everything being destroyed and had turned their despair to thoughts about what it is they love about this fragile planet. In the process, they had created a thing of beauty.

That Sunday in Albany, despite the intermittent rain, a crowd of families and friends picnicked and sang and listened to poems and speeches about peace. Then we circled the capitol building holding the Ribbon in our hands and passed each other, wrapping the Ribbon almost twice around, each panel a small miracle of creativity and beauty. I looked up from the panel into the faces of those others in the long, human chain. They were sometimes wistful, often tearful as the thought of what this was really all about broke through the celebration. Much of the time we grinned at each other, nodded at the panels, commented on the especially moving ones and laughed at the humorous ones.

I was caught up in the sweetness of the moment until (and here comes a rather bewildering confession!) the panels suddenly seemed to reflect, not the depth of our caring, but the limits of our love. It was all too easy. In all this seemingly endless parade of flowery meadows, where was any appreciation of the migrant laborers, the farmers, and field hands who cultivated the crops? In all the images of chubby baby hands, where was the fierce passion of my mad Uncle Harry? For that matter, where was I? The embroidered panels I saw betrayed our failure to hold precious the full range of the world's texture, gesture, and voice—a failure to embrace life itself.

At first I was confused and ashamed of what seemed to be a spoilsport attitude. Wasn't I being too critical? I continued to hold up my part of the Ribbon. I tried to place the source of my disappointment. Then I remembered an experience I'd had two winters before when I had gone Christmas caroling with friends in Manhattan. This group of friends came in all shapes, sizes, ages, colors and sexual orientations. We were singing in the snow, bundled up in our mittens and mufflers, when we were joined by a stranger—a tall, broad-shouldered, African-American man wearing a big, blond, Carol Channing-style wig. The man started waving his arms in grand sweeping motions as though he were conducting us. I was mortified. What would people think? I recalled the graffiti I'd seen in a city restroom:"Toto, I have a feeling we're not in Kansas anymore." Indeed!

But I took a deep breath and looked at the man again. He seemed to be very happy singing with us, with me. We were all singing about love and snowflakes and about good will to all people and great joy and about peace on earth. It took me a while, but slowly I realized that the experience was a gift. The man's bold presence reminded me that talking about peace and love meant nothing at all if I didn't have the guts to stand there and sing Christmas carols with this gathering which was, finally, the very essence of diversity, reflecting the strange and rich variety of human expression. Of the many times I have been Christmas caroling in my life, that one time is by far the most memorable, the most precious. I am thankful to that guy in the big blond wig who was not subtle, not subtle at all.

This is what I remembered that day in Albany as I looked at those lovely, carefully embroidered images of what it is we hold precious about our world. I do not dismiss either the real or the symbolic value of flowers and babies' hands. And I'm not suggesting that there should have been lots of panels in the Peace Ribbon depicting men in wigs. I'm aware that the theme would had to have been formulated very differently for it to have generated the wider range of images. I mean, rather, to suggest that we rarely reflect deeply enough to affirm our inherent beauty, or the way everything in our world is connected. I would have liked more panels devoted to bald men and toothless women, to care-worn faces and hardworking hands, more panels devoted to fat people, spider webs, rain storms, and earthworms. In creating images of what we cherish, we must somehow nurture the notion of the wholeness of creation, the notion of our interconnectedness, and an appreciation of our diversity. This is essential groundwork for any real progress toward peace with justice.

Facing Complicated Truths About Gender

Sometimes, in our fear of anything different from ourselves, we try to make the distinctions neat, logical, orderly. In contemplating male and female behavior, for example, we often draw heavy crayoned lines separating that which we assume to be exclusively male from that which we assume to be exclusively female. The thickest crayons are used by those who intend to maintain the status quo, to limit the range of behaviors, or to reinforce the assumption that there is only one story worth telling. Feminists around the world have been helpful in questioning basic gender assumptions, though sometimes they have employed their own thick crayons.

The first wave of feminists in the United States put great faith in the peace-loving qualities of maternal love and in women's "natural" biological tendencies toward nurturing and gentleness. Charlotte Perkins Gilman, the turn-of-the-century economist, novelist, and theoretician wrote that

> The tendency to "sit" is a sex-distinction of the hen:
> the tendency to strut is a sex-distinction of the cock.
> The tendency to fight is a sex-distinction of males in general:
> the tendency to protect and provide for is a sex-distinction
>   of females in general.

Some suffragists took the idea that women are primarily suited to roles as wives and mothers and turned it into a political platform, claiming that it is precisely because women know how to take care of people that their voices should be heard in the decision-making affairs of the world.

At the beginning of the second wave of feminism in the United States, in the early 1970s, feminists tended to explain gender differences as the consequence of socialization. Boys act tough because we call them "Slugger," and girls are indoctrinated with the desire to become mommies when we give them dolls. Period. Later in that decade, some feminists rode the pendulum back to the other extreme and argued that men's propensity toward violence had to do with their unfortunate abundance of the hormone testosterone and that women were indeed more naturally nurturing.

As we enter the 1990s, most thinking people have put away the heavy crayons and stopped drawing oversimplified sketches of woman-the-nurturer, man-the-fighter. Some warn that the very notion is not only false but dangerous because it plays into the hands of those who would reinstitute female subordination and male superiority. Not only are we leery of the over-simplifications about gender, but we've also done some research. We know more about our history now than we did before, thanks to women's studies programs and serious feminist scholars. We know about the great women warriors, women like Artemisia, who led battles on both land and sea under Xerxes during the Greco-Persian War around 450 Before the Common Era (B.C.E.); Boudica, the fierce Celtic queen, who led the battle against Roman invaders in 60 A.D. in the British Isles; Nzinga, the warrior queen of the Mbundu people (in what is now Angola), who led military campaigns against the occupying Portuguese in the 1600s; and Gertrudis Bocanegra of Mexico, who organized an army of women during the 1810 War of Independence. And we know about another category of fierce women of whom we're not so enamored, the women who cheered at lynchings in slaveholding America and those who helped usher Jews into ovens in Nazi Germany. Not long ago I saw a newspaper photo of a buxom preteen with a pretty smile. The photo was taken at a rally for white supremacists, and the girl in the photo was wearing a T-shirt with the words "THANK GOD FOR AIDS." So much for woman-as-nurturer.

We can no longer afford oversimplified assumptions about gender, blaming socialization, history, hormones, or some combination thereof for the way we act. By embracing the complexity of gender, we can transform the obsolete system of male rule that distorts the lives of both men and women with its heavy-crayoned boundary lines and begin to enjoy the richness of the human experience.

Facing Complicated Truths About Nonviolence

The book series of which this volume is the second is a celebration of women's use of nonviolent action. It is useful here to note, therefore, that just as we must beware of generalizations about gender, so we must beware of oversimplifications about nonviolence. One example of oversimplification is the misguided notion that the philosophy of nonviolence relies upon being extraordinarily nice or meekly turning the other cheek. This confusion may stem from the nonviolent activist's insistence that people can never be reduced solely to their societal function (soldier, boss, landowner). Instead of roughly sorting the world into dualities of good and evil, friend and enemy, the advocate of nonviolence encountering a conflict situation operates on the assumption that a different and better choice could be made by the opponent, that people and circumstances can be transformed, that our stories are not mutually exclusive. At the same time, the advocate of nonviolence refuses to cooperate with at least some aspect of the perceived wrong. Barbara Deming, the activist-writer for whom this book series is named, wrote that nonviolence gives its advocates two hands upon the oppressor, "one hand taking from him what is not his due, the other slowly calming him as we do this." But the hand that takes, that refuses, that resists, is the hand that is often ignored by those who wish to dismiss nonviolence as being too passive.

Once, when fears were running high that Japanese soldiers were about to invade India, a student of nonviolence asked Gandhi, Should one who is nonviolently resisting such an invasion ever give an invading soldier a drink of water? Gandhi's answer reflected the capacity of nonviolence to embrace the complexity of circumstances. He answered that the resisters must refuse to help the soldiers in their function as invaders, "for it is not part of their [the resisters'] duty to help anyone to steal their country." Gandhi went even further to say, "if the Japanese compelled resisters to give them water, the resisters must die in the act of resistance." (Clearly, Gandhi's nonviolence was not a matter of just being nice.)

On the other hand, Gandhi continued, if a man (whose task it is to be an invading soldier) is lost and in need of water, the resister would, of course, give the lost soldier a drink as an act of comfort and compassion, just as anyone would offer water to any person who is lost and thirsty. The action—the nonviolent resister offering a cup of water to an invading soldier—is defined by the context. In his role as invading soldier, the person is denied the water but as a person in need, he is given the water. This is the kind of complexity embraced by advocates of nonviolence.

While those who insist on reducing nonviolence to passivity fall prey to misguided oversimplifications, so too the advocates of nonviolence are sometimes guilty of similar misrepresentations. One such example is the tendency of progressive advocates of nonviolence to assume ownership of nonviolent tactics. It is a temptation that I can claim as my own. Indeed, this book may actually reinforce such a notion. Because I am the storyteller in this book series, I have selected the stories I want to tell, stories that illustrate how women from all around the world have used nonviolent tactics: strikes, physical obstruction, sanctuary, hunger strikes, petitions, protest demonstrations, tax resistance, boycotts, and civil disobedience. But I have specifically chosen stories which illustrate not only particular tactics but that highlight causes that seem to be about empowering people, creating justice, healing, and moving toward wholeness. I have chosen to illustrate women's tactical nonviolence in the service of the Nazi resistance, suffrage activism, and antinuclear work. I have chosen examples from civil rights, labor, and feminist movements, anti-apartheid and Native American struggles, as well as the fight for free speech and peace. This is my bias.

However, the hard truth is that nonviolent tactics are sometimes used by reactionary groups. Just as violent tactics can be used by dictators, fascists and invading nation-states on the one hand and by people's liberation armies on the other, nonviolent tactics are also used by people along a spectrum of ideas. What do we make, for example, of the women who became dupes for the CIA-backed overthrow of the democratically elected Allende government in Chile? Conservative upper middle class women took to the streets banging pots and pans in nonviolent demonstrations to protest Allende's socialist policies that had increased burdens on the middle class. Nonviolent tactics are not owned exclusively by progressives. Such tactics can also be used by conservatives or reactionaries.

Wading Into This River of Courage

We say everything comes back. And you cannot divert the river from the riverbed. We say every act has its consequences. That this place has been shaped by the river, and that the shape of this place tells the river where to go ...

We say look how the water flows from this place and returns as rainfall, everything returns, we say, and one thing follows another ... and everything moves. We are all a part of this motion, we say, and the way of the river is sacred, and this grove of trees is sacred, and we ourselves, we tell you, are sacred.

— Susan Griffin
Woman and Nature

This book is a celebration of the continuity of women's resistance and action on behalf of justice. Women's courage is ancient. Wherever there has been slavery, there have been women fighting against slavery. Wherever poor and working people have starved and suffered while the rich danced, there have been women organizing for economic justice. Wherever there has been terror or censorship or the deprivation of basic rights, there have been women daring to raise their voices, lift their hands. These stories have been left out of history books that tell of kings and conquerors, but the continuity of women's courage has forged its own path like water that wears away rock.

We say look how the water flows from this place and returns as rainfall, everything returns, we say.

The stories of resistance and action are discovered again and again by generations of women who dare to venture forth. The courage that has come before is not lost but flows like a river, cutting through history's bleakest terrains and most barren deserts, its waters feeding us still, sustaining life through our valleys of despair.

This book is for those whose courage has become a part of this ancient river, for those today who seek sustenance from the river, and for those whose resistance to injustice will become part of the legacy.

Pam McAllister

—Pam McAllister
Brooklyn, New York
Summer 1990

1

The Journey Is Our Home

Congressman Wilson: Where do you live?
Mother Jones: I abide wherever there's a fight against wrong!
                                            —*The Autobiography of Mother Jones*

THE GREAT U.S. LABOR ORGANIZER MARY HARRIS JONES, or Mother Jones as she was called by thousands of workers, had an eye for the dramatic in any situation and she knew that nothing was more dramatic than an army of "wild women," women who were hungry, worn-out and fed up. In town after town she would assemble her armies—miners' mothers, sisters and wives—to fight for the union. If a woman showed up in red petticoats, red scarves, wild hair and wild eyes, she'd be the one Mother Jones would call to the front lines. Jones would tell all the women to bring their pots and pans. These became the tools that the women would use to make a ruckus on the picket lines.

On September 25, 1900, Mother Jones organized over two thousand women, miners' wives from McAdoo, Pennsylvania, for a midnight hike through the mountains to the Coaldale Camp in Panther Creek. One hundred and fifty thousand coal miners in that region had agreed to go on strike, but in Coaldale the union organizers had not been able to win the support of the miners. Mother Jones knew it was mostly a matter of getting the word out. The miners had not been permitted to assemble, so they didn't have a clear idea of what was being asked of them or why. The people in McAdoo, on the other hand, were not only organized but enthusiastic about the strike. Mother Jones called on the women of McAdoo to help her win Coaldale.

Mother Jones knew something dramatic was required to inspire the miners to risk what little security they had in order to organize and demand better conditions. They were frightened people, newly arrived in the United States, hoping to find a better life than they had known in Europe. But what they had found were fourteen-hour days, working underground in the darkness of the coal mines, with no laws to guarantee a minimum wage or to regulate safe working conditions. Mother Jones lived with the people and knew their suffering. In her autobiography she wrote:

> Mining at its best is wretched work, and the life and surroundings of the miner are hard and ugly. His work is down in the black depths of the earth. He works alone in a drift. There can be little friendly companionship as there is in the factory, as there is among men who built bridges and houses, working together in groups. The work is dirty. Coal dust grinds itself into the skin, never to be removed. The miner must stoop as he works in the drift. He becomes bent like a gnome. His work is utterly fatiguing. Muscles and bones ache. His lungs breathe coal dust and the strange, damp air of places that are never filled with sunlight.

The miners' families also faced unbearable hardship and hunger in the miserable company-owned shacks they called home. And their children died. Mother Jones remembered, "Often I have helped lay out for burial the babies of the miners, and the mothers could scarce conceal their relief at the little ones' deaths":

> The miner's wife...is overburdened with child-bearing. She ages young. She knows much illness. Many a time I have been in a home where the poor wife was sick in bed, the children crawling over her ...I saw the daily heroism of those wives.

It was to these brave, worn-out women that Mother Jones turned time and again for the drama she needed to inspire the people.

When Mother Jones asked the women to march to Coaldale, the striking men of McAdoo willingly agreed to watch the children for one night. That evening Mother Jones went around to the saloons and asked them to close up early so that the men could get home. She instructed the women to put on their "kitchen clothes" and to bring their mops, brooms, and tin pans. At the appointed meeting time, Mother Jones watched as the women came out of their homes by the hundreds until there were over two thousand women ready and assembled.

They set out into the night, over the Allegheny Mountains, walking one hour, two hours, three hours, all the way beating their tin pans together like cymbals into the cool stillness of the mountain night. Suddenly, at three o'clock in the morning, they came face to face with the militia patrolling the roads to Coaldale.

"Halt!" yelled the colonel.

"Colonel, the working men of America will not halt nor will they ever go back," Mother Jones yelled right back. "The working man is going forward!"

"I'll charge with bayonets!" the colonel threatened.

Mother Jones called back—as she later remembered in her autobiography —"We are not enemies. We are just a band of working women whose brothers and husbands are in a battle for bread. We want our brothers in Coaldale to join us in our fight. We are here on the mountain road for our children's sake, for the nation's sake. We are not going to hurt anyone and surely you would not hurt us."

The militia didn't hurt them, but they did halt the whole procession until the sun came up over the mountain. When the colonel saw the raggedy army of women with their aprons and mops, he shook his head in amazement and laughed. He granted the women permission to continue down the road to the Coaldale camp.

The women reached the town just in time to see the men of Coaldale starting out from their homes to work in the mines. "Join the union!" shouted the McAdoo women over the din of the clanging pots and pans. "Don't scab for the bosses! Join us! Join the union!" The women kept up their shouting until every last bewildered miner had agreed to join the union. Then the women turned their attention to the streetcar drivers and got them to promise not to haul strikebreakers to the mines for the coal companies.

At one point that victorious morning, the nervous town sheriff approached a seventy-year-old woman dressed all in black. He didn't realize he was speaking to Mother Jones herself when he confided in a whisper, "Oh Lord, that Mother Jones is sure a dangerous woman!" To which the amused Mother Jones responded,"Well, why don't you arrest her then?" "Oh Lord, I couldn't," the sheriff answered. "I'd have that mob of women with their mops and brooms after me and the jail ain't big enough to hold them all. They'd mop the life out of a fellow!"

The women had a busy morning, like one they'd never had before, and they had worked up an appetite with all that marching and hollering. As Mother Jones later testified, "The women had nothing but brooms and mops, and they were hungry. The militia had ordered breakfast at some hotel, and I told the women to go in and eat their breakfast and let the state pay for it. So they did."

On their way out of town the McAdoo women yelled at the wives of the Coaldale mine bosses, told them to clean up their men and make decent American citizens out of them. And then they tramped through the mountains, fifteen miles back to McAdoo.

It felt good to be on the road like this again. Yes, it recalled the miles I had walked in the sixties. Our signs speaking in one way. Our feet speaking without words. Speaking our refusal to sit still and let things stay as they are.

— Barbara Deming, 1983
on the Women's Peace Walk from New York City
to the Seneca Army Depot
Prisons That Could Not Hold

WHEN A STRONG TRUTH PULLS, women have sometimes solicited each other as travel companions, forsaking hearth and home for the road and bearing messages of change, rage, hope. Some women have walked alone, women like Peace Pilgrim and Sojourner Truth. Their stories will be told in a future book. In this chapter we will celebrate those who have traveled en masse on sore feet, dusty trains or bumpy motorcades, women who have taken to the road to protest injustice or demand that wrongs be made right.

"Ordinarily a journey takes us over roads that have been well laid out and well traveled, moving steadily toward a destination," wrote feminist theologian Nelle Morton. "But somehow involvement in the woman movement appears to have reversed that process, and road-building becomes inseparable from the journey itself." Traveling for a cause, women have sometimes forged new roads on history's landscape.

* Some women have walked against hunger, like the fish vendors, seamstresses, prostitutes, flower girls, shopworkers and laundresses in 1789 who marched, eight hundred strong, to Versailles to see the king and demand bread for their starving children.

* Some have traveled for their right to a voice in their country's decision-making process. Selina Cooper, a working-class pioneer in the British women's movement, joined thousands of other women for the Suffrage Pilgrimage of June and July 1913. Via eight different routes crisscrossing England, the women trudged through many villages—some of them unfriendly—peacefully witnessing to their

convictions, distributing suffrage literature, and assuaging the fears of those opposed to the vote for women. When they converged on London's Hyde Park—100,000 strong—the women were delighted to find nineteen platforms set up to accomodate the many rousing speakers. By all accounts, the pilgrimage by the nonmilitant faction of pro-suffrage women had a positive impact on the general population and influenced new allies to back the right of women to vote.

  * Still others have traveled to challenge interlocking systems of oppression in the global struggle for justice and peace. In December 1983, one hundred and fifty North American religious women from sixty different denominations and religious orders set out on a "Pilgrimage to Honduras." Their intention was to pray for peace in Central America and to call attention to the misguided priorities of United States foreign aid. They had chosen Honduras, the poorest country in the Americas after Haiti, because, while forty children there were dying of starvation each day, the United States was giving the little country almost forty-five million dollars annually in military aid. The women never completed their prayer Pilgrimage. Most of the women, more than half of whom were Catholic nuns, were not permitted to leave the United States. The rest were stopped at the airport outside Tegucigalpa. But they did make the news. Rev. Karen Ziegler, then pastor of a New York City congregation in the Universal Fellowship of Metropolitan Community Churches (a denomination primarily serving gay male and lesbian Christians), was one member of the Pilgrimage. She remembers:

> When the Miami group left for Honduras our spokespeople were interviewed by TV networks in the airport. We were a conspicuous group, women wearing skirts and blouses and religious symbols, carrying sleeping bags. Finally we reached Honduras, a beautiful country, green and mountainous...As we approached the airport we saw crowds of Honduran people on the second floor balcony. We later learned that there were many international press people there also, and that was why after we circled around the runway the plane was stopped two miles away from the airport...A truck filled with military men and immigration officials pulled up. As United States helicopters circled overhead, about 30 men stood outside the plane, eight or so in uniform carrying automatic rifles. They surrounded the plane. Two of the armed men entered the plane with an immigration officer. They refused even to speak with our leaders. Within 25 minutes we had left Tegucigalpa...

The good news was that the women's attempt to reach Honduras was covered by all three major news networks in the United States. For Rev. Ziegler, however, there was another cause for rejoicing. Before she joined this pilgrimage of religious women, she had been afraid of the reception she would meet as the lesbian pastor of a primarily gay and lesbian denomination. Instead, she found openness and trust. She later wrote:

> Holly Near said once that wherever she goes she finds lesbians and gay men in the forefront of liberation struggles. Perhaps it is partly because we fight for others when we cannot fight for ourselves. Perhaps it is also because, as we learn who we are and experience God's love, we go through a radicalization process which enables us not only to share others' suffering but also to see the deep causes behind that suffering. We must learn to name poverty, racism, repression, and imperialism as "sin." It is also clear that we in MCC have gifts to give not only in the liberation process of our own people, but also in the global struggle for justice and peace.

On our journeys we forge new roads, touching in our own lives new horizons of courage. This journey, for truth and healing, is greater than our sore feet, greater than jet lag. This journey is our home.

IN THE SPRING OF 1922, thirty-five women and their children set out on a journey through the United States to speak the truth of their hardship and despair. They came from midwestern cornfields and New England factories. Theirs was a journey of storytellers, poor and hard-working women telling the world about their husbands, brothers, and sons and the rest of the one hundred and thirteen men who were imprisoned for the crime of political dissent in a land which boasted freedom of speech.

Their stories were about working men—tenant farmers, factory workers, lumberjacks, miners—union men, most belonging to either the Industrial Workers of the World (IWW) or to the Working Class Union. They were members of a working-class movement which sought to abolish the system of capitalism. The Preamble of the IWW constitution, written in 1905, spelled it out: "The working class and the employing class have nothing in common. There can be no peace so long as hunger and want are found among millions of working people, and the few, who make up the employing class, have all the good things of life." Later, someone stated the goal even more clearly—"The IWW is organizing for porkchops in the present and for a new social system."

When World War I was declared (and even before), the IWW opposed the war, calling it a capitalist folly in which workers were being sent to the slaughter just to line the pockets of the rich. One IWW spokesperson explained the internationalist position taken by the IWW:

> In a broad sense, there is no such thing as a foreigner. We are all native-born members of this planet and for members of it to be

divided into groups or units and taught that each nation is better than others leads to clashes and world war. We ought to have in the place of national patriotism (the idea that one people is better than another) a broader concept—that of international solidarity.

But, inevitably, war requires patriotic fervor. Union members' antiwar statements were met with community hysteria, raids by homegrown vigilantes, and charges by employers who claimed that the union workers were a threat to "the national security." When the United States Congress passed the Espionage Act, signed by President Woodrow Wilson in June 1917, it became illegal for any citizen to express "disloyalty" when the United States is at war. In its vagueness and ambiguity, this Act became a tool used to imprison anyone who spoke or wrote against the war as well as a tool against unionism, the labor movement, and socialism in general. In September 1917, government agents raided union meeting halls, seizing literature and arresting union leaders for antiwar conspiracy. Over one hundred union leaders were found guilty and jailed, some with sentences of up to twenty years. One, Ralph Chaplin, a poet and the author of the workers' anthem, "Solidarity Forever," was sentenced to twenty years for having once edited a labor magazine.

Kate Richards O'Hare, a socialist and mother of four, was arrested that year too, in July, for giving an antiwar speech in North Dakota, the same speech she had delivered in at least seventy other towns and cities. In her speech, she said that "the women of the United States were nothing more nor less than brood sows, to raise children to get into the army and be made into fertilizer." For this she was found guilty by a jury made up predominately of bankers and businessmen. She entered prison in 1919, but even there, O'Hare continued her work and became popular among the inmates for organizing on behalf of basic rights for prisoners.

The families the imprisoned union men left behind were poor and friendless, subject to ridicule and harassment in their neighborhoods. The wives and mothers of the men jailed for their beliefs sent endless petitions to the President, pleading the case for amnesty. In 1922, Kate O'Hare, now out of prison, began to agitate for amnesty for these political prisoners. Then O'Hare came up with the idea of sending the President a "living petition"—the wives and children of the imprisoned—who would travel to the White House and, along the way, would tell people about the plight of the imprisoned men. The media-conscious organizers called it the "Children's Crusade for Amnesty," hoping that the mention of children would catch the headlines they needed and perhaps the sympathy, too. And so it was that the "Children's Crusade for Amnesty" stepped off from St. Louis, Missouri, on April 16, 1922. En route to Washington the women stopped in Cincinnati, Toledo, Dayton, Detroit, Cleveland, Chicago, Buffalo, and New York City. Everywhere they told their stories.

One woman told the story of her two sons. At the beginning of the war, one of her sons had come to her and said, "Mother, I know how you feel about killing, but I've got to go." He enlisted and was sent to fight in France. Her other son, Clyde, had come to her and said, "Mother, I've been studying over it all night and I made up my mind. I can't kill anyone. I'm not going to register." He turned himself in for a jail sentence. While he was in jail someone remembered that Clyde had once belonged to a woodworkers' union for a few months. The day Clyde got out of prison for refusing to go to war, he was arrested again, this time under the Espionage Act. At first he thought it was an April Fool's joke until he was slapped with a new, five-year prison sentence. His mother told this story in city after city. "I stood it all right for a long time," she said, "but then I got sick and got to thinking about Clyde in the night, and I could not stand it, and I took to crying. I cried and cried and could not stop crying for days, thinking of my Clyde. It was too much. One boy in France and the other in jail."

Another woman who told her story on the crusade was Mrs. Hicks, a frail and sickly woman who clutched a three-year-old she'd named Helen Keller after the famous blind and deaf socialist. Mrs. Hicks' husband, a pacifist and a socialist, was a descendant of the founder of the Quaker Hicksites. In 1912, Mr. Hicks had written a letter to a friend in England about the possibility of war and the detrimental effects such a war might have on working people. When the antiwar sentiments he had expressed in the letter somehow became known, he was put in prison under the Espionage Act. With her husband in prison and seven little children to feed, Mrs. Hicks had turned for help to the county. But the county judge was merciless; he took away one of her toddlers and threatened to take away her other children.

By the time the thirty-five storytelling women and their children arrived in New York City, they had experienced a range of responses to their Crusade. In Indianapolis, the American Legion had opposed their visit and the city officials had refused to let the children march or pass out literature. In Cleveland, on the other hand, two thousand people had greeted the weary women and joined in calling for the release of all political prisoners. In New York City, the women were permitted to parade from Grand Central Station up Madison Avenue with their banners, "A HUNDRED AND THIRTEEN MEN JAILED FOR THEIR OPINIONS!" and "IS THE CONSTITUTION DEAD?" and another sign, carried by a young girl, "MY MOTHER DIED OF GRIEF." When she saw the parade in New York, Mary Heaton Vorse, the great labor journalist and feminist, called it a "grief parade." She wrote:

Men and women of America, look at these reticent mountain women. Look at these shrinking young girls staring straight ahead of them...Look at the tired babies. And realize what desperation has sent them on this crusade through your cities...These women from mountain villages and their children come of a breed which closes its mouth on grief. Their difficult lives do not allow them such soft habits as the indulgence of tears. One thing they had: They had their privacy...The proud instinct for seclusion is in the marrow of them...Understanding this, I want to say to them:

"I know you should have been left to bear the hardships of your lot with your austere dignity...But the civilization in which we live has made the violation of these sacred things necessary. That is why you left your home. That is why you came on your crusade. That is why I must write..."

The women and children walked to the headquarters of the Amalgamated Food Workers where they found tables decked with flowers and gifts for the children. The hungry travelers sat down to a meal especially prepared for them by French and Italian chefs from New York's most exclusive hotels and restaurants.

That afternoon, while some of the children were taken to a circus at Madison Square Garden, the women went to tea at a Fifth Avenue mansion cradling their babies and telling their stories to a sympathetic audience. In the evening, the women were once again on stage, this time at a mass meeting at Webster Hall. Elizabeth Gurley Flynn, the fiery labor organizer known as "the rebel girl," was there that night. In her autobiography she wrote:

But I remember most vividly Kate O'Hare, tall, gaunt, standing there speaking while she held Helen Keller Hicks asleep in her arms. There were no loudspeakers then, but Kate's powerful ringing voice filled every part of the hall. "This," she said of the sleeping child, "is a petition they cannot throw away!"

The next day they went on to Philadelphia for another round of storytelling.

The crusaders arrived in Washington, D.C., on April 29, exhausted but determined to meet with President Harding. The President chose instead to keep his appointment with Lord and Lady Astor that day. When he was still busy the next day and the next, the women and their solemn children decided to picket the White House. They had come too far and been through too much to turn back now. Besides, they continued to successfully generate publicity for the cause of amnesty. *The New York Times* ran an article with the headline, "Convicts' Children Picket White House" and described the "bedraggled little ones."

The women and their children picketed the White House through weeks of an uncommonly hot Washington summer. A house was rented for them where they stayed until they won their demand. On July 19, President Harding groaned, "I can't stand seeing those kids out there any longer!" While some of the women and their children picketed the west entrance of the White House that day with banners calling on the President to take action, other women from the delegation met with him in person and handed him an amnesty petition with a million signatures, collected by the General Defense Committee of Chicago. Harding expressed his sympathy for the prisoners and their families, and, although he refused to grant a general amnesty, he agreed that each case should be reviewed. As promised, he instructed the Department of Justice to do this within the next sixty days. Having completed their mission, the women and their children were able to return to their hometowns with honor, carrying bundles of gifts from well-wishers.

As the world grew chilly in the shadow of the cold war, women in Britain decided to act as witnesses for peace. With the terrors of war still fresh in their memories and nationalistic hatreds still festering, they decided the time was right for Women's Caravan of Peace. The idea for the Caravan was credited to Dora Russell, a longtime activist once married to the world-famous Bertrand Russell. Her contacts with Soviet peace efforts had made her unpopular even with the progressive press of the day, and her status as a woman didn't help. "We were so tired of seeing how, in everything that we touched, the opinions of women counted for so little," she later wrote. "I complained that women were always on the outside looking in...My own conscience moved me to persevere in our efforts to make those in power listen to the voices of mothers, now being raised in all corners of the world."

Russell and her friends drafted a letter of invitation to women in organizations across Britain. The letter was also carried in a number of newspapers, although one paper refused to run even a paid advertisement of the Caravan. The letter of invitation read in part:

> Women especially are impatient at the absence of any initiative by the statesmen, and many of us feel that the time has come for us to act and to make a practical gesture of goodwill from the West to the people of the East...

> Women want an end to these intolerable anxieties which haunt them. We cannot wait for our politicians, we ourselves must act. We need trade and peace and a secure future for our children. Do not the mothers in all countries feel the same? Those who join the Women's Caravan of Peace can find out for themselves.

Women responded enthusiastically to the idea of the Caravan, although no one came forward with financial support. Russell managed to secure an old bus and a Ford truck as well as several tents and some food. Banners proclaiming "WOMEN OF ALL LANDS WANT PEACE" were prepared in English, French and German as well as leaflets which spelled out the women's demands:

> This is a mission of Peace and Friendship among all nations! Women of the West are on this mission of peace and goodwill to the women of the East.

> We PROTEST against the manufacture, testing and stockpiling of nuclear weapons and the building of rocket sites.

> We DEMAND that planes carrying nuclear bombs shall not fly overhead.

> We PLEDGE ourselves to urge our Governments to negotiate immediately for TOTAL Disarmament.

> We call upon the UNITED NATIONS to ACT energetically for peace and disarmament.

> We APPEAL to women of all lands to join with us! WOMEN must help to create a united world at PEACE!

The Caravan departed from London on May 26, 1958, with approximately twenty women aboard. In the next three months, they toured fifteen countries from West to East, finding in every land women like themselves eager to raise their voices for a peace of substance. In Brussels, Belgium, they visited the pavilions of the great International Exhibition. Russell wrote:

> A great ball, symbol of the atom, was poised above all. There it shone brilliant and golden in the sunshine, like an immense question mark over Europe—for peace or war?

In Paris, they attended a conference called Women's Responsibility in the Atomic Age with women from across Europe. In Germany, they visited a cemetery where, beside the German dead, there were buried 10,800 British soldiers and airmen, many forever unnamed, with gravestones inscribed with the words, "Known to God Only."

In Switzerland, whose parliament was then discussing a motion to provide the Swiss armed forces with nuclear weapons and to regard as treason any protest, the Caravan women supported local demonstrations by the local Swiss women. When they held up their banners, the Caravan women were taken immediately to a police station. After several hours, they were released with the warning that they must not make any speeches. As Russell put it, "Switzerland was a peaceful country, they said, not in need of people talking about peace."

Then it was on to Italy and after that to the countries on the other side of the Iron Curtain—to Albania, Yugoslavia (Belgrade seemed "like a fairy tale," wrote Russell, "with goose girl and flock, storks on the roofs, men returning from work shouldering shovel and pick"), Bulgaria and Romania. Everywhere they were greeted by women from the villages hurrying up to the bus with flowers and cakes and jugs of hot tea. In a small town in Hungary where they stopped at one a.m., halfway to Budapest, the exhausted Russell had a remarkable experience.

> A woman teacher rose to speak of the function and duties of women in political life. This unknown ally in the heart of a troubled and unknown land was voicing the hopes and beliefs underlying most of my adult life. Such moments of psychic fusion are like bright jewels, almost mystically illumining the past, the present and the future. As I stood up to give her an answer in almost her own words, it seemed to me as if there were present in the room with us a great company of women who had set themselves free and would make their impact on the world.

It was on to Czechoslovakia and then Poland where the women visited the site of the death camp at Auschwitz where whole families of Jews had been incinerated.

At each place along the way, the Caravan women carried a book in which the women they met could record their greetings of peace. This book was presented to the Soviet Women's Committee in Moscow during a three-day meeting. On their way back home, the Caravan traveled through East Germany, stopping in Dresden to remember the Allied bombing raid that had wreaked such havoc there. By September they were home again. Russell wrote:

> Although we were tired, we were still exalted, carrying back with us the memory of so many different friendly faces; courteous speeches from many men; and from women words that moved us so deeply because they fully echoed the aspirations and hopes within our own hearts.

IT WAS NO EASY MATTER to launch a women's movement in Ireland—a country that, in 1970 and in the context of a long and bitter war, still outlawed contraception (not to mention abortion), constitutionally prohibited divorce, recognized husbands as the legal heads of their households, and did not mandate equal pay for equal work. The oppression of women was highlighted in graphic relief.

The ban on birth control seemed to one group of feminist activists a good place to begin. They developed a plan: several women who lived just fifty miles south of the border would take a train (dubbed the "Pill Train") into Northern Ireland, buy contraceptives in a pharmacy there, and smuggle them across the border back into Ireland. The plan hinged on the women deliberately allowing themselves to be caught and arrested with the contraband, enabling them to take full advantage of the media. As Nell McCafferty, one of the participants, explained:

> It was the fervent hope of those who embarked on that Pill Train that the Irish government would arrest us on our return, making us instant martyrs and obliterating all our sins. If you want to progress socially in colonized Ireland, we told ourselves, the first thing you have to do is go to jail.

But the plan was not without its serious political complications. What sort of statement would they be making about their country, so heavily influenced by the Roman Catholic Church, regarding the colonial rule in Northern Ireland, where women at least had access to birth control? They worried that the action, appropriate in the pursuit of women's reproductive rights, would be misunderstood in the context of the war between the two blood-soaked Irelands. Nevertheless, they made the decision not to put women's oppression on the back burner any longer, but to go ahead with the action.

On the appointed day in 1970, the small group boarded the "Pill Train" and crossed the border into Northern Ireland. As soon as they reached their destination, they headed for a drug store. These women had been born and raised Roman Catholic and had been denied access, not only to contraception, but to information about it. Their understanding of birth control was sorely limited. Unaware of the extent of their ignorance, they boldly entered a pharmacy and demanded coils, loops, and birth control pills. The pharmacist coolly explained that medical consultation was required before they could purchase those forms of birth control. The women had to settle for condoms, creams, and jellies.

They also bought a lot of aspirin. They had prepared for the action with an emergency back-up plan.

Upon their return to Dublin they were immediately confronted by customs officials, railway representatives and the police, just as the women had hoped. They boldly seized their moment in the spotlight. As onlookers gaped, the women waved tubes of contraceptive creams and jellies over their heads. They began to read aloud from an informative article on birth control they had clipped from a magazine. And they scattered what looked like birth control pills throughout the station. (It was, of course, only aspirin.) The condoms they kept well hidden for their own personal use later.

With national and international television reporters in tow, the women insisted on marching to a police station. There they declared again that they had possession of illegal birth control devices and were consciously breaking the law. They challenged the authorities to arrest them, but the action fizzled when the police refused to act. Two days later the Prime Minister assured parliament members that the contraceptives had been confiscated and that all was well. The government men were relieved.

It is difficult to say what impact the Irish women's action had on the general population or whether it helped anyone think about a previously closed subject. We do know that the Pill Train action tore open the shaky new women's movement in Ireland as feminists were moved to struggle with the competing and overlapping claims of the right to birth control, women's right to autonomy and self-determination, and issues of nationalism. As McCafferty later reflected on the action:

> The Pill Train was the last cohesive, radical, officially sanctioned gesture of a united women's movement in Ireland. Women took seriously the issues raised by the Pill Train—nationalism, control of fertility, pluralism, and even capitalism (because contraception was available to the bourgeoisie, regardless of legalities, and what did that tell us about class politics?).

N ATIVE (MALISEET) WOMEN OF THE TOBIQUE RESERVE in New Brunswick, Canada took to the road in 1979 with a one-hundred-mile walk to call attention to their plight. But before walking 100 miles they tried a range of other actions. Theirs was a long struggle.

The women of the Tobique Reserve had lived without secure housing rights for so long it was a way of life. Before the 1950s no one had needed a deed or title to establish entitlement to land on the reserve. After 1951, however, when the 1876 Indian Act was amended, titles to land on the reserve were made out in the name of the male heads of households. Eva ("Gookum") Saulis remembered the startling effect of this change:

> Before the 1950s there was no such thing as title. There was no deed or paperwork, it was just your land; you cleared it, and everybody respected that land as your property. When I first noticed women being evicted out of their homes and having a hard time was in the 1950s. I seen a lot of that…People would make fun of those women, "So and so is moving out again!" People laughed at them. Especially before we started making our protests…
>
> I felt so bad, seeing this kind of thing happening to the women and children. It got worse as time went on. The men kicked their families out and then they'd move their girlfriends in.

Glenna Perley dreaded weekends because every Saturday night she was sure to hear the screams of women being beaten by their husbands.

> Every Monday morning we would see a truck going by, some woman got kicked out or couples had separated. All the men would be standing outside the band tribal office laughing...

This was life for women on the Tobique Reserve and it seemed there was nothing to be done. But Juanita Perley changed that when she and her ten children were kicked out of their home in the fall of 1976. Juanita, like Glenna, had witnessed years of women's misery. "This business about women being kicked out of their homes, it goes way back," she said. But in the fall of 1976, she made history.

> It is just that nobody ever really made an issue of it until I got kicked out. Then all hell broke loose. There used to be women out on the streets even when I was a little girl. What has stood out mostly in my mind is women being beaten by their husbands...

> I remember my daughter's twentieth birthday. That was the first time the kids and I got thrown out of our home. My husband had became an alcoholic and things just went from bad to worse. I had ten children and a grandson by then and I thought, where in the world would I take my children? Where's a place big enough? Then I thought, there is the band office. Nobody lives in the band office, they only work there. So we moved in.

It was the first time any woman had occupied a public building and demanded the right to housing for herself and her children. This action inspired women throughout the reserve to talk with each other and compare notes. They went from house to house and discovered that they had a lot in common. The more they talked the angrier they became as they realized the extent of the injustices they faced, not as unlucky individuals, but as women.

Some of the Tobique women decided to act. First, they documented their grievances; they collected personal statements and sent them to the Indian Affairs office in Ottawa, but no one paid attention. They circulated a petition demanding property rights for women and sent it to the minister of Indian Affairs, but it never reached his desk. In July, a number of women traveled to Fredericton, the capital of New Brunswick, to lobby the Indian Affairs office and the Human Rights Commissioner, but it seemed no one was interested. After lobbying, the women tried demonstrating in front of the Indian Affairs office and picketing at the band office on the reserve. In spite of everything they had done, no one would take the time to listen to the women. That's when they began to occupy the band office. Bet-te Paul was there:

> We didn't really move in; we were just going to sit there until we got a meeting with the chief and council. That's actually how the

occupation started. Never once did we tell them we were going to throw them out. The kids were always with us; well, where are you going to put your kids?...

We all sat in the reception area and said, "No, we're not leaving." So they just left us there; like they'd come in the morning to work and we'd still be there. After a while they moved out, couldn't take it, I guess. But all we were trying to do was get a meeting with the chief.

Some people on the reserve were supportive of the women and children throughout the three-month occupation. They offered cooked meals and words of encouragement. Other people were angry. They called the women "troublemakers" and "women's libbers" and subjected them to endless harassment. The women endured threatening phone calls and rocks thrown at the windows.

The three-month occupation won media attention for the first time in the women's struggle for justice. During one interview, several women realized they were talking about something larger than the issue of housing; they were also talking about how women were being deprived of their native Indian heritage. According to the Indian Act, a woman born with Indian status relinquished that status and its privileges if she married a non-Indian man. On the other hand, if an Indian man married a non-Indian woman, he not only retained his Indian status, but his wife was granted Indian status as well. As early as the 1950s, Mary Two Axe Early of Caugnawaga, Quebec, had protested Section 12(1)(b) in the Indian Act, but most native women didn't realize the law existed until it was too late.

In 1949, when Mavis Goeres was fifteen, she met and married a white man and moved to the United States. Her husband didn't permit her to speak her native Maliseet language nor was she allowed to teach it to any of their nine children. In 1975, after a divorce, Goeres moved back to the reserve.

I leave in 1949, come back in 1975 and all of a sudden somebody tells me, "You know, you're not an Indian any longer." I say, "I'm not?" I find out that white women are Indians now, but I'm not. Honest to God, I was shocked. I couldn't believe it...

The question of native status became the foundation for the women's struggle for justice. Goeres explained:

I think what really kept us going is our determination to seek what is rightfully ours. And that is our heritage. We all know that no government agency, be it white or be it Indian, was going to tell us we were no longer Indian, when we know we are Indian. Here the Canadian government was making instant Indians out of white women. You might as well say they were trying to make instant white women out of us Indians. And it cannot be, because being Indian is our heritage: it's in our blood. I think that is our determination right there, it's because we are Indian. We were fighting for our birthright.

The women decided to demand property rights for women and the immediate reinstatement as Indian of all women who were former band members as well as their first-generation children.

On December 29, 1977, the women asked Sandra Lovelace, who had lost her Indian status through marriage, if she would be willing to file a complaint against the Canadian government with the United Nations Human Rights Committee in Geneva, Switzerland. Lovelace agreed, and in the long process became the most interviewed spokeswoman for the Tobique women's struggle. Meanwhile, the women continued to organize.

By the spring of 1979, the housing situation for women on the reserve hadn't changed. The chief and his councillors tried to keep the women away from the housing allocation meeting that year, for good reason. Only one woman was granted a house. This time, the women's rage found a new expression. Just a few months earlier, some of them had participated in The Longest Walk, a march from California to Washington, D.C., to publicize the grievances of native peoples. Why, they wondered, couldn't the women from the Tobique Reserve use the same tactic?

The women got to work, planning their route and destination, arranging for any necessary permits, and publicizing the walk in the hope that other women would join them along the way. They also managed to raise enough money to buy food, sneakers, foot powder, and disposable diapers. They also found money to pay for a bus and driver to get them to the Oka Reserve near Montreal in Quebec, where they would begin their one-hundred-mile walk to Ottawa.

Even in the planning stage, the walk was threatening to many people. Almost immediately the organizers who had phones suspected that their phones were being tapped. Priests that the women contacted for possible accommodation during the walk refused to offer the use of their churches. Several women who decided to join the walk were beaten by their husbands. All the women endured the jeers of their neighbors. Sandra Lovelace remembered the morning the women left the reserve.

> When we started out on the walk, getting on the bus here on the reserve, you should have seen the men. They were standing outside laughing at us, saying, "You fools. What are you going to accomplish?" Oh, we were angry. That is when we were determined to do that walk.

The women arrived at the Oka Reserve and were greeted by French-speaking reporters. Already the media was responding, a good sign. But not everyone was supportive. The women had planned to stay overnight in a Catholic retreat house that had lots of empty rooms, but at the last minute the priest denied them entrance, so they slept instead on the floor of the little town hall.

The next day, July 14, 1979, the women and children began the first stretch of their one-hundred-mile walk in one-hundred-degree heat. As they turned their backs on New Brunswick where their only support had come from a few feminist groups, the Tobique women found a lot of support from the French-speaking people of Quebec. Townspeople as well as farming families came out of their homes to greet the walkers. They came bearing sandwiches, cold drinks and freshly baked cakes. That night people offered their homes so that only a few women were forced to sleep on the bus.

The next morning, a case of beer was found with the women's belongings; it was clear that several of the young women had been drinking. The rest of the women confronted them, pleading that the younger women understand what bad publicity could do to their cause. Several of the young women agreed not to drink again until they got home, but others talked back defiantly. They were promptly put on a bus back to the reserve.

The second day of the walk was as hot as the first, but more women from other reserves showed up to join the effort. Messages of encouragement reached the women from the Northwest Territories, British Columbia, and even from faraway Yukon Territory. A few men joined in, too. Again, well-wishers along the way came out of their homes with sandwiches and juice. But the walking was hard. Lilly Harris, who at sixty-two was the oldest walker, remembered the sore feet:

> Oh, but our feet. At one place it was so hot and we had to stop because our feet and ankles were swelling up. Somebody got powder and we washed our feet right on the street. Reporters were taking pictures of us putting on the powder.

The next night they slept in a hockey arena in Hawksbury, Ontario, where they were permitted to cook supper in the cafeteria. The children were overjoyed, making full use of the public pool and the roller skating rink. The women, however, spent much of their time either being interviewed or attending planning meetings. One woman remembered, "We had meetings and meetings. Walking during the day and meetings at night. We'd have meetings to decide whether we should have a meeting!"

During the next few days, the walkers continued to battle heat, exhaustion, and sore feet. Several of the children were taken to a hospital to be treated for bronchitis, and one walker sought medical attention for a bad sunburn. And people needed to be fed. Caroline Ennis was one who faced that challenge:

Every morning Glenna and I would have to get up ahead of the crowd, after walking all day and then meeting till all hours of the night. With about two hours of sleep, we'd get up early and try to find breakfast for everybody. Sometimes there was no restaurant and we'd have to buy rolls, juice and stuff like that and bring back tons of it. Every day I went out and found a drug store to get more bandaids and foot powder.

Then there were the flaring tempers. Karen Perley remembered:

I think I heard Glenna say one time that she hated everyone during the walk. Which is true. Everybody hated everybody. Everybody talked about everybody. But we did it—we kept going. We were all so tired, the heat, the kids, everything. We weren't sure—"Why are we doing this? We're crazy!" I used to like to walk with Sandra because we'd walk at the same pace with our shorts and knobby knees.

As the women walked, they began to receive invitations to meet with important decision makers, including the prime minister of Canada and the minister of Indian Affairs. The women learned about the power of the media. Caroline Ennis recalled:

When we started getting on national television, people at home who'd thought we were crazy or something really changed their attitude toward us. Somehow I guess being on The National [the CBC's ten p.m. in-depth news program] made the walk legitimate.

The Tobique women developed a carefully worded position paper explaining their situation and their goals. Ennis described the process:

Each night we would work on the position paper. Anything we wanted the government to do was in that paper, all our complaints. Altogether we listed twenty-one concerns, ranging from housing and education to health and the right to be buried on reserves. Theresa Nahanee who is a writer lined it up really nice to present to the prime minister and the minister of Indian Affairs.

As the women approached Ottawa, their excitement built. Women from the offices of the National Indian Brotherhood (NIB) joined the walk in NIB T-shirts and high heels. Reporters swarmed around the marchers and sought out Sandra Lovelace for updated information about her case at the United Nations. And the numbers continued to increase. When the women had started out from Oka, they had been a tight group of about fifty from the Tobique Reserve, ranging in age from three months to over sixty years. Now the walk had swelled to over two hundred women, including non-Indian supporters. Crowds lined the streets of Ottawa. Many people held up signs identifying whole groups of people who had heard the Indian women's grievance and were there to support the cause, people from gay liberation, feminist, Marxist-Leninist, and antiwar organizations as well as several religious groups. The Tobique women were amazed at the response. Karen Perley described their entry into Ottawa.

> At the end of the walk it was another terribly hot day. We were coming up the hill and all the news media were coming down from Parliament Hill, getting ready to greet us. A whole crowd of people was applauding while we were walking. Oh jeez, it was emotional. Tears coming down our eyes, crying. I hadn't realized that we had made such an impact, but we did. I'd thought, here we are walking all this way and nobody cares, but they did.

In the days that followed, meetings were held with the prime minister and other officials. Three hundred thousand dollars in extra housing money was granted to the Tobique Reserve, and the Native Women's Association of Canada was given a major funding increase as well. But the women's struggle was far from over. The women faced several more years of lobbying, petitioning, and demonstrating. Even after July 1981, when the United Nations Human Rights Committee embarrassed the Canadian government by finding Canada guilty of sexual discrimination in its Indian Act, several more years of persistent struggle were necessary. Finally, on June 28, 1985, a law was passed eliminating sexual discrimination from the Indian Act and offering full reinstatement to all those born with Indian status. Lilly Harris wrote:

> It was a long struggle, but it was worth it. We would probably never have got back in—been reinstated—if we hadn't gone on the women's walk or demonstrated. Before the walk nobody ever listened to us—you had to do something outstanding so that people would take notice. I always thought we had a good cause and that people needed to pay attention…Oh, I can't describe how it felt when the change [to the Indian Act] finally came through!

AN AMBULANCE DRIVEN BY TWO WOMEN pulled away from a Berkeley, California curb at dawn on May 2, 1982. Like other ambulances that day, it was moving fast, on its way to the place of an emergency. But where other ambulances raced that day to rescue injured people, this one, driven by women, was racing to rescue planet Earth. In the next month, a handful of women would drive the ambulance across the United States in a ceremonial journey to each of twelve nuclear weapons sites. At each base, they planned to dig into the threatened, injured earth with their hands and shovels and gather it into special pillowcases decorated with words or drawings depicting the dreams and nightmares of women today.

The Earth Ambulance was the vision of performance artist Helene Aylon. Just two years earlier, in 1980, she had been working, isolated in her studio, creating "paintings" made of linseed oil in a series she called "Formations Breaking." The oil, poured onto huge panels on the floor, would be left to dry for several months until the top layer formed a skin. Then friends would be invited to act as midwives to the artwork by lifting the panel off the floor onto the wall. Gravity would pull the oil underneath the skin into a kind of membrane sack that inevitably burst open, and the liquid would be released, birthed—cascading, gushing, oozing, dribbling.

Sometime in 1980, Aylon attended a lecture by Dr. Helen Caldicott, the famous antinuclear activist from Australia, who told the listeners to "use where you are in your life to stop the arms race." Aylon realized that she could no longer remain isolated in her studio, that her art must bring people together to heal the earth. She continued to work with the sack image, fascinated by its power and its associations. "I used to collect these old war photos," she said, "and you always see the men are going off to war, and the women are fleeing with their bundles. They salvage what they can, and then they run." The women in the newsreels too, she noted, escape places of danger with their babies in one arm and cloth sacks full of only their most precious possessions in the other.

Aylon began to use the sack image most powerfully in conjunction with performance art ceremonies involving the earth. She brought together pregnant women, women with infant sons, and women with teenage boys who all swore to discourage their children from entering the military. Together, they gathered sand from the beaches, sand later poured from various heights while an audience listened to the sounds each grain of sand made in the process. Another time she brought together over five hundred women to move ten tons of sand in sacks, performance art that dramatized Aylon's belief that women were willing to carry the burden of earth's survival. Still another time she brought together Arab women and Jewish women in Israel who gathered sacks full of stones together as they recited, "These stones were here before the Jew, before the Arab." Then the women laughed as they said, "Let us leave these sacks for the police to find. They will think these are bombs, and when they pull apart the knots and look inside, they will discover women's unity." Later, sacks of soil were gathered for a ritual of healing at the border of Israel and Lebanon. The earth itself had become the artist's canvas.

The Earth Ambulance, then, was a part of a longer experiment, a dream, an ongoing vision. In planning the trip, Aylon knelt on her kitchen floor beside Fay Sellin, an activist mother of two daughters, to determine the itinerary. They knelt over a map of "Nuclear America" published by The War Resisters League, that had pink dots to indicate the Strategic Air Command bases where weapons are stored and stars to indicate places for weapons research, weapons stockpiles, nuclear waste sites, and reactors. Aylon remembers thinking that the United States looked ill covered with these stars and pink dots, almost as if it had the measles. And there were so many pink dots to choose from—where should they begin to select only twelve during this, the planet's twelfth hour? Sellin suggested they take the scenic route along the Pacific coast to a base at the foot of the Grand Canyon, a healing stop in the Hopi and Navajo land of Big Mountain, then along snow-peaked mountains and on to other bases. After charting their course, the women rented a truck, covered it with white contact paper, and drew blood-red crosses on the two sides: the Earth Ambulance.

Aylon then wrote to women along the proposed route, inviting them to participate and asking for their hospitality along the way. In her letter she urged women not to "cringe from the visionary, the utopian." And the women didn't cringe. Right away one woman who heard about the idea persuaded several hospitals to donate the hundreds of pillowcases that were needed. Another woman wrote a song for the Caravan. Others signed up to go along as drivers.

The Earth Ambulance and its caravan left at sunrise on May 2 from the Lawrence Laboratory in Berkeley, a laboratory once known for the findings of its medical scientists but now used for nuclear research. Members of Nurses for Social Responsibility came forward wearing their white uniforms and caps and bearing the first pillowcases. They repeated again and again the women's diagnosis: "Emergency! The Earth is in grave danger of becoming terminally ill." As the Earth Ambulance inched down the mountainside, women danced and clapped their hands, running in front of the ambulance in a noisy send-off. The journey to sound a warning and to seek healing had begun.

The caravan made its way to the Livermore Laboratory where weapons are designed, as well as to other laboratories, plutonium factories, waste burial sites and Air Force bases in California, New Mexico, Colorado, Kansas, Missouri, Ohio, Pennsylvania, New Jersey, and New York. In Wichita, Kansas, the travelers were joined by a woman with cerebral palsy who struggled patiently to explain that her brother had died in Vietnam. And they were joined by Native American women and by feminist activists and by mothers with young children.

At each place more women gathered. They came to listen to the earth crying, to sing together, to tell their dreams and nightmares, and to press their palms flat against the earth in gestures of healing. At each place, they asked questions of those employed at the military centers and answered the questions asked by curious onlookers at each gas station. At each place, they collected pillowcases full of soil that were then loaded into the Earth Ambulance. Playing with acronyms, they noted that they met at SAC (Strategic Air Command) sites with their pillowcase "sacks" and their prayers that the planet might Survive And Continue. Then, with their sacks of precious earth, they fled the places of danger and drove cross-country in search of a place of healing, hope, reconciliation, and sanctuary.

The women's Earth Ambulance and caravan made it to New York City in time for the historic June 12 disarmament demonstration in which one million people participated. The women parked the ambulance near the United Nations and unloaded the eight hundred pillowcases full of rescued earth onto old army stretchers that had been used in the Vietnam and Korean wars. Then, in solemn procession, they carried the heavy stretchers to the base of the Isaiah Wall and opened the pillowcases. They poured the ailing earth into twelve grave-length, transparent boxes, each box neatly labeled for the soil it held: sandy soil from Vandenberg SAC in Southern California; clay-colored earth from Los Alamos, New Mexico; dark, reddish-brown earth from an atomic lab near Pittsburgh. These were earth paintings, works of art, each a different color and texture. Passersby stopped to look at the planet's soil, awed by its beauty.

A year after the demonstration, in 1983, the emptied pillowcases were hung like laundry on clotheslines that stretched the long block from one New York City avenue to another, filling Dag Hammarskjold Plaza. Months before, women from the United States had exchanged pillowcases with women from the Soviet Union, acknowledging that "we all dream the same dreams." Now these were added to the eight hundred pillowcases from the Earth Ambulance. For fourteen days they hung there, women's dreams and nightmares for the planet waving in the breeze. At night, women from all over the world came to the Plaza and camped out on the sidewalks in sleeping bags, with the dream-laden sacks over them as shelter. The police looked on, mistakenly assuming that official permission had been granted for all this activity. Eventually, the pillowcases were hung up for an eventful summer at the Seneca Women's Peace Encampment in upstate New York, where more dreams and nightmares were recorded.

SOURCES

Mother Jones and the McAdoo Women

Jones, Mary Harris. *The Autobiography of Mother Jones.* Mary Field Parton, ed. Chicago: Charles H. Kerr Publishing Company, 1925/1980.

The Children's Crusade for Amnesty

Bird, Stewart and Peter T. Robilotta. *The Wobblies: The U.S. vs. Wm. D. Haywood, et. al. (a play).* New York: Smyrna Press, 1980.

"Convicts' Children Picket White House." *The New York Times.* April 30, 1922.

Flynn, Elizabeth Gurley. *The Rebel Girl: An Autobiography/ My First Life (1906-1926).* New York: International Publishers, 1974/1955.

"President States Amnesty Policy." *The New York Times.* July 20, 1922.

Vorse, Mary Heaton. "The Children's Crusade for Amnesty." In *Rebel Pen: The Writings of Mary Heaton Vorse.* Dee Garrison, ed. New York: Monthly Review Press, 1985.

Zinn, Howard. *A People's History of the United States.* New York: Harper & Row, 1980.

British Women's Caravan of Peace

Russell, Dora. *The Tamarisk Tree,* Vol. 3: *Challenge to the Cold War.* London: Virago Press, 1985.

Ireland's Pill Train

McCafferty, Nell. "IRELAND(S): Coping with the Womb and the Border." In *Sisterhood is Global: The International Women's Movement Anthology.* Robin Morgan, ed. Garden City, NY: Anchor Press/ Doubleday, 1984.

Native Women's Walk

"Native Women's Walk." *off our backs* (Oct. 1979).

"Native Women Walk for Rights." *New Women's Times* (September 14-27, 1979).

Tobique Women's Group. *Enough is Enough: Aboriginal Women Speak Out* (as told to Janet Silman). Toronto: The Women's Press, 1987.

Earth Ambulance

Aylon, Helene. "On Common Ground." *Heresies* no. 23.

Aylon's personal collection of papers, correspondence, journals and artist's notes.

Other

Deming, Barbara. *Prisons That Could Not Hold: Prison Notes 1964-Seneca 1984.* San Francisco: Spinsters Ink, 1985.

Liddington, Jill. *The Life and Times of a Respectable Rebel: Selina Cooper, 1864-1946.* London: Virago Press, 1984.

Morton, Nelle. *The Journey Is Home.* Boston: Beacon Press, 1985.

Ziegler, Karen. "Pilgrimage to Honduras Blocked." *Journey* (Feb. 1984).

2

Huggers, Sleepers, And Breastfeeders

WHILE SOME WOMEN HAVE TAKEN TO THE ROAD WITH THEIR GRIEVANCES, refusing to sit still with their rage or their hope, others have stubbornly refused to move, planting their feet squarely in the middle of the places they are not wanted. Women around the world have experimented with the sit-in, lie-in, sleep-in, die-in, stand-in, dance-in, pray-in, pee-in, and breastfeed-in. They have chained their bodies to fences and wrapped their arms around sacred trees to save the trees from lumberjacks' saws. Women have claimed the spaces from which they've been denied access and interfered with business-as-usual to call attention to a wrong.

Breastfeed-In

With their breasts bared, fifty toronto women boldly set their babies to suck in the middle of the Cumberland Terrace shopping mall one April afternoon in 1981. The event was a "breastfeed-in," staged to protest an incident a few days earlier when a young mother had been forced to leave the mall after she was found discreetly breastfeeding her two-month-old son. At the time, she had been selling antiques at a table in front of a boutique. According to reports, the boutique owner who witnessed the breastfeeding rushed out of her store shouting, "Oh God! She's breastfeeding. I don't believe it. What kind of pig would do that?" The nursing mother was forced to leave the mall.

"Babies are the only members of society who are now required to have their dinner in the toilet," one of the protesters explained to reporters. Like others who came to the demonstration that day, the protester was outraged that such a fuss had been made about a woman who had used her breasts to feed her baby, when every newsstand displays magazine covers on which women's breasts are exposed for the profit of pornographers and for the sexual entertainment of men.

It seemed to the bare-breasted women in the mall that only when breasts are exposed to feed children do some people find them offensive. As a consequence, nursing mothers and their babies are forced to hide in public washrooms. The breastfeed-in drew a crowd of curious shoppers, most of whom agreed with the women.

Pram-In

In 1970, women in a Copenhagen suburb took over a busy parking lot by barricading the entrance with baby carriages full of wide-eyed tots. When bewildered motorists drove up to the gate, the Danish women passed out fruit juice and biscuits and talked with the drivers about the shortage of decent nursery schools for the little ones and the proliferation of parking lots. The women who stood that morning under a banner "CHILDREN BETTER THAN CARS" called themselves "Thilde's Children" or simply "the Thildes" in memory of Mathilde Fibiger, a nineteenth-century pioneer of the Danish feminist movement.

Sleep-Ins

Two sixty-eight-year-old women marched into the Pacific Power and Light (PP&L) offices in Portland, Oregon, one chilly afternoon in February, 1975, prepared for a "sleep-in." Julia Ruutila and Martina Curl brought with them their sleeping bags, a little food, and a thermos of coffee. "At least we might get a warm night's sleep," they said. "It's pretty cold at home."

The women were protesting PP&L's high rates and the company's request for yet another rate increase. They were already feeling the pinch; they prepared only one hot meal a day and took fewer hot showers in order to save money on the electric bill. But what bothered Julia Ruutila the most was that she was so cold at night that she shivered; she could no longer enjoy her life-long habit of reading in bed. "Taking a book to bed at night is one of the few pleasures left to an old lady," she joked.

The women settled down for the sleep-in when the PP&L offices closed at five p.m and were promptly arrested. As they were carried out of the building they chanted, "Roll back the electric rates!" At the county jail they were booked, fingerprinted, and photographed. The women refused to post bail and were detained for five hours in a dirty holding cell. Ruutila's medication for asthma and ulcers was taken from her as extra punishment. PP&L was very unhappy about the bad publicity and dropped charges against both women. The company did not, however, drop its rates.

Women in South Africa have also experimented with the sleep-in tactic. In March 1987, twelve women moved into the men-only barracks that housed nearly three thousand coal miners near Witbank. The men who worked in the mines were required to sign one-year contracts in order to live and work there. Under the perversion of the apartheid system, by which the minority white population maintains a police state to rule the majority indigenous African population, the black workers were forced to live in dorms, separated from their wives and children who lived in distant "homelands." Only the white miners were provided with family housing during their term of employment.

The sleep-in was organized by the National Union of Mineworkers, the biggest union in the country's black labor movement. Throughout the occupation, more than one hundred black women moved in to live with their husbands every weekend. The women gained the sympathy and cooperation of the tribal heads appointed by the company management to guard the entrances of the hostel to keep the women out.

The company management was taken by surprise by the women's action; they protested the radical action but did nothing more. A representative of the Anglo American Corporation that owns the mine whined, "I think it is the wrong way for the union to make its point. There is a forum for this to be discussed, and I am surprised the union has gone into this kind of confrontation instead." A company manager wrote an open letter to the women warning them of the "unpleasantness" that could result from their action and informing them that they were not entitled to housing or food. But the women were already well acquainted with "unpleasantness." And as for the women not being entitled to the space or the food provided the husbands by the company—well, that was the point of the action.

Outside the red brick barracks women hung their laundered bras and skirts beside their husbands' overalls. Elmon Mbokodo, the head of the local union, told reporters, "We are beginning to live like normal human beings instead of [like] schoolboys." The sleep-in activists demanded an end to the migrant labor system and insisted that the companies provide both permanent work and family housing for the miners' families. One union official noted the awkward position in which the sleep-in action placed the mining companies: "It would look bad," he said, "if they were to fire a man for living with his wife."

The action was successful. Not only did it gain worldwide attention and dramatize yet another aspect of apartheid's insanity, but it forced a change in the policy of the targeted company. The Anglo American Corporation pledged to begin to provide housing for the families of 24,000 black miners near four of its mines.

Pee-In

Flo Kennedy called it a "protest pee-in on the Harvard Yard." Florynce Kennedy, one of the first African-American women to graduate from Columbia Law School, was well known in 1973 for her outrageous ideas and her eagerness to act on them. In her fights against racism and sexism, she had established a solid reputation as "radicalism's rudest mouth." Kennedy had gained notoriety as the author of some of the decade's most memorable mottos ("Don't agonize, organize") and truisms ("If men could get pregnant, abortion would be a sacrament") and for clever terms such as one referring to the U.S. military spending as "Pentagonorrhea." So when the women applying for admission to previously all-male Harvard University wanted to find a way to dramatize the discrimination they faced, they called in Flo.

One of the women's primary objections was the agonizing lack of toilet facilities permitted to women at Harvard. Prospective students had to take their entrance exams in Lowell Hall, an old building with only one bathroom—for men. Women with full bladders were forced to be excused, dash across the street to another building, find the women's room there, and then run back—a trip that generally took fifteen minutes away from the exam. In addition, the campus was teeming with female secretaries who, as Flo later pointed out, though destined to be nameless and faceless to the Harvard establishment, were still born with bladders.

On June 7, 1973, the invincible Kennedy led a small number of women through the rain-dampened streets of Cambridge chanting, "To pee or not to pee, that is the question!" As the marchers repeatedly circled Harvard Yard, their numbers grew. At last, they came to a stop on the steps of Lowell Hall where Flo explained the women's objections. She said that restricting bathrooms was a way to reinforce the superior-inferior relationship of different segments of a community just as public bathrooms had been used to reinforce racial division for years in the South. Noting the sign one marcher carried, that read, "IF GOD MEANT WOMEN TO HAVE PAY TOILETS, WE WOULD BE MADE WITH EXACT CHANGE," Kennedy further pointed out that in most public bathrooms women still had to pay a fee. While men always had the option of a urinal or an inconspicuous corner, women who couldn't or wouldn't pay usually only had the option to use the one free toilet "that either has no door or no paper or a puddle or something just to remind you you're a nigger." ("Nigger" was a word Kennedy used to describe anyone being oppressed, regardless of their color.)

After making her comments, the crowd was entertained with a reading of a poem titled "To the Pay Toilet," which Marge Piercy had written for the occasion. Then, at a signal from Flo, several women came forward with glass jars and splashed bright yellow liquid onto the steps of Lowell Hall. Some of the onlookers cheered, but the symbolic action wasn't enough for one woman who cried out in an outraged Southern accent, "You ain't going to pee? I thought you-all were going to pee. I'll pee! I'll pee right on the steps of old Lowell Hall!" Thinking fast, Flo raised the clenched fist of protest and shouted, "Let the Dean of Harvard be warned. Unless Lowell Hall gets a room for women so that women taking exams don't have to hold it in, run across the street, or waste time deciding whether to pee or not to pee, next year we will be back doing the real thing."

Later, when asked her reaction to the day's events, Kennedy said,

> First: It was more fun than most of us ever expected to have on any single day of our lives. Second: We have helped some smart women to cross the Harvard gender line. Third: On this day, in this place, women have taught the Harvard power structure their first lesson about Women's Liberation.

Sit-In

Sit-ins, pee-ins, die-ins, and the like are actions intended to be visually dramatic and are deliberately designed to have an impact on the public imagination. Because of their visual drama, these events also tend to make good news copy and delight photojournalists. The photos that result often leave powerful afterimages and a lasting impression on the public debate.

In one unforgettable photo from the United States civil rights movement, three young people—an African-American woman, a white woman, and a white man—sit at a segregated lunch counter in Jackson, Mississippi, on June 12, 1963. The counter is recognizable. I've seen ones like it a hundred times and worked behind one as a waitress during my own college days, wiping the formica clean and filling the salt and pepper shakers and the napkin dispenser. But in this photo, the three people seated at the counter look miserable yet brave as they are crushed by a solid wall of young, white men. The white boys with hard, hate-filled faces crowd the diner. They are are laughing as they pour sugar, ketchup, and mustard over the heads of the students. The young civil rights activists, by doing nothing more than sitting at a lunch counter, were changing history. I wonder, as I look at the photo, if they knew it. I wonder, too, if any of those with the hate-filled faces recognized courage when they saw it.

Diane Nash was a young African-American student at Fisk University in Nashville when she signed up for a workshop in nonviolent action. "During the workshops we had begun what we called 'testing the lunch counters,'" remembered Nash later. "We sent teams of people into department-store restaurants to attempt to be served. We had anticipated that we'd be refused, and we were." Nash herself took part in the sit-ins.

> The first sit-in we had was really funny. The waitresses were nervous. They must have dropped $2,000 worth of dishes that day....It was almost like a cartoon...we were sitting there trying not to laugh [but] at the same time we were scared to death....I was wall-to-wall terrified.

Her fear was legitimate. White segregationists tormented the students, hitting and pushing them, pouring food over their heads, and extinguishing lighted cigarette butts on their backs. Then the police would arrive and arrest those sitting passively at the counters. As Nash described it:

> The police said, "Okay, all you nigras, get up from the lunch counter or we're going to arrest you." [Then] they said, "Everybody's under arrest." So we all got up and marched to the wagon. Then they turned and looked around at the lunch counter again, and the second wave of students had all taken seats...then a third wave. No matter what they did and how many they arrested, there was still a lunch counter full of students there.

By sitting at "white-only" lunch counters, the students broke the silence that had sustained years of business-as-usual racism and spoke with their bodies the shame of segregation and the truth of their rage and their dignity. The sit-ins were a major source of irritation and endless inconvenience to white segregationist business establishments as well as an embarrassment to Southern cities. The actions, though nonviolent, scared away occasional shoppers, discouraged steady customers, and resulted in loss of revenue for the store owners. The arrests filled the jail cells and caught national media attention. Furthermore, the sit-ins did not happen in a vacuum but rather added to the mosaic of memorable civil rights actions which included pickets, "Freedom Rides," "Freedom Marches," and boycotts.

Die-Ins

Thumbing through my history books, I find another dramatic photo. In it, women are staging a "die-in" in front of London's Stock Exchange. The photo was taken on June 7, 1982, the same day President Ronald Reagan was visiting the financial district. In the photo, peace activist women lie sprawled across the pavement in mock death while high-heeled women and gray-suited men carrying briefcases hurry by.

During the London action, women lay "dying" on all five roads leading to the Stock Exchange, an institution chosen by the protesters to highlight the vast amounts of money spent on nuclear weapons. Some women participating in the well-orchestrated demonstration stood by with leaflets explaining the action. The leaflets read:

In front of you are the dead bodies of women. Inside this building men are controlling the money which will make this a reality by investing our money in the arms industries who in turn manipulate governments all over the world and create markets for the weapons of mass destruction to be purchased again with our money.

President Reagan's presence here today is to ensure American nuclear missiles will be placed on our soil. This will lead to you lying dead.

As women we wish to protect all life on this planet. We will not allow the war games, which allegedly protect some whilst killing others, and lead to nuclear war which will kill us all.

Gillian Booth, a lesbian mother in her early forties who had struggled with the violence in the world as well as the violence in her most intimate relationships, was there that day. Later she wrote about what she had experienced, beginning with her amazement at having to play dead at seven o'clock in the morning. "I had fried egg and potatoes," she wrote, "and toast too because I couldn't die on an empty stomach." She continued:

We know this much, that the die-in which our particular group is doing will not be on the main drag, as some groups will be, but down a side street that motorists might use as an escape route. We come up the street, our leader rushes ahead. Arlene looks pale, my stomach kills, knees feel woolly....As we cross a street, suddenly we are engulfed by a huge grey wave of office workers, military provision of skirts and tailored trousers, and ah, those many pointed umbrellas. Dear god, it was all this time a tyre crushing in my head I was fearing, not to be confronted by irate pedestrians with pointed missiles....I'm with a group of women striding through the early morning heat... getting looked at by 100 passers-by who could be inhabitants of another planet they seem that different but who I know will burn and shrivel up the same as me if the bomb fell in the clear light on such a Monday morning.

A year before this action, on International Women's Day, 1981, three thousand women in Ramstien, West Germany, marched to a NATO airbase for a die-in. They lay down on the ground in silence to simulate the effect of a nuclear attack, and they released balloons into the air, each balloon carrying the message, "We hope you will never be reached by radioactive fallout. That is why we are resisting the deployment of Cruise missiles and Pershing II. Women for Peace."

Dance-In

In another memorable photo, we see police cars and a fence topped by circles and circles of razor wire that protect a strange mound—a missile silo at the Greenham Common military base in England. The silo houses United States-owned weapons intended for World War III. On top of the death mound is another circle, this one not razor wire but forty-four women holding hands and dancing in the soft rain of the dawn on New Year's Day, January 1, 1983. In *Greenham Common: Women at the Wire*, Bee Burgess recalled that morning:

> The sky would be lighting at 7:30 and not all the women had arrived. We wait, nerves tender, excitement spinning through our bodies.... At last everyone is here. The ladders are found, we discard their camouflage and start moving towards the fence. The silos loom threateningly in the half-light of dawn. We knew that now, standing before the fence, we would need to be so quick. Two ladders are propped successfully against the fence, with carpet laid over the top barbed wire, and another ladder is dropped down the other side. The atmosphere is frantic.

> There is a flash of light from behind us, an over-zealous reporter more concerned for his story than for our safety and the success of our action. We start clambering over. There are headlights coming towards us from inside the base while it seems like an endless stream of women are crossing the barriers of destruction. As we jump from the ladders on the other side, we crouch for a moment, waiting for the other women, wondering, "Will we get there?" In the next second we've joined hands. Suddenly two policemen are there, aggressively shoving the ladders and wrenching them away from the inside of the fence, leaving two women on top of the barbed wire...they jump.... We begin singing and walking quickly, almost at a run, towards the silos. Our hearts are beating and our voices ring out clearly. The sky is light and it's raining softly on our faces.

> We scrambled up the mud-drenched slopes to the top of the silos. Unbelieving—but knowing—we cheered, waved, jumped up and down, hugged each other in what seemed like an endless amount of energy! We had brought with us a huge piece of cloth with "Peace 83" painted across it which we held for the women to see, for the tv cameras who would then take it back to broadcast into living rooms all over the country. For an hour we danced, sang and made women's peace symbols with the stones that lay on the surface.

Chains

Sometimes women have not been satisfied with merely occupying a forbidden space but have taken the action one step further and secured themselves to that space.

"SUFFRAGETTES IN CHAINS" blasted the London newspaper headlines on January 17, 1908. It was the year's first Cabinet Council, and all the Ministers had headed for 10 Downing Street to review the season's legislative program. The press corps was in tow, seeking polite statements to fill the evening newspapers. The Ministers and the men of the press should not have been surprised to find suffrage activists congregating on Downing Street as well; the women had been trying to persuade the male-run government to consider the issue of women's suffrage for decades. Their motto was, "Deeds, not words."

As three or four suffragettes approached the Cabinet Ministers to request an interview, the women were roughly pulled aside by the police, prevented once again from voicing their concerns. At that moment, activist Edith New began to address the crowd, explaining the urgency and frustration the women felt. Her voice carried over the press corps, the onlookers, and the police. Her speech could even be heard inside 10 Downing Street where the Ministers had assembled. To the dismay of the police who rushed to silence her, New had chained herself to the railings beside the Prime Minister's front door and could not be quickly carted away. While the police had their hands full with New, Olivia Smith, suffrage activist and nurse, quietly pulled heavy chains out of her bag and also attached herself to the Prime Minister's railing. With two women chained to the property, the police got edgy. How many more chain-wielding women planned to follow suit? As they struggled to dislodge the suffrage orators, the police failed to stop Flora Drummond from hopping out of a cab and rushing past the chained women into 10 Downing Street. She was stopped just before she reached the Council Chamber, dragged to the door, hurled down the steps, arrested for disorderly conduct, and sent to prison for three weeks. Six months later, Edith New returned to 10 Downing Street to throw the first stone in the window-smashing campaign of the militant suffragettes.

Across the Atlantic Ocean seventy-three years later, on August 26, 1981, United States feminists chained themselves to the White House fence in celebration of Women's Equality Day, the sixty-first anniversary of women's suffrage. They were demanding passage of the Equal Rights Amendment (ERA) which would add to the United States Constitution these words: "Equality of rights under the law shall not be denied or abridged by the United States or by any state on account of sex."

The action began at eleven a.m., when ten women from the Congressional Union, named and modeled after the suffrage activist organization, gathered in Lafayette Park across from the White House. They were dressed in white with purple sashes, and each woman had heavy metal chains wrapped around her waist. Beneath sunny skies they sang as the crowds of onlookers, police, and press gathered. They had made up their own verses to familiar tunes like "The Battle Hymn of the Republic" and "My Country 'Tis of Thee." They continued to sing as they walked out of the park, up the sidewalk to the street light, and across the street to the White House. The police and press tumbled over each other, trying to stay one step ahead of the women. Then, one woman spoke calmly above the singing. "Gentlemen," she said, grinning, "some of you might want to go over there to get pictures of some of the rest of us who are also participating in this action." She pointed down the block.

The chained singers had just been a decoy team. A little way away, twenty-one women had quietly chained themselves to the fence and to each other. They, too, were dressed in white, but their purple sashes bore the names of the states that had not yet ratified the Equal Rights Amendment. The "UTAH" sash was worn by Sonia Johnson who had gained notoriety a few years earlier when she was excommunicated from the Mormon Church for her support of the ERA. As the news reporters hurried to the scene of the action, the women delivered speeches. They explained, "The Equal Rights Amendment was introduced in 1923. It's been fifty-eight years, and we're tired of waiting."

The police remained befuddled as the women sang, gave interviews and made speeches. Suddenly, the women pulled little keys out of their pockets, unlocked their chains from the fences, and, still chained to each other, proceeded to the White House driveway where they settled in for a sit-in. Here the women again chanted and sang as other women stood nearby with signs reading, "JUSTICE HAS NO GENDER," and "NEVER ANOTHER SEASON OF SILENCE." Author-activist Charlotte Bunch read the 24-point platform of the National Plan for Women's Equality, Union, and Justice, that had been adopted at the 1977 women's convention in Houston.

Then, still not arrested, the women stood as a group and marched to the middle of Pennsylvania Avenue where they blocked lunch hour traffic as they sang "We Shall Not Be Moved." Since the women were now on city turf (instead of park or White House property), Washington D.C. police in riot gear descended on the group, one of whom carried a three-foot red chain cutter. The arrests began. One by one the women were unchained and escorted to a paddy wagon. They were taken to the Second Precinct Station, charged with obstructing traffic, and fined $50 each. That night they celebrated at an organizer's house where they watched themselves on the evening news.

In Toronto, the day before the 1980 seal hunt, three women chained themselves to desks in the federal Department of Fisheries office and had to be cut loose by firefighters. The women used their chains to protest the annual slaughter of baby seals. Though the Department of Fisheries was not directly involved in regulating the seal hunt, it is the most closely related department located in Toronto and therefore a convenient arena for protest.

Every year, the Canadian harp seal hunt colored the waters of the northwest Atlantic with the blood of 180,000 week-old seal pups and filled the fur traders' pockets with money. By 1980, the clubbing to death of baby seals was generating public fury. Animal rights activists, downplaying mere sentimentality in favor of a deeper claim of basic animal rights, had developed a range of tactics to stop the slaughter that turned baby seals into fashionable fur coats. In addition to chaining themselves to office furniture, activists had interfered with the hunt by spraying a harmless green dye on the pups' coats, rendering the fur worthless to the club-wielding sealers.

Five months later, another six protesters (one man and five women, one of whom had a three-month-old nursing baby) chained themselves together in the same office. One held a sign which read, "AMERICA'S WATERGATE—CANADA'S SEALGATE." The six protesters, members of the International Fund for Animal Welfare, were protesting the jailing of Brian Davies, the organization's director, who was imprisoned for landing a helicopter within half a nautical mile of the annual seal hunt and disrupting the event.

One of those in chains that July afternoon was Harriet Schleifer, the executive director of the Montreal-based Animal Liberation Collective. She claimed that the government was creating a police state and violating civil liberties with its policy of prohibiting the public and the media from attending the event. As Schleifer was talking about a police state, the officers who came to remove the protesters asked the news reporters to leave the room. The protesters began to chant "Freedom of the press! Freedom of the press!" Police had to borrow a chain cutter from the fire department before they were able to remove the demonstrators from the office.

The united and persistent efforts of the many animal rights activists who had obstructed the seal hunt over the years eventually paid off. In 1983, the European Economic Community banned seal imports, an action that helped to curb, though not end, the hunt.

Tree Hugging

The forests are sold,
The earth is helpless,
As the tree tiger prowls
A danger is born,
All because of the forest auction.
From whence shall the snow fall on mountains?
Our rain forests have been felled.*

Amrita Devi was already an old woman in 1730 the day the axmen came to the small village of Khejarli. Even after they told her that the Maharajah of Jodhpur wanted wood for the lime-burning necessary for building a new palace, she didn't understand. To her it was unthinkable that anyone, even the Maharajah, could order the trees to be cut down.

The trees were a blessing to the villagers, their very source of life. The only spot of green in an otherwise barren and cruel landscape, the forest shielded them from the surrounding desert, provided the village with food, and protected the fragile water supply. And didn't the forest yield fodder for the poor cattle and produce twigs to make the cooking fires? The forest meant life itself to the village. Furthermore, as followers of the Bishnoi, a Hindu sect, the villagers were required to protect the trees and wildlife. It was their sacred duty.

As the Maharajah's axmen approached the threatened forest, Amrita Devi tried to reason with them. She explained again how essential the trees were to the existence of the village and that it was against the villagers' faith to allow the trees to be injured. But the axmen had orders to follow: they were to bring back trees for the building of the new palace.

Amrita Devi was as unmoved by the axmen's purpose as they were by hers. The villagers agreed with Amrita Devi: they could not allow the precious trees, their lifeline, to be cut. But what could they do? All reasoning with the ax-wielding men had failed. They were eyeing the trees as they prepared their tools. They were ready to get to work.

Suddenly, without a word, Amrita Devi stepped up to a tree and stretched her thin arms around it. The axmen were perplexed. This crazy old woman was in their way, making a nuisance of herself. They pulled Amrita Devi away from the tree and threw her to the ground, but as soon as she got up she hugged the tree again and informed the axmen that they'd have to kill her before they could cut down the tree.

These verses are from a Garhwali folksong by Ghyanshyam
* Sailani, often sung by women of Uttarakhand.

What is the life of an old peasant woman to men who are bound to obey the orders of a maharajah? The axmen began to cut through Amrita Devi to get to the tree. When she fell to the ground, her three daughters ran up to embrace the tree in her place. Each was killed by the axmen. The other villagers began hugging the trees, and the forest echoed with screams as the axmen reaped their bloody harvest. In all, more than three hundred and sixty people are said to have been murdered in the forest that day.

When Maharajah Ajit Singh later heard what his axmen had done, he was appalled. He had never intended, never even imagined, such a thing would happen. In reparation for the tragic loss of life, he declared a permanent injunction against felling the trees or killing the wildlife in the area of the massacre and exempted the villages of that region from all land taxes. Today, Amrita Devi's home is a green and beautiful preserve filled with animals and birds in the otherwise desolate Rajasthan Desert, and her name has become a legend, a beacon of courage to the many in India's "Chipko" (tree-hugging) ecology movement who continue to put their bodies between the tree and the ax.

> And from whence shall the spring come?
> Rainy months are lost forever,
> the trees felled,
> Streams have run dry.
> Who shall lessen the villager's misery?
> From whence shall the snow fall on mountains?
> Our rain forests have been felled.

How can I, a woman living in the United States, understand what trees might mean to the women of the Himalayas? If I'm thirsty, I turn the tap, and clear, drinkable water comes out. If I want to cook my dinner, I turn another knob and a small, controllable ring of fire appears on my stove top. But the women of the Himalayas spend eighty percent of their time walking miles to get firewood and water. For them, quenching their thirst or preparing dinner for their families is back-breaking. I was not encouraged to regard the trees as my spiritual partners, but the women of the Himalayas worship forest gods and goddesses, speak of the forest as "maika" (mother's home).

In 1730, Amrita Devi and three hundred and sixty other villagers braved the Maharajah's axmen, but other tree cutters were to follow years later with more sophisticated tools. Since the beginning of the twentieth century, developers have descended on the forests of the Himalayas. Seeking only short-term profit, they have chewed up vast forests. Today the deforestation has accelerated to a rate of almost 3.2 million acres of forest a year. One of Mohandas Gandhi's closest disciples, Mira Behn, moved to the Himalayan region in the late 1940s and observed the devastation:

> I witnessed a shocking flood: as the swirling waters increased, [there] came first bushes and boughs and great logs of wood, then in the turmoil of more and more water came whole trees, cattle of all sizes and from time to time a human being clinging to the remnants of his hut. Nothing could be done to save man or beast from this turmoil.... Merciless deforestation as well as cultivation of profitable pines in place of broad-leaf trees was clearly the cause.

Years later, scientific environmental studies verified Mira Behn's analysis of the cause of the floods that plagued the impoverished people of the Himalayas. Where the trees had been felled, landslides gashed the mountainsides. The indigenous oak trees, that held water and gripped the mountainsides with their deep roots, had been felled to make way for landing strips and roads. In place of the oaks, cash crop forests of faster growing and commercially profitable pine and ash had been planted. These trees, not useful to the mountain people, did nothing to restore the delicate ecological balance of the Himalayas, but they yielded the kind of wood that makes terrific tennis rackets for people who live far away from the mountains. In 1970, the monsoon rain flooded the Alakhnanda River, and the surrounding valley suffered unprecedented damage. Five major bridges were washed away as well as thirteen suspension bridges, hundreds of cows, and acres of timber. Two hundred people died, and hundreds of homes were destroyed. The commercial lumbering that had been done in the region was the major cause of this flood.

In response to the devastation of the forest resources, the mountain people began to organize. One of their leaders was a young man named Chandi Prasad Bhatt, who had grown up in a small village in the mountains and understood the links between the floods and the lumbering profiteers. He was also a Sarvodaya activist, a student and believer in the nonviolent ideology of Gandhi. Bhatt resurrected the idea of hugging the trees and helped the people organize into nonviolent action teams. Pockets of resistance to the tree cutters began to spring up in remote mountain villages. The resistance became a movement known as "Chipko."

In March 1974, in the small village of Reni near the Indo-Tibetan border, the state forestry department marked three thousand trees for felling that would be auctioned to a contractor. On March 26, the government lured the men from the region to a nearby district to be paid some compensation they were owed. The women were left alone. One little girl tending the village cattle saw men marching into the forest with axes. She ran to tell Gaura Devi, a widow in her fifties who was one of the strongest and most respected leaders of the people.

Within minutes, word spread through the village, and a small troop of women headed toward the forest. Gaura Devi addressed the men:

> Brothers, this forest is our maternal home. From this we satisfy so many of our needs. Do not destroy it. If you do, landslides will ruin our homes and fields.

The workers had been given alcohol; some were drunk. One swaying man pulled out a gun and pointed it at Gaura Devi. She remained calm. "Shoot us," she said with a steady, low voice. "Only then will you be able to cut down this forest which is like a mother to us." Ashamed, the men left the forest untouched. The women of Reni stayed by the trees all night until their brothers, husbands, and sons returned the next day.

> Nature's laws broken,
> Seasons have turned unkind.
> Barren are the fields,
> The earth shall shed her tears,
> Seeds shall not sprout now.
> From whence shall the snow fall on mountains?
> Our rain forests have been felled.

In November 1977, six hundred and forty trees in the Advani Forest were marked for cutting. A timber company had purchased them from the state forest department; a contractor and two dozen laborers had been hired to do the job.

As the two trucks and three police jeeps came up the forest road, however, no one in the chain of command was surprised to find five hundred people, almost all of them women, waiting in the pale, dawn light at the edge of the forest—no one, that is, but the workers. They had been brought from distant regions where they would not have heard the story of Amrita Devi or of the long history of resistance to tree cutting in the Himalayas.

The village women had already caused enough trouble and had promised more. For days, groups of women had walked through the forest singing, removing from each tree the forest department's iron blades, used in resin tapping, and then bandaging the wounded pines. They had tied "rakhee" (sacred threads) around the trees signifying their promise to protect the trees with their very lives. The women had also argued with the forestry officer who visited their village. He had claimed that the trees of the forest would yield resin, timber, and foreign exchange. But the women had responded that the forest would also yield soil, water, and pure air, the bases of life itself.

On this morning, the women watched cold-eyed as ever. The day before, they had seen the men with rifles strutting up and down the road to the forest in a show of force meant to scare the women away from interfering with official business. And the women knew that this time the district officials had sent along some of those men, armed with rifles and bayonets, to see that the women kept back. A woman shivering in the morning air called out, "The Himalayas will awake today: the cruel ax will be chased away!" The other women immediately picked up the chant, lifting their voices to greet the approaching trucks. Surely this was the day for a confrontation, but guns would not stop them. The blood pounded in each woman's chest, and the children huddled a little closer, many of the older children carrying babies on tiny, jutting hips. In the crowd, too, were some of the men of the village who had not gone to the plains seeking work.

As the workers piled out of the trucks, the contractor told the men to get to work and to ignore the women. But when the men entered the forest, the women and children did, too. When the men approached the marked trees, the women did also. Three or four women with children tugging at their skirts encircled each tree, patiently explaining, "If the ax falls on the trees, it will fall on our bodies first. The forest is the lifeline of our village. You may not cut down these trees. Go home." The contractor hollered, and the men moved deeper into the forest, but the women moved with them, encircling the trees as they went. Again and again they explained patiently, knowing that the workers, poor people like themselves, were potential allies in the struggle.

Now the police were as perplexed as the workers. Why weren't the women afraid of the guns? Why didn't they run on home? No one really wanted to shoot the women and children, did they? The women could be arrested, but there were so many of them they would never fit in the available jail space. The village people chanted for the police:

> No matter what the attack is on us,
> Our hands will not rise in violence!
> The policemen are our brothers,
> Our fight is not with them.

After several hours, the frustrated contractor called off the effort, and the tired laborers and sheepish police left the forest.

> My village sister, get ready,
> You elderly ones too,
> You fairies of the hills,
> Incarnations of power!
> Your mothers' land is being raped,
> The forests of butter and milk
> Are being looted.
> From whence shall the snow fall on mountains?
> Our rain forests have been felled.

SOURCES

Breastfeed-in

Gaskin, Ida May. "The First Canadian Suck-In." *New Women's Times* (Oct. 1981).

Pram-In

Dahlsgard, Inga. *Women In Denmark: Yesterday and Today.* Copenhagen: Det Danske Selskab, Danish Institute for Information About Denmark and Cultural Cooperation With Other Nations, 1980.

Pee-In

Davall, Irene. "To Pee or Not to Pee..." *On the Issues,* vol. 15 (Summer 1990).

Frankfort, Ellen. "Urinary Politics." *Village Voice* (June 7, 1973).

Kennedy, Flo. *Color Me Flo: My Hard Life and Good Times.* Englewood Cliffs, NJ: Prentice-Hall, 1976.

Sleep-Ins

"South Africa: Some Families May Be Reunited." *off our backs* (Nov. 1987).

Sparks, Allister. "Miners' Wives Stage 'Sleep-In'—S. African Union Protests Black Workers' Isolation." *The Washington Post.* April 17, 1987.

"Two 68-Year Old Women Arrested while Staging 'Sleep-In' At Utility Company Offices." *WIN Magazine* (May 22, 1975).

Chains

"Chained to a Cause." *The Toronto Star.* March 14, 1980.

"Controversy Flares Over Fate of Newfoundland's Seals." *The Animals' Agenda* (June, 1986).

Dykstra, Peter. "Setbacks for Sealers." *Greenpeace* (Spring 1982).

Fithian, Nancy. "Women Control Chain of Events at E.R.A. Demo." *off our backs* (Oct. 1981).

Klug, Brian. "Animal Rights: The Slogan and the Movement." *Agenda: News Magazine of the Animal Rights Network* (Mar./Apr. 1984).

Mackenzie, Midge. *Shoulder to Shoulder.* New York: Alfred A. Knopf, 1975.

Moira, Fran. "Congressional Union Gets Into Heavy Metal." *off our backs* (Oct. 1981).

"Police Eject Seal Crusader's Backers." *The Toronto Globe and Mail.* July 17, 1980.

Photo Series

Cook, Alice and Gwyn Kirk. *Greenham Women Everywhere: Dreams, Ideas and Actions from the Women's Peace Movement.* Boston: South End Press, 1983.

Harford, Barbara and Sarah Hopkins, eds. *Greenham Common: Women at the Wire.* London: The Women's Press, 1984.

Quistorp, Eva. "Starting a Movement: Women for Peace, West Germany." In *Keeping the Peace.* Lynne Jones, ed. London: The Women's Press, 1983.

Starhawk. "We Are the Hope That Will Not Hide." *Women of Power.* no. 10 (Summer 1988).

Williams, Juan. *Eyes on the Prize: America's Civil Rights Years, 1954-1965.* New York: Penguin Books, 1987.

Tree-hugging

Albert, David. "Hugging Trees: The Battle to Save the Indian Himalayas" (unpublished paper).

Albert, David. "Hugging Trees: The Growth of India's Ecology Movement." *WIN Magazine* (Nov. 22, 1979).

Anand, Anita. "Saving Trees, Saving Lives: Third World Women and the Issue of Survival." In *Reclaim the Earth: Women Speak Out for Life on Earth.* Leonie Caldecott and Stephanie Leland, eds. London: The Women's Press, 1983.

Hegde, Pandurang. *Chipko and Appiko: How the People Save the Trees.* London: Quaker Peace & Service, 1988.

Philipose, Pamela. "Women Act: Women and Environmental Protection in India." In *Healing the Wounds: The Promise of Ecofeminism.* Judith Plant, ed. Philadelphia: New Society Publishers, 1989.

Shepard, Mark. *Gandhi Today: The Story of Mahatma Gandhi's Successors.* Cabin John, MD: Seven Locks Press, 1987.

Shiva, Vandana. *Staying Alive: Women, Ecology and Survival in India.* London: Zed Books, 1988.

3

The Strike Of a Sex

> If enough women ever really went on strike—refusing the roles that have been assigned to us, insisting on roles of our own choosing—everything, everything would have to change.
>
> —Barbara Deming
> "Remembering Who We Are"

RODNEY CARFORD WANDERED INTO A STRANGE TOWN one day. He instinctively felt that something was wrong with the town but he couldn't quite put his finger on it. The men he saw all looked dazed and disheveled; buttons were missing from their clothes. Their houses were dusty and the curtains hung crooked. Only after making careful note of these details did he realize he hadn't seen any women or children in the whole village. "Where are the women?" he asked one pitiful, woebegone man. "Oh," came the reply, "the women have barricaded themselves and the children in a fortress up on the hill and they won't come down. The women have gone on strike."

"They say," explained one bedraggled husband, "that the chains which have bound them for unnumbered ages, although artfully garlanded with flowers and called by sentimental and endearing names, are older and more galling than those of any bondspeople on the globe. They have decided that the time has come to throw off those chains."

"But what do the ladies want?" asked Rodney, totally bewildered by the notion of a gender strike. "Do they want the vote? The right to own property? To be eligible for civil office? A right to material advantages? Equal wages for equal work?"

The men shook their heads. "No," they told Rodney. The women had asked for all of these things and the men had given in to every demand—every demand but one. There was a chill in the air, and the men trembled as they silently thought of the one demand they could not fathom granting.

"But, what is it?" Rodney demanded to know. "What is the one awful demand that has caused the women to stay on strike? For heaven's sake, what do the ladies want?"

And the answer came: Each woman wants "the right to the perfect ownership of her own person."

The women in this novel, *The Strike of a Sex,* written in 1890 by George Noyes Miller, fought men's control of women's bodies by removing themselves from their own homes, depriving the men of women's company and labor. From their self-imposed exile, they published a newspaper, *Bitter Cry.* The men suffered without the women to sew on buttons and straighten the curtains, but both sides held out.

Finally the women tried one last, all-out tactic to win the final demand. They came down from their sanctuary and paraded through the streets so that the men could see for themselves the hard lives of their mothers, sisters, daughters, wives. First the unmarried women passed by and, as if in a dream, the men could truly see the impoverished women whom they had taunted and ridiculed. Then the prostitutes, invalids, and assorted "victims" passed by in their misery. Next came the great hordes of unhappily married women, and again, the men could suddenly see the truth of the hardships the women had endured. To the men's chagrin, only a handful marched under the banner of "happily married women." Finally, the bright and high-stepping young girls danced by full of innocence, facing nothing but misery and heartache ahead. The full impact of their destiny overwhelmed Rodney. He passed out cold.

The next day, when the female strikers called for a future for "the new man and woman, neither oppressing nor oppressed," the men agreed. This story ended happily, with the women's final demand willingly granted by the newly enlightened men.

STRIKES BY WOMEN who identify themselves as a gender-class have been as rare in history as they are in literature and have usually been planned as symbolic, one-day actions to dramatize a specific concern.

The idea for one such strike began in the Washington, D.C. home of Dagmar Wilson. One evening in mid-September 1961, Wilson read a news account of an action taken by Bertrand Russell, the winner of the 1950 Nobel Prize for Literature and a philosopher whom some called the spiritual leader of the civil disobedience movement in England. According to the account, he had committed civil disobedience at an anti nuclear demonstration and was on his way to prison. He had explained that he felt compelled to take this drastic action because all his writings and lectures had failed to rouse the people to act for peace. "I cannot bear the thought of this beautiful planet spinning timelessly in space—without life," he said. Dagmar Wilson heard the anguish and the urgency and recognized it as her own.

The next morning she called five friends and asked them to join her for coffee in the garden. They discussed their frustrations with the latest insanity: the Soviet Union and United States had accused each other of breaking a moratorium on nuclear testing. The women didn't care who was breaking it. They cared about what the radioactive strontium 90 was doing to their children, and they were outraged with the government's promotion of a fallout shelter program, as though the program was a serious, logical response to the threat of nuclear annihilation. Something had to be done.

Before the women had brewed a second pot of coffee that morning, they were preparing lists of names to be called announcing a women's strike against the bomb. "We decided it was up to the women," Dagmar Wilson later told a *New York Times* reporter, "because the men are trapped in the course of daily events."

A few weeks later, as she distributed mimeographed sheets calling on women across the country to strike for peace, Wilson was asked about her expectations regarding the action. "I haven't a clue how many will turn up," she told reporters. "I just started this because I thought that there must be something that women could do. You know how men are," she continued. "They talk in abstractions [about the]...technicalities of the bomb, almost as if this were all a game of chess. Well, it isn't. There are times, it seems to me, when the only thing to do is to let out a loud scream." The women in Dagmar Wilson's garden didn't want to form an organization, with board meetings, dues, membership lists, and committee minutes. All they wanted was one action that would be the equivalent of a scream loud enough for the whole world to hear.

Six weeks after the garden coffee klatch, on Wednesday, November 1, 1961, women across the United States—homemakers and factory workers, clerical workers and waitresses—interrupted their daily routines and took to the streets in the Women's Strike for Peace. That day the women didn't make the beds or pack the lunches. They didn't type the bosses' letters or file any papers. They didn't milk the cows or work on their dissertations. The women went on strike for peace. Fifty thousand women in over sixty cities, from Miami Beach to Portland, Oregon and from Yuma, Arizona to Madison, Wisconsin, called on the world's governments to "end the arms race, not the human race."

In Washington, D.C., over one thousand women picketed the White House, leafletted, and sent delegations to the Soviet Embassy. Letters were dispatched to Mrs. John F. Kennedy and Mrs. Nikita Khrushchev. The First Ladies were invited to join the Women's Strike for Peace to end the arms race. The identical letters read:

> Think what hope would gladden the world if women everywhere would rise to claim the right to life for their children and for generations yet unborn. Surely no mother today can feel that her duty as a mother has been fulfilled until she has spoken out for life instead of death, for peace instead of war. The fate of all humanity is now one fate. The life of all nations is now one life. Join with us—make the survival of mankind the one great cause of our time.

That night throughout the country, women with tired feet returned to their homes to find that they had made front page news. A Berkeley, California paper announced: "300 MARCH ON CITY HALL, URGE END TO ATOM RACE." It described the overflow of women delegates who had pushed into the office of the man in charge of Berkeley's civil defense. There were even a few women peering in through his ground floor windows. An *L.A. Mirror* reporter described the demonstration by two thousand local women as "part of a wave of feminine determination which swept the country today." An article in *The San Francisco Chronicle* began, "Plodding doggedly through a faintly radioactive drizzle of rain, 200 San Francisco women carried their plea for world disarmament to city, federal and school offices here." The article in Philadelphia's *Evening Bulletin* was headlined "WOMEN QUIZ 2 SENATORS DURING 'PEACE STRIKE' HERE."

Though it was conceived as a one-day action, the Women's Strike for Peace (WSP, or WISP, as it was sometimes called) continued long past November 1, 1961. Rather than get bogged down in the trappings of an organization, WSP mobilized women to join already established peace groups and to spread their influence on a local level through the Parents and Teachers Associations (PTA), churches and bridge clubs. The participants conceptualized WSP not as an organization but as a movement; through it, they organized such actions as pickets, demonstrations, and letter-writing campaigns. They also promoted nationwide boycotts of fresh milk after every atmospheric nuclear test to protest contamination of milk from fallout.

Amy Swerdlow, a founder of the New York WSP, watched the tone and style of the movement change over the years. Remembering the early years of WSP, she told a *New York Times* reporter:

> In a sense, we used the 'feminine mystique' to our advantage. We used the fact that we were housewives and mothers, women stepping out of our acceptable sphere. We were doing a job of being good mothers by becoming involved in political action for the sake of our children's survival.

But then the war in Vietnam became an anguished focal point, and the women's movement brought about a new energy as well as new horizons of political activity for women. According to Swerdlow, women in WSP changed with the times.

We became expert draft counselors, we got involved in civil disobedience, in sitting down in Congress and in front of trains carrying napalm. We chained ourselves to the White House, blocked ships, lay down on the street pretending to be dead Vietnamese, and went to Hanoi.

In 1967, a *New York Times* headline blared, "2,500 WOMEN STORM THE PENTAGON TO PROTEST WAR." The women who had once gone on strike in 1961 were finding new ways to make the world hear their scream.

IN MARCH 1970, BETTY FRIEDAN, author of *The Feminine Mystique*, stepped down from the presidency of the National Organization for Women (NOW). In her farewell speech, she shocked the NOW leadership and other women's movement organizers by spontaneously committing the movement to a one-day, nationwide strike by women. The Women's Strike for Equality was intended to call attention to the limitations and inequalities faced by women living under a system of patriarchy in which men determine the mythologies and the rules that govern daily life. The date chosen for the action was August 26, 1970, the fiftieth anniversary of the passage of the Nineteenth Amendment, that gave women the vote. Friedan proclaimed:

> I propose that the women who are doing menial chores in the offices as secretaries put the covers on their typewriters and close their notebooks and the telephone operators unplug their switchboards, the waitresses stop waiting, women stop cleaning and everyone who is doing a job for which a man would be paid more, stop. When it begins to get dark, instead of cooking dinner or making love, we will assemble and we will carry candles alight in every city to converge the visible power of women at city hall. Women will occupy for the night the political decision-making arena and sacrifice a night of love to make the political meaning clear.

Organizers of the Women's Strike for Equality used the heightened public attention to women's issues to focus on three specific demands: free abortion on request, 24-hour day-care centers for the children of working mothers, and equal educational and employment opportunities. They also proclaimed a women's boycott of four products: Silva Thins, advertised with the slogan "Cigarettes are like women: the better ones are thin and rich"; *Cosmopolitan* magazine, dubbed by strike organizers as the misguided counterpart to *Playboy*; Ivory Liquid, because it overemphasized the youth cult in its ads; and Pristeen, a "feminine hygiene deodorant" that exploited the women's liberation movement in its ads by associating the product with "women's new freedom."

On August 26, women across the country took the day off to participate in a variety of symbolic actions. In Syracuse, New York, women held a "baby-in" at city hall to advocate for child care by dramatizing how difficult it is for women to accomplish anything with children claiming their attention. In Miami, members of NOW threw pieces of broken coffee cups into a trash can to symbolize their desire to make policy, not coffee. In Boston, women marched down the streets chained to typewriters and cleaning tools, carrying a coffin in memory of the women who had died after illegal abortions.

In Washington, D.C., women used the day to initiate a lobby and petition campaign for passage of the Equal Rights Amendment. Some senators were supportive of the women's efforts. Birch Bayh, a Democrat from Indiana, asked the men on his staff to answer phones and type memos for the day. Other senators were threatened. A West Virginia senator, in a speech on the floor of the Senate, denounced the women involved in the strike as "a small band of braless bubbleheads." Though very few of the women were bubbleheads, some were indeed braless. Women working at the Pentagon filled a trash basket with discarded bras, pink panties, and girdles, identifying these as items women were encouraged to wear to make themselves sex objects.

Around the country women held "teach-ins." Activists in some cities called on women to "liberate food" from the supermarkets and occupy the welfare offices. Three women in Manhasset, Long Island, took over a country-western radio station for two hours and discussed feminism on the air. The management of WBAB in Babylon, Long Island turned over the entire radio station to women employees for the day.

The Women's Strike for Equality was celebrated in New York City with a variety of actions. Sixty women invaded the offices of the Katherine Gibbs Secretarial School protesting an ad which suggested that female college graduates must have secretarial skills to get a good job. At the Random House offices, eighty women attended a lunch-hour "rap session" to discuss equal employment. *Newsweek* magazine chose that day to sign a pledge that it would accelerate its recruitment and promotion of women. Some women picketed on Wall Street at the Stock Exchange, while others rallied at City Hall Park with signs that read "Repent, Male Chauvinists, Your World is Coming to an End." Leaflets titled "You and Your Marriage" that spelled out legal inequalities concerning married women, were handed out to women standing in line at the marriage-license bureau.

At five-thirty p.m. came the highlight of the day: a march by close to fifty thousand women down New York City's Fifth Avenue, setting a new record for the largest women's demonstration in United States history. The women had been denied permission to use the full Avenue because, city officials explained, they would block rush-hour traffic. When fifty thousand women showed up, however, Friedan realized both the folly and the insult of trying to relegate them to a mere portion of the Avenue. She shrugged and said, "I'm sorry. This is *our* hour of history, and we're going to take it!" And take it they did. The *New York Daily News* reported:

> As the march began, a leading phalanx of women spread all across the avenue holding hands and ignoring police barriers erected to confine them to one and a half lanes of the route. As harried cops saw the mass of women approaching across the width of the street, they quickly dragged the barriers away and let the ladies have their all-or-nothing way.

Women from the Black Panther Party, the Emma Goldman Brigade, and lesbian groups joined hands with airline flight attendants, veterans of the suffrage movement, members of NOW, and Men for Women's Rights. Later, Marcia Cohen described the feeling of the event:

> What no one can miss, what taps and clicks under each marching foot, is a jazzy rhythm, an emotion few have ever before associated with the women's movement.

> Joy.

> It sweeps up in the summer sun of Manhattan like the cry of a hundred shiny trombones, the ring and crash of a forest of timpani. Women—all kinds, all classes, all shapes and sizes—have come together here. From distance. From isolation.

Newspapers across the country headlined the Women's Strike for Equality, though they worked hard to discredit the feminist cause. The *New York Times* reported that Betty Friedan had been twenty minutes late for her first speaking engagement of the day because she was getting her hair done at the Vidal Sassoon Salon. "I don't want people to think Women's Lib girls don't care about how they look," she was reported to have said. The *Times* that day also featured an article titled "Traditional Groups Prefer to Ignore Women's Lib" and, in the name of journalistic objectivity they quoted Mrs. Saul Schary, executive secretary of the 23-million member National Council of Women as saying, "There's no discrimination against women. Women themselves are just self-limiting. It's in their nature." About those who participated in the strike, Schary could only say, "So many of them are just so unattractive." The *New York Daily News*, too, offset its featured article "Gals Liberate 5th to Cheers, Jeers" with an article about Dorothy Frooks, a sixty-nine-year-old ex-suffragette who worried, "Why, if we're not careful, the men might get fed up with the whole thing and leave us to go fishing." But the strike had brought women's concerns into the spotlight and served as a catalyst for a range of women's actions. Some journalists began to take note. A reporter for the *Washington Star* wrote, "Despite the humorous outlook that prevails when the boys talk it over, the drive for women's equality is a serious political movement that could have a profound effect on American life."

In Paris that day, French women organized a demonstration in solidarity with their sisters in the United States. They carried a banner to the Arc de Triomphe which read, "MORE UNKNOWN THAN THE UNKNOWN SOLDIER: HIS WIFE." This banner and the new term, "women's liberation," made Parisian newspapers' front-page headlines.

"YOU CAN'T MAKE FUNDAMENTAL CHANGES in society without the occasional mad act," said Thomas Sankara, president of the West African country of Burkina Faso (formerly the Republic of Upper Volta). In September 1984, with Sankara's blessing, the women in the Committee for the Defense of the Revolution called for a one-day women's strike and "Market Day for Men."

The people in the capital city of Ouagadougou were given fair notice of the event in a media campaign organized by the Ministry of Health and Family Welfare, headed by Josephine Ouedaogo. Ouedaogo was only one of the women who had been appointed to high government position in the days before President Sankara was assassinated. There was even a woman placed second in command at the Ministry of Defense. It was a time of great change in a country that had always known a strict division of labor along gender lines.

In Burkino Faso, women have to go to the market daily, rain or shine, because there is no way to preserve food from day to day. They leave early in the morning, often walking long distances to a marketplace. There they select the produce and haggle with the vendors in order to get the most out of the food money which is doled out to them each day by the men. The women then carry their heavy loads back home and prepare the family meal.

The Native American adage, "You must walk a mile in my moccasins to understand my journey," aptly describes the intent of Market Day for Men in Burkino Faso. In this case, however, the journey was generally longer than a mile and light years long in consciousness. The women who organized Market Day for Men urged community leaders—priests, imams (Muslim prayer leaders), teachers, and news reporters—to encourage support for the experiment. The date was kept a secret so that women would not do extra shopping the day before to spare their husbands a day at the market.

At eight p.m. on a Friday night the word came: the strike was to be the next day, September 22. The next morning the men got up early. The women handed them the lists of food to be bought that day and the men were on their way—in a torrential rain. At each market place, the men were greeted by teams of militant women from the Committee for the Defense of the Revolution, there to prevent women from entering the markets unless the women were single or had husbands who were ill that day.

The marketplaces proved alien to the men who wandered in confusion as if they were lost on a strange planet. They asked about prices and were alarmed at the figures quoted. Not adept at bargaining, they handed over the money and hurried on to buy the next item on their lists. Finally they carried their heavy loads home, realizing from their aching backs, tired feet, and pounding heads the frustrations and fatigue the women lived with daily.

Josephine Ouedaogo later wrote of that day:

> The atmosphere was fantastic, as much for those who "played the game" as for those who found it "absolutely ridiculous." It was well worth it. It provoked unexpected debate in all quarters. The revolution had burst into the family and pointed an accusing finger at the masculine conscience!

B UNDLED IN COATS AND SCARVES, twenty thousand women crowded into the main square of Reykjavik on October 24, 1985, chanting, "We dare, we can, we will!" Throughout Iceland, women walked out of the fisheries, the wool processing plants, the banks, and the hospitals in a nationwide "Day Off for Women." The phone system and the schools were paralyzed. Day-care centers and supermarkets closed for lack of business. Only the cafes reported doing a booming business as hungry husbands sought breakfast and dinner.

Even Iceland's President, Vigdis Finnbogadottir, made up her mind to stay at home in solidarity with the strike action. She was harassed by the prime minister, however, who appeared on her doorstep and wouldn't leave until she'd signed emergency legislation ordering Icelandair flight attendants back to work. Despite her reluctant signature, the airline attendants refused to return to work until the following day.

In part, the women who went on strike in 1985 were commemorating a successful Day Off for Women held ten years earlier. An estimated ninety percent of Iceland's women had participated in the strike that year in celebration of the United Nations' "Women's Decade" and in protest of women's economic inequality.

W HEN THE BLACK WOMEN in the South African township of Port Alfred were pushed too far, they decided to fight back with a women's "stayaway strike." The first week of May 1986, had been devastating for the women of the community. First, police had terrorized their children. School students had marched down the street singing in an effort to collect money for school funds. But the police had arrived with teargas and rubber bullets, and five schoolgirls had been detained for two weeks. The violence and arrests made no sense to the residents.

The second event of the week that pushed the women to call a strike was the rape and mutilation of a fifty-nine-year-old woman. The woman was taken to the hospital with knife slashes across her thighs and stomach. She identified the rapist, and he was arrested by police. A few hours later the man was released from the police station without being charged. This was not the first time he had been arrested for rape and assault, nor was it the first time he had been let off without charges. The women were outraged.

At the next day's meeting of the Port Alfred Women's Organization (PAWO), the women decided it was time to act. They would stay away from their jobs as domestics and factory workers. They also decided to invite the local white women to contact them. Koleka Nkwinti, an activist in PAWO, explained:

> All women, whether black or white, fear rape. We felt that white women would be sympathetic. We hoped that those with husbands in the police would be able to explain to them, and help them to understand, what releasing a known rapist means to us.

The next day, several thousand black African women stayed away from work. The women in the nearby "colored" (mixed-race) township offered no support. Nor did the white women come that first day of the stayaway to learn about the black women's demands.

But the second day of the women's strike, a white female journalist arrived in the township. The black women told her about the recent terrorizing and imprisonment of their children and about the known rapist who had been dismissed without charges. They took the white woman to meet the rape survivor and showed her the woman's injuries.

Even when the evidence was presented, it seemed to the women in PAWO that the white women for whom so many of them worked were not sympathetic at all. Instead, the white women seemed to be angry. They were angry, not that the five schoolgirls were still imprisoned or that a rapist had once again gotten off, but that they were having to do their own housework.

On Saturday morning, one week after the rape, several white women met with PAWO, but they could not bring themselves to believe that things were as bad as the black African women said they were. The white women believed that the rapist had been charged and was out on bail. Again and again the black women tried to correct this misinformation, but they were not believed. They were not really surprised by the white women's attitude. Many of the local white families were people who had moved out of Zimbabwe (formerly

Rhodesia) after the revolution in fear that they would have to live under black rule. It was, the black women were well aware, a reactionary community.

Again on Monday, harried white women arrived at the black township, promising to listen. Women from PAWO took the white women on a tour of their township and tried, again, to explain the recent horrors and why they were on strike. This time the white women seemed interested in establishing some sort of ongoing contact with the women in the black township.

On Tuesday morning, however, the black women were dealt a serious blow. Four members of PAWO as well as the chairwoman of the Port Alfred Youth Congress were "detained" by the police. In addition, eight men of the black community were also detained. All of the women were released the following day except Koleka Nkwinti, who was interrogated about the stayaway. Later she told reporters:

> The police asked me who was behind the stayaway. They couldn't believe women organized it themselves. They detained the male activists because they think men are behind everything women do.

During the time that Nkwinti was in prison in Alexandria about fifty miles away from the township, the women of PAWO hired a car so that they could visit her and take her food. The Port Alfred Residents' Civic Organization, as a demonstration of support, launched a consumer boycott of several stores for as long as Nkwinti was detained.

By the time Nkwinti, the other activists, and the five schoolgirls were released, the boycott ended, and all the women had gone back to work, the community itself was changed. The women in the newly-formed PAWO were amazed that they had been able to have such an impact. They had used their one trump card, the collective withholding of their labor, to force people of all races to talk seriously about sexual assault as a *common* fear, a *common* reality. In the black township, the men stood in bold solidarity with the women, articulate in the conviction that women do not provoke rape but that the crime lies with the attacker. The women had become a force to be reckoned with.

The man accused of the rape was eventually arrested, but he left the township when his house burned to the ground. PAWO continued to grow, and the women turned their attention to building a nursery school and self-help center.

L YSISTRATA, A FICTIONAL CHARACTER in Aristophanes' bawdy play by that name, written in 411 B.C.E., was desperate to stop the war that took husbands from their beds and that shed the blood of fathers and sons. But those who make the wars were not interested in what Lysistrata thought. She was a woman. She had no voice in the decision making. There was no consequence to her opinion or to her despair. She shifted the balance of power, however, when she put her finger on one commodity that was hers, as a woman, to offer or withhold: her function as a heterosexual partner in the marriage bed.

Realizing the bargaining power of wives, Lysistrata called together the women of Greece—women from Athens, Sparta and Thebes—whose husbands were battling each other. They felt the desperation of all women who wait through wars and the frustration of women who are powerless to have any impact. But Lysistrata had a plan:

> If we should sit around, rouged and with skins well creamed, with nothing on but a transparent negligee, and come up to them with our deltas plucked quite smooth, and once our men get stiff and want to come to grips, we do not yield to them at all but just hold off, they'll make a truce in no time. There's no doubt of that.

Lysistrata's plan, in other words, was for each woman to sexually entice and arouse her husband but then refuse any lovemaking until men, as a group, agreed to end the war. The women were, in effect, on strike, withholding their bodies, their tenderness, their comfort, their sexual playfulness.

The "Lysistrata action" is a specific type of gender strike. It is a uniquely female tactic of noncooperation that involves women's withholding of heterosexual sex or childbirth for the purpose of making an impact, not on just one man, but on the larger society. Sexual abstention is an action hard to document; it is usually only mentioned briefly in passing, in footnotes and sidebars, as a curiosity. Only in fiction are we likely to find on record any extended defense of the notion or a treatise on how women imagine such a strike might work.

In the play *War Brides*, written in 1915 by socialist playwright Marion Graig Wentworth, a woman proposes a Lysistrata action to end war. The storyline centers on young Hedwig, pregnant and alone. Her beloved husband Franz has gone to war. She knows the agony of those who wait. She knows too the absurdity of war. She has become radicalized by her own despair and argues forcibly, with anyone who will listen, against the current government pressure on women to marry and bear children. Her argument is crystalized in the following dialogue with Hans Hoffman who, ready to go off to war, has proposed marriage to Hedwig's sister Amelia who stands by his side.

> *Hoffman:* We are going away—the best of us—to be shot, most likely. Don't you suppose we want to send some part of ourselves into the future, since we can't live ourselves?...
>
> *Hedwig:* [Nodding slowly.] What I said—to breed a soldier for the empire; to restock the land. [Fiercely.] And for what? For food for the

next generation's cannon. Oh, it is an insult to our womanhood! You violate all that makes marriage sacred! Are we women never to get up out of the dust? You never asked us if we wanted this war, yet you ask us to gather in the crops, cut the wood, keep the world going, drudge and slave, and wait, and agonize, lose our all, and go on bearing more men—and more—to be shot down! If we breed the men for you, why don't you let us say what is to become of them? Do we want them shot—the very breath of our life?

Hoffman: It is for the fatherland.

Hedwig: You use us, and use us—dolls, beasts of burden, and you expect us to bear it forever dumbly; but I won't! I shall cry out till I die. And now you say it almost out loud, "Go and breed for the empire." War brides! Pah!

This speech convinces the listening Amelia not to marry Hans. Suddenly, the men of the community notice that there are fewer and fewer war brides every day. They begin to suspect that Hedwig is spreading her "anti-breeding" propaganda too effectively. They understand that by discouraging these potential child-bearers, Hedwig is guilty of treason by working against the fatherland and the best interests of both church and state. They threaten to put her in jail if she doesn't stop talking.

Hedwig proposes a truce. She'll stop discouraging the war brides and even encourage more child-bearing, if the men, in turn, will promise that there will be no more war, that the sons will no longer be sent forth to murder and be murdered.

"Ridiculous!" the men respond. "There will always be war." To which Hedwig responds:

Then one day we will stop giving you men. Look at mother. Four sons torn from her in one month, and none of you ever asked her if she wanted war....You tear our husbands, our sons, from us,—you never ask us to help you find a better way,—and haven't we anything to say?

The men laugh. No, they say, war is men's business. Hedwig responds:

Who gives you the men? We women. We bear and rear and agonize. Well, if we are fit for that, we are fit to have a voice in the fate of the men we bear. If we can bring forth the men for the nation, we can sit with you in your councils and shape the destiny of the nation, and say whether it is to war or peace we give the sons we bear.

Herr Captain laughs, but in truth he is not amused. He threatens again to lock up Hedwig if she doesn't stop interfering.

Suddenly word comes that Hedwig's beloved Franz has been killed in battle. Calmly, Hedwig sits at a writing table and pens a brief message. It reads, "A Message to the Emperor: I refuse to bear my child until you promise there shall be no more war." She exits. After a moment of silence the audience hears a gunshot. The play ends with the local military officer tearing up Hedwig's message to the emperor and promising Hedwig's mother that he will hush up the suicide, saying only, "She was mad."

War Brides, like *Lysistrata*, considers women's refusal to bear children for the purpose of gaining a voice in the matters of war and peace. As we will see, there have been occasions in history when women have actually propsed such a scheme. Lysistrata actions have been proposed for another purpose as well: to deprive an oppressor-class of its slaves, a use articulated in *Rachel*, a three-act play written by Angelina Weld Grimke in 1920.

Grimke, a playwright, was an African-American descendant of the same family as the well-known white feminist abolitionists Sarah Grimke and Angelina Grimke Weld. When Sarah and Angelina's brother Henry, a widower, took as a lover his slave Nancy Weston, three sons were born. The oldest, Archibald Grimke, considered to be of African descent, eventually escaped the slaveholding white Grimkes, established a mutually beneficial relationship with the Grimke sisters in the North, graduated from Harvard Law School, and became an abolitionist leader in his own right. He practiced law in Boston, where he married Sarah Stanley. When Archibald and Sarah had a daughter, they named her Angelina, in honor of her famous aunt.

Angelina Weld Grimke became a teacher of English in Washington, D.C., and a poet, often dedicating love poems to women. A successful dramatist, her play *Rachel* was produced in March 1916 by the Drama Committee of Washington's National Association for the Advancement of Colored People (NAACP). The intent of its African-American author and producers was made clear in the program notes: "This is the first attempt to use the stage for race propaganda in order to enlighten the American people relative to the lamentable condition of ten millions of Colored citizens in this free republic."

As the curtain rises, Rachel Loving is a positive and hopeful young woman of a genteel African-American family living in the North. Her attitude begins to change when she learns the truth: that her father and brother had been lynched ten years earlier in the South.

> *Rachel:* And the little babies, the dear, little, helpless babies, being born today—now—and those who will be, tomorrow, and all the tomorrows to come—have that sooner or later to look forward to? They will laugh and play and sing and be happy and grow up, perhaps, and be ambitious—just for that?

> *Mrs. Loving:* Yes, Rachel.

> *Rachel:* Then, everywhere, everywhere, throughout the South there are hundreds of dark mothers who live in fear, terrible, suffocating fear, whose rest by night is broken and whose joy by day in their

babies on their hearts is three parts pain. Oh, I know this is true....Why, it would be more merciful to strangle the little things at birth. And so this nation—this white Christian nation—has deliberately set its curse upon the most beautiful, the most holy thing in life—motherhood! Why—it—makes—you doubt—God!

Mrs. Loving: Oh, hush! little girl. Hush!

But Rachel doesn't hush. She begins to see more clearly that racism in the United States is not confined to the overt brutality found in the South. Neither she nor her brother Tom, both educated, can get the jobs for which they are qualified. She begins to see ever more subtle cruelties of racism and how it silently kills the dreams of the children and instills in them fear and despair. One incident in particular stands out: when seven-year-old Jimmy, a child she cares for, comes to her crying that some white boys had chased him, throwing stones at him and calling him "nigger." After Rachel comforts Jimmy and sends him away with cookies, she contemplates the lynchings, stone throwings, and name-callings. From the street below her window she can hear the sounds of children's laughter. As she tries to regain her composure and arrange some rose buds in a vase, she speaks aloud:

Once I said, centuries ago, it must have been: "How can life be so terrible, when there are little children in the world?" Terrible! Terrible! That's the reason it is so terrible. (The laughter reaches her again. She listens.) And, suddenly, some day, from out of the black, the blight shall descend, and shall still forever the laughter on those little lips and in those little hearts. And the loveliest thing—almost, that ever happened to me, that beautiful voice, in my dream, those beautiful words: "Rachel you are to be the mother to little children." Why, God, you were making a mock of me; you were laughing at me. I didn't believe God could laugh at our sufferings, but He can....You God! You terrible, laughing God! Listen! I swear—and may my soul be damned to all eternity if I do break this oath—I swear that no child of mine shall ever lie upon my breast, for I will not have it rise up, in the terrible days that are to be and call me cursed. (A pause, very wistfully; questioningly) Never to know the loveliest thing in all the world—the feel of a little head, the touch of little hands, the beautiful utter dependence—of a little child? (With sudden frenzy) You can laugh, Oh God! Well, so can I. (Bursts into terrible, racking laughter)

The play ends with Rachel, nearly mad with grief, sending away the man she loves and promising her unborn children that she will protect them from the racism of her society by never giving birth to them.

Rachel and *War Brides* address two different political motivations for women's refusal to fulfill their societal obligations as sexual partners and child-bearers. There is, in fact, historical evidence that women have proposed such plans in various circumstances, though there is little data to substantiate the results of proposed Lysistrata actions.

* In 1530, when the Spanish governor of Nicaragua established a slave trade there, indigenous Nicaraguan women proclaimed a "Strike of the Uterus." They vowed to stop sleeping with their husbands in order to prevent their children from being born into slavery.

* Around 1600, women of the Iroquois Indian nation threatened to abstain from sexual interactions with men, and, consequently, to forego child-bearing until men conceded some of their decision-making powers, admitting the women who produced the warriors to the council of war.

* In 1913, in Germany, Rosa Luxemburg joined with France's Anatole France in proposing a "birth strike" in order for working class women to stem the flow of exploited laborers into the capitalist state. This proposal spurred a debate among European radicals and socialists. Luxemburg's argument was also noted by birth control advocate Margaret Sanger a year later when she published an article in her paper, *Woman Rebel*, advocating the use of contraception by the working class as a way to frighten the "capitalist class."

* In 1919, following the horrors of World War I, the French feminist, socialist, and orator Nelly Roussel was appalled by post-war pro-natalist propaganda. She called for a "strike of the wombs" to counter the climate of forced maternity.

* Also in France, in the early 1900s, the unconventional Arria Ly created havoc wherever she went by preaching "virginal feminism." Men's sexual passions kept women in a constant state of subjection, claimed Ly, who advocated that women wage a permanent strike against the marriage bed. Marriage itself was an act of "shameful compromise" argued Ly, who lived with her mother, dressed in men's clothes, and cut her hair short.

* In the early 1920s, women in the Bryansk province of the Soviet Union went on a sex strike to protest battery and physical abuse by their husbands.

* In the 1940s, Chinese Communist women, active in local politics, often had to fight for the right to vote in the elections. In one village where the women had been denied suffrage, the Women's Association urged women not to sleep with their husbands. As a consequence, a second election was called, and the women were allowed to vote. They elected a woman as deputy village head.

* In September 1977, Italian feminists circulated a "Lysistrata Petition," and promoted it at an international feminist march from Rome to Seveso. Seveso was chosen as the rallying point because it was the town where the release of a poisonous chemical had resulted in miscarriages and the births of many babies with stunted limbs. The Lysistrata petition indicted the global systems of "patriarchal, phallocratic power,

whether capitalist, socialist or other" for "running the world on death."
It condemned the men's "little chess games in which some billions of
human beings are pawns." It warned,

> We will refuse from this day on to give life that you will slaughter.
> We won't raise children so that you can teach them to kill and die.
> The land we live on belongs to us, the air we breathe belongs to us;
> we will not concede any more rights to you until you respect them.
> We don't know what to do anymore with the killing mania that
> characterizes you and which you have imposed on us for the last
> 5,000 years...From this day on we will begin to spread among women
> the idea of a STRIKE AGAINST CHILDBIRTH and, if necessary, a
> STRIKE AGAINST SEXUAL RELATIONS WITH MEN until our
> demands are realized.

* On Mother's Day, 1979, in Lower Saxony, West Germany, over one
thousand women joined in a nationwide antinuclear campaign,
pledging not to bear any more children "as long as the ruling powers
are not ready to give up nuclear weapons and nuclear power plants."
The pledge statement proclaimed, "No future without children, no
children without a future." To dramatize the action, the Lower Saxony
women called for an Easter Sunday pilgrimage of mothers and
children to the town of Gorleben, where the West German government
had consented to allow a nuclear waste disposal area. There, the
women planted Easter Lily bulbs to be enjoyed year after year—a
symbol of hope and resurrection, of new life in barren soil and barren
times. Ilona Wagner, a spokesperson for the campaign organizers, told
reporters, "We are doing this because we are *for* children."

* In October 1981, Sicilian women reacted to the proposed positioning
of cruise missiles in the town of Comiso. They issued a statement in
which they pointed out the connections between war and rape and
called for the end of the exploitation of one nation over another, of one
class over another, and of one sex over another. It was no coincidence,
they said, that "the gruesome game of war" mirrors the stages of a
traditional sexual relationship: aggression, conquest, possession, control.
"Of a woman or a land," they said, "it makes little difference." In their
statement, they denounced the myth of the "angel of the home," a myth
that keeps women looking after husbands and raising children for the
sake of the nation. Confronted with the missiles, they said, women
could no longer be patient, sweet, or resigned. The Sicilian feminists
called for unilateral disarmament immediately, "because we firmly
believe in the utopia of common sense." Finally, they issued their
ultimatum:

> We have to shake off the habit of accepting war; it is the first step
> towards avoiding certain death. War is neither natural nor
> unavoidable. Otherwise, what is the sense of giving birth, that

experience which for many of us is our only creative outlet and source of identity? Faced with such unnatural options, why should we continue to believe in the "natural" meaning of motherhood? Our answer to nuclear death, paradoxical as it may seem, could be a conscious refusal to give life....

Let military budgets be invested instead in a better quality of life. This is the message of women. If it is not heeded—we stop MOTHERHOOD!

* In 1985, at the prestigious St. Stephens College in New Delhi, India, women students vowed to avoid "any and all relations" with men until the end of the semester. They were protesting six years of harassment by male students. "We are at war with this woman-abusing culture," one woman was quoted in a news article. The incident that precipitated the Lysistrata action was a panty raid in which male students had invaded the privacy of the women's dorm rooms, stolen hundreds of pairs of underpants, and hung them from a large cross on campus. While the men considered it a prank, the women believed it was more serious than that. "The panty raid was not an isolated incident, but a link in a chain of practices that has relegated women to second-class status," said one woman.

* In December 1986, women in Finland circulated a Lysistrata petition. Proclaiming "No Natal for No Nukes!" they collected four thousand signatures. The women who signed the petition promised not to bear children until the government of Finland changed its pro-nuclear policies.

Gender-class strikes, by their very nature, force us to look at our most taken-for-granted, everyday behaviors as if they were in graphic relief. The most common tasks and the most intimate gestures become larger than life, and the gender bias of our actions is revealed. And, underlying each call for a gender strike or each threat of one, is the bewildering realization that, as Barbara Deming pondered, if enough women ever *really* went on strike and refused their assigned roles, "everything, everything would have to change!"

SOURCES

The Strike of a Sex

Miller, George Noyes. *The Strike of a Sex.* New York: G. W. Dillingham, 1890.

McAllister, Pam. "Women in the Lead: Waisbrooker's Way to Peace." In *A Sex Revolution.* Lois Waisbrooker, auth. Philadelphia: New Society Publishers, 1985.

Women Strike for Peace

Brozan, Nadine. "Women's Group Began as One Day Protest 4,215 Days Ago." *The New York Times*. May 16, 1973.

Gage-Colby, Ruth. "Women Strike for Peace." *New World Review* (June, 1963).

Hunter, Marjorie. "Women's Peace Campaign Gains Support." *The New York Times*. November 22, 1961.

McGrory, Mary. "A 'Hue and Cry' Is Raised." *Washington Star*. October 26, 1961.

Raymond, John. "300 March on City Hall, Urge End to Atom Race." *Berkeley Daily Gazette*. November 1, 1961.

Shuster, Alvin. "Close-up of a 'Peace Striker'." *The New York Times Magazine*. May 6, 1962.

Swerdlow, Amy. "WSP's Long March." *Journal of Women Strike for Peace*. 1979.

Tucker, Sheila. "Sisters United Against Militarism." *Hagborn: A Radical Feminist Newsjournal* (Spring 1981).

"2,500 Women Storm the Pentagon to Protest War." *The New York Times*. February 16, 1967.

"2,000 L.A. Women Join March to Keep Peace." *Los Angeles Mirror*. November 1, 1961.

Waite, Elmont. "200 S.F. Women In City Hall Plea." *San Francisco Chronicle*. November 2, 1961.

"Women Quiz 2 Senators During 'Peace Strike' Here." *Philadelphia Evening Bulletin*. November 2, 1961.

Wyatt, Sophia. "One Day Strike for Peace." *Manchester Guardian*. April 12, 1962.

Women's Strike for Equality and the Netherlands Strike

Charlton, Linda. "Women Seeking Equality March on 5th Ave. Today." *The New York Times*. August 26, 1970.

Cohen, Marcia. *The Sisterhood: The Inside Story of the Women's Movement and the Leaders Who Made It Happen*. New York: Fawcett Columbine, 1988.

Fosburgh, Lacey. "Traditional Groups Prefer to Ignore Women's Lib." *The New York Times*. August 26, 1970.

"General Strike by U.S. Women Urged in August." *Women: A Journal of Liberation* (Summer 1970).

Johnson, Haynes. "'Equal Rights Now,' Exhort Women Protesters." *The Washington Post*. August 27, 1970.

Kalter, Eleanor and John Murphy. "Gals Liberate 5th to Cheers, Jeers." *New York Daily News*. August 27, 1970.

Levine, Suzanne and Harriet Lyons, editors. *The Decade of Women: A Ms. History of the Seventies in Words and Pictures.* New York: G.P. Putnam's Sons, 1980.

"Leading Feminist Puts Hairdo Before Strike." *The New York Times.* August 27, 1970.

Levy, Claudia. "Women Rally to Publicize Grievances." *The Washington Post.* August 27, 1970.

Lichtenstein, Grace. "For Most Women, 'Strike' Day Was Just a Topic of Conversation." *The New York Times.* August 27, 1970.

"Lobby Campaign Begun in Capital." *The New York Times.* August 27, 1970.

Meyer, Karl E. "Women's Lib Asks Boycott of 4 Products." *The Washington Post.* August 26, 1970.

Modzelewski, Joseph. "Ex-Suffragette Votes No." *New York Daily News.* August 27, 1970.

Morgan, Robin, ed. *Sisterhood Is Global: The International Women's Movement Anthology.* Garden City, NY: Anchor Press/Doubleday, 1984.

"Women March Down Fifth Avenue to a Rally in Bryant Park in Drive for Equality." *The New York Times.* August 27, 1970.

Market Day for Men and Time Off for Women

Ouedaogo, Josephine. "The Feminist Venture in Burkina Faso." *Isis: Women's International Cross-Cultural Exchange,* no. 16 (Dec. 1987).

"Time Off for Women!" *Peace News.* (Sep. 1987).

Iceland and South Africa

Forrest, Kally and Karen Jochelson. "South Africa: Uniting Against Rape." *off our backs* (Mar. 1988).

"Iceland: Strike." *off our backs* (Dec. 1985).

Messing, Suzanne and Pat De La Fuente. "Strike Shows Strength." *New Directions for Women* (Jan./Feb. 1986).

Lysistrata actions

"Against Nuclearisation and Beyond: Statement of Sicilian Women." In *Reclaim the Earth: Women Speak Out for Life on Earth.* Leonie Caldecott and Stephanie Leland, eds. London: The Women's Press Limited, 1983.

Aristophanes. *Lysistrata.* Donald Sutherland, trans. San Francisco: Chandler Publishing, 1961.

"Birth Strike: No More Kids." *New Women's Times* (Nov. 23-Dec. 6, 1979).

"Birth Strike Protests Nukes." *off our backs.* (Jan. 1980).

Davis, Angela Y. *Women, Race & Class.* New York: Random House, 1981.

"Doing It For Ourselves." WBAI Radio Broadcast. Dec. 8, 1986.

Grimke, Angelina Weld. *Rachel: A Play in Three Acts.* Boston: The Cornhill Company, 1920.

Hause, Steven and Anne Kenney. *Women's Suffrage and Social Politics in the French Third Republic.* Princeton, NJ: Princeton University Press, 1984.

Kennedy, David M. *Birth Control in America: The Career of Margaret Sanger.* New Haven, CT: Yale University Press, 1970/1976.

Lerner, Gerda. *The Grimke Sisters from South Carolina: Pioneers for Woman's Rights and Abolition.* New York: Schocken Books, 1971.

"Lysistrata Petition." *My Country is the Whole World: An Anthology of Women's Work on Peace and War.* Cambridge Women's Peace Collective. London: Pandora Press, 1984.

Miller, Jeanne-Marie. "Black Women Playwrights from Grimke to Shange: Selected Synopses of Their Works." In *All the Women Are White, All the Blacks Are Men, But Some of Us Are Brave: Black Women's Studies.* Gloria Hull, Patricia Bell Scott and Barbara Smith, eds. Old Westbury, NY: Feminist Press, 1982.

Marks, Elaine and Isabelle de Courtivron. *New French Feminisms: An Anthology.* Amherst, MA: University of Massachusetts Press, 1980.

Morgan, Robin, ed. *Sisterhood Is Global: The International Women's Movement Anthology.* Garden City, NY: Anchor Press/Doubleday, 1984.

Sharp, Gene. *The Politics of Nonviolent Action: Part Two—The Methods of Nonviolent Action.* Boston: Porter Sargent Publishers, 1973.

Weekly World News. (Unsigned, untitled news item about India.) May, 7, 1985.

Wentworth, Marion Graig. *War Brides: A Play In One Act.* New York: Century Company, 1915.

Wilkerson, Margaret B., ed. Introduction to *9 Plays by Black Women.* New York: New American Library, 1986.

Women's Encampment for a Future of Peace & Justice. *Resource Handbook.* New York: Seneca Army Depot, 1983.

4

A Tale Of Two Days

Mother's Day

> Why do not the mothers of mankind interfere in these matters,
> to prevent the waste of that human life of which they alone bear
> and know the cost?
>
> —Julia Ward Howe, 1870

MOST HISTORIES OF MOTHER'S DAY credit Philadelphia's devoted daughter Anna Jarvis for its conception. In 1907, she proposed that the second Sunday of May be set aside to honor mothers, reasoning that, "The common possession of the living world is a mother. Everyone has—or has had—a mother." On that day, a red carnation was to be worn if one's mother was alive or a white one if she had died. Though she probably didn't know it, Jarvis was actually reviving a centuries-old holiday known as "Mothering Sunday" which was celebrated on the fourth Sunday in Lent throughout rural Europe. In 1914, Jarvis's one-woman campaign of letter-writing to governors and legislators paid off: President Woodrow Wilson signed a resolution recommending the official observance of Mother's Day. The following year, he proclaimed a national Mother's Day, that has since benefited greeting card companies, chocolate manufacturers, and florists. To her credit, Jarvis detested the commercialization of the day and even threatened, in 1923, to bring a lawsuit to stop a New York City Mother's Day celebration she thought too profit-oriented. It is this commercialized day that is widely celebrated around the world today.

There was, however, another Mother's Day, an earlier celebration based on an entirely different premise. This day was the brainchild of Julia Ward Howe, who lived rather unhappily in the shadow of her famous abolitionist-reformer husband, Samuel Gridley Howe. In February, 1862, the *Atlantic Monthly* published her poem "Battle Hymn of the Republic," which, when set to a popular folk tune, became the semi-official battle song of the Union army during the Civil War and made Howe famous overnight. After the Civil War, Howe became increasingly involved in the women's suffrage movement.

In 1870, her life took a new turn. She was, that year, overcome by grief because of the outbreak of the Franco-Prussian war. In her reminiscences she wrote:

> As I was revolving these matters in my mind, while the war was still in progress, I was visited by a sudden feeling of the cruel and unnecessary character of the contest. It seemed to me a return to barbarism, the issue having been one which might easily have been settled without bloodshed. The question forced itself upon me, "Why do not the mothers of mankind interfere in these matters, to prevent the waste of that human life of which they alone bear and know the cost?" I had never thought of this before. The august dignity of motherhood and its terrible responsibilities now appeared to me in a new aspect, and I could think of no better way of expressing my sense of these than that of sending forth an appeal to womanhood throughout the world, which I then and there composed.

Sitting at her desk in September 1870, Julia Ward Howe once again picked up her pen, as she had so often in the past, but this time she wrote for an audience she had never before addressed: the women of the western world (specifically, at first, Christian women, though she would later modify her call to address women of all religions). Because it has been lost to us these many years, it is included here in its entirety:

AN APPEAL TO WOMANHOOD THROUGHOUT THE WORLD

Again, in the sight of the Christian world, have the skill and power of two great nations exhausted themselves in mutual murder. Again have the sacred questions of international justice been committed to the fatal mediation of military weapons. In this day of progress, in this century of light, the ambition of rulers has been allowed to barter the dear interests of domestic life for the bloody exchanges of the battlefield. Thus men have done. Thus men will do. But women need no longer be made a party to proceedings which fill the globe with grief and horror. Despite the assumptions of physical force, the mother has a sacred and commanding word to say to the sons who owe their life to her suffering. That word should now be heard, and answered to as never before.

Arise, then, Christian women of this day! Arise, all women who have hearts, whether your baptism be that of water or of tears! Say firmly: "We will not have great questions decided by irrelevant agencies. Our husbands shall not come to us, reeking with carnage, for caresses and applause. Our sons shall not be taken from us to unlearn all that we have been able to teach them of charity, mercy and patience. We, women of one country, will be too tender of those of another country, to allow our sons to be trained to injure theirs." From the bosom of the devastated earth a voice goes up with our own. It says: "Disarm, disarm! The sword of murder is not the balance of justice." Blood does not wipe out dishonor, nor violence indicate possession. As men have often forsaken the plough and the anvil at the summons of war, let women now leave all that may be left of home for a great and earnest day of counsel.

Let them meet first, as women, to bewail and commemorate the dead. Let them then solemnly take counsel with each other as to the means whereby the great human family can live in peace, man as the brother of man, each bearing after his own kind the sacred impress, not of Caesar, but of God.

In the name of womanhood and of humanity, I earnestly ask that a general congress of women, without limit of nationality, may be appointed and held at some place deemed most convenient, and at the earliest period, consistent with its objects, to promote the alliance of the different nationalities, the amicable settlement of international questions, the great and general interests of peace.

Howe had the Appeal translated into French, Spanish, Italian, German, and Swedish and arranged meetings and speaking engagements to promote her idea of a women's global peace gathering. In a letter to the American Peace Society, she boldly claimed, "The issue is one which will unite virtually the whole sex."

In December 1870, a planning meeting took place in New York City for the proposed "World's Congress of Women in Behalf of International Peace." At the meeting, a number of important activists, including Lucretia Mott, John Stuart Mill, and Harriet Beecher Stowe, lent their support in the form of addresses and letters. In her opening statement, Howe voiced her frustration with the role into which women were socialized.

Patience and passivity are sometimes in place for women—not always. I think of this when I go to women, intelligent and charming, who warn me off with white hands, unaccustomed to any graver labor than that of gesticulation. "Don't ask me to work," they say; "I cannot do it. God always raises up a set of people to do these things, like the Anti-Slavery people, and they set to work to do them." And then I want to say to these friends: "God can raise you up too, and I hope He will...." If women did not waste life in frivolity, men would not waste it in murder.

It was her hope, she said, that her call and cry to women to engage in the work of world peace would "pierce through dirt and rags...through velvet and cashmere."

Sadly, her call would pierce through very little, let alone both rags and cashmere. Nevertheless, the next two years were years of hard work and organizing. In 1871, she became the first president of the American branch of the Woman's International Peace Association, organized in Boston that spring. On May 26 of that year she wrote enthusiastically in her diary:

> I am fifty-two years old this day and must regard this year as in some sense the best of my life. The great joy of the Peace Idea has unfolded itself to me...I have got at better methods of working in the practical matters at which I do work, and believe more than ever in patience, labor, and sticking to one's own idea of work. Study, book-work, and solitary thinking and writing show us only one side of what we study. Practical life and intercourse with others supply the other side. If I may sit at work on this day next year, I hope that my peace matter will have assumed a practical and useful form, and that I may have worked out my conception worthily.

A year later, in the spring of 1872, Howe went to England to arrange for a Woman's Peace Congress in London. She addressed audiences in Birmingham, Manchester, Leeds, London, Bristol, Liverpool, Cambridge, and Carlisle, but she frequently encountered resistance. The English Peace Society denied her a platform on the grounds that women had never before been permitted to speak at their meetings. Undeterred, Howe rented the drawing room at Freemason's Tavern for a series of Sunday afternoon meetings, where she spoke and led discussions for several weeks.

Howe also traveled to Paris to attend a peace congress as an American delegate. Upon arriving, however, she was told that, being a woman, she would have to make her address only to the officers of the society after the public meeting had been adjourned. Howe played by the rules. She later wrote, "I accordingly met a dozen or more of these gentlemen in a side room, where I simply spoke of my endeavors to enlist the sympathies and efforts of women in behalf of the world's peace."

Returning to London, she attended a women's peace meeting in St. George's Hall, an occasion she had worked hard to organize but which, though attendance was good, was nevertheless a great disappointment to her. She later said of that day:

> The ladies who spoke in public in those days mostly confined their labors to the advocacy of women's suffrage and were not much interested in my scheme of a world-wide protest of women against the cruelties of war.

She returned to the United States exhausted by her efforts. In her diary she wrote:

> I am here at my table with books and papers, but feel very languid. My arms feel as if there were no marrow in their bones. I suppose this is reaction after so much work, but unless I can get up strength somehow I shall not accomplish anything. Weakness in all my limbs.

Her call for a women's peace conference had been met with very little enthusiasm, but she was not ready to let the matter rest. Abandoning the idea of a conference, Howe began instead to promote a festival which would be called "Mother's Day." June 2 of every year would be set aside for women's advocacy of peace.

The first Mother's Day was held on Monday, June 2, 1873 in over eighteen cities and towns. In Boston, Howe attended the celebration in Mechanic Hall, which was decorated with wreaths, baskets of flowers, and a white dove of peace flying above the festivities.

An account of the day appeared in the next day's Boston *Daily Globe* beneath the headline "Universal Peace: A Woman's Festival Held in This City." According to the article, the women who celebrated the first Mother's Day prayed, read scripture, sang and listened attentively to Howe's report of the sympathy and encouragement she had received from people around the world for the initiation of Mother's Day. The meeting adjourned for the afternoon and reconvened at seven-thirty p.m. for an evening program. Again, Howe spoke and read from letters from women around the world.

> Mrs. Howe then read an essay in relation to the subject before the convention. It spoke of how illogical is the reasoning which leads to war whose aim it is to see how many lives, precious and invaluable to mankind, it can destroy. Women appreciate peace, for they know too well the pains of maternity to encourage that which destroys what they produce.

Rev. Tilden spoke next in support of women's peace work, calling on women of all classes to work toward the success of the movement and offering the New South Free Church for regular, monthly meetings of the Boston women. He promised that "God and his holy angels" were surely with the women. The renowned abolitionist William Lloyd Garrison also spoke that evening, sharing his belief that all the world was his country and all the world's people his countrymen. He looked forward to the day when the dove of peace would replace the eagle. After the speeches and several violin solos, a series of resolutions was presented and approved, endorsing other such festivals in the future. The celebration ended with hymns led by singers from the Home for Little Wanderers.

Though she couldn't know it then, that day's festival may well have been the highlight of Howe's Mother's Day efforts. Later, in her room, she confided to her diary that she had begun to doubt her effectiveness as an organizer and wondered if she should have stayed with her writing career:

> Oh joy! joy! I have been sometimes of late wondering whether I have done well to forsake the paths of literary distinction. I am answered now.

For a few years, Mother's Day was celebrated as a women's peace advocacy day in Boston, New York, Edinburgh, London, Geneva, and, according to one report, at least once in Constantinople. It was also celebrated in Philadelphia where, in 1876, it was the occasion for an international peace meeting with delegates from France, Italy, and Germany. When the meeting conveners suddenly realized that none of the foreign delegates spoke English, Howe came to the rescue, standing beside the delegates and translating each speech "to the delight of the delegates and the admiration of all."

Despite the initial enthusiasm in activist circles, the idea of a women's annual peace-focused celebration never took hold in the general population. Howe's Mother's Day faded into obscurity, replaced by Anna Jarvis's holiday. The U.S. was not the only country to spawn a highly commercialized and sentimentalized Mother's Day. In Germany, in 1922, Dr. Rudolf Knauer began to promote the idea of Mother's Day as a project of the Association of German Florists. The business underpinnings were purposely camouflaged by nationalistic rhetoric honoring "family" women. It was mothers, the advertisements claimed, who cultivated "the true spirit of joy in work, responsibility and selfless devotion to the fatherland." The florists linked arms with anti-abortion and pro-family groups, and soon the churches, schools, and clubs became vehicles for promoting motherhood as a service to the nation. By 1933, as Hitler rose to power, the florists' association was incorporated into a Nazi organization, and Mother's Day propaganda promoted the women's duty toward "racial origins." Aryan mothers became the Mothers of the Nation. Few had the courage to protest the propaganda, but one newspaper, *Forward*, published a poem in 1931, during the height of the global depression, and challenged the blithe celebration of mothers. It read in part:

> Mother's Day? A salvation you said?
> When we haven't got diapers,
> Not to mention a bed?
> Neither mother nor child can celebrate
> When motherhood is a helpless fate.
> Mothers are deserted, left high and dry
> While society shuts its purse and its eye,
> And pregnant women must be afraid
> Because there's no financial aid.

So, once a year, we're honored right,
Once a year, we're a moving sight,
And otherwise it's pretty sad,
We're forgotten because it's just an ad.
People make a wonderful fuss
And then collect high profits from us.
They set up a day when mothers' value is high
And then buy and buy and buy and buy!

Around the world, Mother's Day celebrations have primarily been used by family members to honor their mothers and by church and state to honor the notion of motherhood. But in the late twentieth century, small pockets of feminists reclaimed the day as a day for women's resistance, social action, protest, and organizing.

In 1980, women in Peru chose Mother's Day as a day to protest against all the forces that keep women powerless. In Lima and other towns and cities across Peru, women organized Mother's Day protest actions, where they spoke out on the need for health care and child care, freedom from government repression, and freedom from violent spouses.

Again in Lima, in 1984, women who had formed an ongoing study group called "Telitha Cumi" (Woman, Arise), specifically to discuss issues of faith and feminism, wrote and published an essay entitled "Reflections on Mother's Day." In it they extended Mother's Day greetings to their sisters throughout Peru and noted that it was sad that the women who are given flowers, poems, and gifts on this day endure all the other days of the year in self-denial and sacrifice, working against hunger and unemployment. The women of Telitha Cumi presented a number of their concerns in an open letter to the biblical heroine Judith.

Dear Judith:

You have been in heaven a long time now. You should be in good company, right?—with Abraham, Moses, Isaiah, Peter and Paul, Saint Augustine, Thomas Aquinas—in short, with all of the great men of faith. But we suspect that you may have a little corner there where you can talk with your compañeras, with Sarah and Miriam, Rebecca, Rachel, Deborah, Esther, Naomi, Ruth, Mary, Mary Magdalene, Joan of Arc, Teresa of Avila, Catherine of Siena and all the other women who have played key roles in the liberation of their people, women who, because they were not deemed important by men, are missing from the pages of Sacred Scripture and from the Church's list of the saints. Perhaps you've even started a mother's club or a feminist organization up there....

When you all gather together, what do you say about us, your compañeras here on earth? Hopefully, you see valiant women like yourselves, because they do exist; yes, indeed they do: women, liberators of their people, like our heroic sisters of Nicaragua; Salvadoran women; and women in Guatemala who wage battle against the modern-day Pharaoh in order to save their people from slavery. Then there are the mothers from Chile and Uruguay, the Madres de la Plaza de Mayo....

From there, do you see the great numbers of nameless but courageous women who struggle day after day to feed their families, to earn enough to put a bit of bread on the table?...Do you see the women who gather wood and sweet potatoes with their babies on their backs, laden down, as well, with the sorrows of the eternal oppression of the poor? Do you see these sisters and weep for them?

And what do you think of this special day the world has set aside for honoring its mothers, celebrating their wombs, their breasts, those hands that change diapers, the legs that run here and there looking for medicines, school books...whole bodies that, according to what they tell us, should be spent, drop by drop, cell by cell, in fulfillment of the exalted vocation of motherhood....

It would be marvelous if this distorted celebration of Mother's Day could become an occasion for honoring the courageous women of the past, the present, and those who are still to be born. For example, we could designate the day to commemorate all of you, our foremothers, reflecting on your faith, your fidelity to God's call, your total involvement in the liberation process of your people....

Listen to us, dear sisters. Help us, your descendants, to break the chains of oppression that enslave us and rob us of our identity. From here below, we continue to push forward, in spite of everything, with the subversive hope that the world can be different. We know that liberation takes place again and again through the hands of a humble woman, of millions of humble women on the march, who propose from the depths of their being to be the saviors of our people.

Like their European and South American sisters, feminists in the United States also began to reclaim the holiday as a time to demand something more substantial than sentimentalized greeting cards or chocolate candy. In 1978, lesbians in Seattle called on women throughout the country to hold special Mother's Day demonstrations to call attention to the custody battles being fought by lesbian mothers and to protest the blatantly anti-lesbian prejudice of the courts. They hoped the demonstrations could be used to link the oppression faced by lesbian mothers with other infringements on women's control over their own lives, such as the forced sterilization of Native American and Puerto Rican women and legislative restrictions on abortion.

Also in the Seattle area that year, a group calling itself the Mother's Day Brigade used Super Glue to seal shut the doors of a movie theater because it ran films the group considered anti-woman. The Brigade left behind a note which read, "STOP VIOLENCE AGAINST WOMEN. HAPPY MOTHER'S DAY."

In 1981, over seven hundred women in Washington, D.C., marched through the rain to Lafayette Park, across from the White House, for a peace rally, where they protested the Reagan administration's increased military budget. Beulah Sanders, former chairperson of the National Welfare Rights Organization, was one of the speakers that day. She wished Nancy Reagan a happy Mother's Day but then noted the extreme differences in the First Lady's life from the lives of most women in the United States. "Nancy doesn't have to worry about a decent house, heat, or hot water," Sanders told the cheering crowd. "She doesn't have to worry about a job or food. But here on Mother's Day, a lot of us are sad because we don't have it."

The Mother's Day Coalition for Nuclear Disarmament, that sponsored the protest, distributed a brochure about the escalating arms race and asked, "Is this the last Mother's Day?" Throughout the day, Coalition members also repeated a suggestion made by Dr. Helen Caldicott, an Australian doctor famous for her antinuclear work, that women should change their babies' diapers on congressmen's desks until the lawmakers listen to what women are saying.

In 1987, Clergy and Laity Concerned (CALC), a national, interfaith peace and justice organization, called for a Day of Mourning on Mother's Day that year, in response to the United States-sponsored war against Nicaragua. Only a week earlier, Benjamin Linder, a young North American peace activist, had been killed in Nicaragua by United States-backed contras. Sister Barbara Lupo, CALC Coordinator, said,

> In keeping with the original spirit of Mother's Day, we honor the mothers of Nicaraguans killed by the contras; we honor the mothers of North Americans working in Nicaragua; and we call for an immediate and permanent cutoff of contra aid, both covert and overt. We mourn the death of Benjamin Linder. We mourn, also, for the thousands of Nicaraguans who have died as a result of the U.S.-sponsored contra war.

Also that year on Mother's Day, over three thousand people, three-quarters of them women, gathered at the Nevada Test Site, north of Las Vegas, for a day of protest and nonviolent civil disobedience, calling for a comprehensive nuclear test-ban treaty between the United States and the Soviet Union. Seven hundred and forty protesters were arrested for trespassing on the site, where test bombs are regularly detonated once every two to three weeks. The demonstration, organized by women from groups across the United States, was colorful and lively. One group had created and brought a huge, pink butterfly that they carried on four tall poles as they climbed over the fence in a civil disobedience action. Protest organizer Susan Constantine told reporters, "We had this beautiful butterfly wandering across the desert until [the women] were arrested."

International Women's Day

International Women's Day is a contribution of the American workers to the world labor movement.
—Mother Ella Reeve Bloor
Labor organizer

UNLIKE MOTHER'S DAY, International Women's Day has retained much of the political focus and vitality that marked its inception over eighty years ago. Grounded in the merger of women's liberation and socialism, there is nothing frivolous or whimsical about the day. The only thing fanciful about International Women's Day is the current mythology in feminist and labor communities about its origins. According to the legend, the celebration was founded to commemorate a March 8 demonstration in 1857, when women garment workers on New York City's Lower East Side took to the streets to protest their deplorable working conditions. In fact, there is no record of such a protest on that date. Quebec historian Renée Côtè believes there was a women's protest in New York on or near March 8, 1837, and wonders if the confusion is due to a mere typographical error. Another feminist historian, Temma Kaplan, believes that the legend originated in France. She writes, "In a curious development, an apocryphal story surfaced in French Communist circles in the 1950s. Allegedly, a brutally repressed New York strike of female textile workers on March 8, 1857, had led to a rally in commemoration of its fiftieth anniversary in 1907. Neither event seems to have taken place."

What we do know is that the official holiday had its modest beginnings in 1908. That year in the United States, the Socialist Party appointed a Women's National Committee to Campaign for the Suffrage. After meeting, this Committee recommended that the Socialist Party set aside a day every year to campaign for women's right to vote, a big step for socialists and one welcomed by women working for suffrage.

Socialists in the United States were not as rare in the early 1900s as they are today. In 1912, Eugene Debs, the leader of the Socialist Party, received 900,000 votes when he ran for president. "The issue is Socialism versus Capitalism," he said. "I am for Socialism because I am for humanity. We have been cursed with the reign of gold long enough. Money constitutes no proper basis of civilization. The time has come to regenerate society—we are on the eve of a universal change." His dream was powerfully articulated. By 1914, Oklahoma had twelve thousand dues-paying members of socialist organizations and had elected six socialists to the Oklahoma state legislature. In Texas, Louisiana, Arkansas, and Oklahoma, there were fifty-five weekly socialist newspapers. Such famous persons as Helen Keller and Jack London were not afraid to be identified as socialists. Before the United States government linked forces with corporate interests to erase socialism from the political spectrum, thousands of hardworking farmers, factory laborers, miners, railroad workers, office workers, immigrants, intellectuals, and progressives joined the socialist movement.

On the issue of women's suffrage, however, socialists in the United States and Europe were still dragging their feet. They feared that women, if given the vote, would use it to endorse politically conservative views. Nevertheless, when women's suffrage seemed inevitable, and pressure mounted to endorse women's rights, socialist parties began to respond affirmatively. On March 8, 1908, Branch No. 3 of the New York City Social Democratic Women's Society sponsored a mass meeting on women's rights. This was just the beginning.

In 1909, American socialists agreed to designate the last Sunday in February as "National Woman's Day," and that year socialist women throughout the United States held mass meetings. In New York City, two thousand people gathered at the Murray Hill Lyceum to hear orators like garment worker and union organizer Leonora O'Reilly and others call for equal rights for women. Metta Stern made an impassioned speech proclaiming that, "Every Socialist is in favor of woman's suffrage...because Socialism stands for true democracy, and true democracy is impossible without equal rights." In Brooklyn, a rousing mass sing was reported that day at the Labor Lyceum meeting. The congregation of Parkside Church was addressed by writer and lecturer Charlotte Perkins Gilman, who said in her speech, "It is true that a woman's duty is centered in her home," but, she clarified, "home should mean the whole country and not be confined to three or four rooms or a city or a state."

Inspired by the dramatic uprising of the twenty thousand shirtwaist workers, socialists in the United States celebrated National Woman's Day 1910 again on the last Sunday in February. In New York City, a crowd gathered inside Carnegie Hall to sing the rousing "Marseillaise" and to listen to speeches by Rose Schneiderman, Charlotte Perkins Gilman, and Metta Stern. The February 27 issue of the *New York Call*, a socialist newspaper, included a special section for women in its Sunday magazine. In that issue, Lena Morrow Lewis wrote:

> Woman's Day...is not a day in which we celebrate anything....The battle for economic and political freedom is yet to be fought out.

> Woman's Day in the socialist movement is, therefore...in every essential, AN ANTICIPATION DAY.

In a prophetic greeting to American women, German socialist August Bebel wrote, "I wish your national Woman's Day may attain international importance."

Apparently American women agreed with Bebel because in May 1910, at the national Congress of the Socialist Party, the Women's National Commission recommended "that our delegates to the International Congress be instructed to propose the last Sunday in February as an International Women's Day." Other women were thinking the same thing. In Copenhagen, at the Conference of Socialist Women that August, Luise Zietz proposed internationalizing the American Woman's Day. The dynamic German socialist leader and fighter for women's rights, Clara Zetkin, generally given credit for making the motion, seconded the proposal, and it passed unanimously among the women as it did a few days later in the general International Socialist Congress. And so International Women's Day was born. According to an account by Russian delegate Alexandra Kollontai, the slogan of the new International Women's Day was, "The vote for women will unite our strength in the struggle for socialism."

The day had been named, a slogan had been chosen, but a date was never specified. Consequently, until 1917, International Women's Day was celebrated on different days throughout the world. In the United States, International Women's Day continued to be celebrated in February.

In Boston, in 1911, socialist women joined suffrage activists (all dressed in white in the style set by British suffragettes) in an outdoor rally and meeting, while in New York's Carnegie Hall, Bertha Fraser gave an antiwar speech in which she claimed that women would use the ballot "to make war impossible." In March of that year, over three hundred International Women's Day celebrations and demonstrations were held throughout Europe.

In 1915, with the outbreak of World War I, Clara Zetkin called on socialist women from neutral as well as warring nations to use the day to protest against the war. In March, women met in Berne, Switzerland to participate in an antiwar demonstration. In September of that year, many of these women met again to draft a manifesto urging women to work for peace and proclaiming, "Workers have nothing to gain from the war. They have everything to lose, everything that is dear to them."

In 1917, International Women's Day became a day of protest against the shortages of food resulting from the war. In Turin, Italy, women hung placards in working class neighborhoods:

> Hasn't there been enough torment from this war? Now the food necessary for our children has begun to disappear. It is time for us to

act in the name of suffering humanity. Our cry is "Down with arms!"
We are part of the same family. We want peace. We must show that
women can protect those who depend on them.

But the International Women's Day protest that changed the world
occurred that year in Russia. The women had planned a day (March 8
by Western reckoning, February 23 on the Gregorian calendar) of
speech-making, leafletting, and general protest, but the spirit of the day
carried them beyond these simple plans. Coming on the rise of long
struggle and many strikes, International Women's Day inspired
thousands of women to leave their homes and factories to protest the
terrible shortages of food, the high prices, the war, and the increased
suffering they had so bitterly endured. In ten years, rent had more than
doubled; the cost of rye bread had risen from three kopeks to eighteen;
and the price of soap had risen two hundred and forty-five percent.
That day the women went on strike. Trotsky wrote in *The History of the
Russian Revolution*:

> A mass of women, not all of them workers, flocked to the municipal
> *duma* demanding bread. It was like demanding milk from a he-goat.
> Red banners appeared in different parts of the city, and inscriptions
> of them showed that the workers wanted bread, but neither autocracy
> nor war. Thus, the fact is, that the February revolution was begun
> from below, overcoming the resistance of its own revolutionary
> organizations, the initiative being taken of their own accord by the
> most oppressed and down trodden part of the proletariat, the women
> textile workers, among them no doubt many soldiers' wives.

The women had inadvertently inspired the last push of a revolution.
A general strike spread through Petrograd, and, within a week, Czar
Nicholas II was forced to abdicate.

After 1917, and in honor of women's role in the Russian Revolution,
International Women's Day secured its place on March 8 on socialist
calendars. The date became official in 1921, when Bulgarian women
attending the International Women's Secretariat of the Communist
International made a motion that the day be uniformally celebrated
around the world on March 8.

In the early days of its observance, International Women's Day was
celebrated as a socialist holiday honoring working women. With the
resurgence of feminism in the late 1960s came a renewed interest in
International Women's Day. Feminists found it a ready-made holiday
for the celebration of women's lives and work and began promoting
March 8 as such. These efforts resulted in a revitalized holiday in
countries where it had traditionally been celebrated and inspired new
interest in a number of countries where the holiday had previously not
been observed.

International Women's Day became a catalyst for a variety of events, a day for conferences, cultural events, special commemorations, and new beginnings. In 1982, the United States Congress proclaimed the national observance of a week honoring women; March 8 was incorporated into the week, its labor origins neatly buried. International Women's Day is also used as a day of nonviolent protest. On any given year, there are hundreds of marches and demonstrations around the globe on that day. The listing included here can only suggest the day's importance in women's history.

AUSTRIA: On March 8, 1918, despite a ban on all demonstrations, three thousand socialist wives and mothers in Austria marched in small groups past the parliament demanding peace.

SPAIN: In 1936, Dolores Ibaurri, a leader of the Spanish Communist Party who went by the name La Pasionaria, led thousands of women in a demonstration in Madrid for progress and liberty and against the growing fascist threat.

CHINA: Communists in China began celebrating International Women's Day in 1922. In 1938, the Women's National Salvation Association of the Chinese Red Army banged on pots and pans, bravely celebrating March 8 despite Japanese occupation of their country. In the 1950s, women in the new People's Republic of China proudly named their work teams in honor of International Women's Day and used the day to demonstrate cooperative skills. China's first squadron of women fliers celebrated March 8, 1952, by flying in formation over cheering crowds. In 1955, a dozen women organized a "March 8 Tree-Planting Team" and, in three years, planted over one hundred thousand trees on sandy wasteland. In 1958, the women of Changtzu Island in Liaoning Province, China, formed a March 8 unit of fishing boats, dedicating their work to the revolution. They rebuked those who said it was impossible for women to do the hard work of going to sea with the retort, "We fear neither hardship nor death to fish for the revolution." In their first decade of operation, (with a female captain, first and second mates, and engineers), the "March 8" women caught over three thousand seven hundred tons of fish for the state. In 1970, women electricians formed a March 8 team in the Pearl River delta of south China.

VENEZUELA: In 1944, women celebrated International Women's Day for the first time by presenting the Venezuelan congress with a petition with more than eleven thousand names of women demanding the right to vote.

INDONESIA: On March 8, 1955, five hundred thousand women throughout Indonesia took to the streets in massive demonstrations demanding their rights. By contrast, in the United States McCarthyism had put a damper on the socialist-based holiday.

CUBA: On International Women's Day in 1975, Cuba's revolutionary "Family Code" was made official. Activist-writer Margaret Randall wrote approvingly, "The sense of the new Code rests entirely on mutual respect between women and men, and respect on the part of the parents for their children."

CHILE: In 1979, in spite of severe political repression by the brutal military government, the Union of Housemaids sponsored a March 8 celebration. Thousands crowded into the Caupolican Theatre. Male union leaders presented women with flowers, and greetings of solidarity were read from workers' unions. One greeting came from the "Committee for the Disappeared"; when the greeting was read, the crowd rose to its feet shouting over and over, "¡Libertad!" (Freedom!) Despite the police posted at every door, a group of musicians performed a song by Victor Jara, the martyred folksinger who had dared sing of justice. They sang another song by Patricio Manns, a composer who had been forced into exile. The crowd began to chant "Matilde, Matilde," calling for the widow of Pablo Neruda. Crying, she was ushered to the stage and gave greetings to people in struggle everywhere. Onto the stage of this already emotionally charged event appeared a group of women of all ages, relatives of *los desaparecidos* ("the disappeared"). They sang a song by Violetta Parra, "Ay, que tristeza, Ay que dolor." ("Oh, what sorrow, oh what pain.") And then the group began to perform another song, "En un tiempo fui dichosa," ("I once was happy.") Three young women came forward to dance to this song. They each danced alone, conveying beyond the words the agony of the grief they felt for their missing partners. Again, the theater filled with applause, tears, and shouts of "Freedom! Freedom!" before the crowd hurried away into the night, back into the cruelty and ignorance of life under dictatorship.

IRAN: The March 8 event of 1979 that made headlines was the demonstration by thousands of women in Iran. They had planned to celebrate the February overthrow of the Shah and the years of repression they had suffered under his rule, but already the new regime of the Ayatollah Khomeini had imposed a fundamentalist Islamic regime. In a matter of weeks, Khomeini had banned co-education, divorce, abortion; had ordered women government workers to wear the full length chador; and had suspended laws prohibiting polygamy. As the women marched from Teheran University, they chanted, "In the dawn of freedom, there is no freedom."

NICARAGUA: On International Women's Day, 1980, just eight months after the Sandinista revolution, women arrived in Managua from all parts of Nicaragua to celebrate their part in creating a new society. They marched through the streets chanting, "We'll create the New Woman!" "Power to the people!" and "Se siente, se siente, la mujer esta presente!" (You can feel it, you can feel it, woman is here!)

At the rally that followed the march, honorary awards were given to women who had been leaders during the revolution: guerilla fighters, those imprisoned during the Somoza dictatorship, and the mother of one of the first women guerillas killed in battle. Gloria Carrion, General Secretary of the Association of Nicaraguan Women, spoke passionately about women's new role in the reconstruction of the government and the Association's goal of abolishing all laws that discriminated against women.

IRELAND: Every year on March 8, women from England join their Irish sisters to picket outside the Armagh women's jail in Northern Ireland. The demonstrators shout out the name of each prisoner followed by a lusty chorus of "WE SUPPORT YOU!" Sometimes, as happened in 1983, the imprisoned women are able to signal that they hear the tribute by throwing a dress out a window.

SICILY: In 1983, hundreds of women from many countries—Italy, the United States, England, Switzerland, Germany, France, and Holland gathered on International Women's Day at the Comiso, Sicily, peace camp for a week of nonviolent actions to protest the deployment of cruise missiles. Two-thirds of the population of Comiso had signed a petition urging their government to cancel the missiles to no avail. Fifty women from the international gathering chose to stage a sit-down protest at the Magliocco air base. They sat in a circle, wove a mammoth multicolored web of yarn, and taught each other peace songs in their many languages. The circle of women stood, holding their beautiful web over their heads. But when they moved toward the gates of the base, the police, rushing to shut the gates, became entangled in the web. At first the police laughed, but they quickly became irritated and embarrassed; freeing themselves, the police threw the rainbow-colored web into a large puddle, poking at it with their feet. That night, six hundred women marched in a noisy demonstration through the streets of Comiso, setting the stage for the next morning's nonviolent blockade of the base, an action that would result in police brutality and many arrests.

ANGOLA: That same day in 1983, in Luanda, the capital of Angola, the Organization of Angolan Women (OMA) concluded its first Congress with a well-attended peace march. Beginning at the newly inaugurated Square of the Heroines, delegates from the Congress marched with government leaders and the people of Luanda under a banner proclaiming "WOMEN DEMAND PEACE." They marched to the city's huge sports stadium, where they listened to speeches honoring International Women's Day and watched a colorful dance and gymnastics performance.

UNITED STATES: On March 8, 1984, approximately one hundred and fifty women converged on the Presidio Army Base in San Francisco. While some women set up a picket line outside the main gate, other women marched into the base through several entrances and met at the headquarters of the Sixth U.S. Army division chanting:

> We're angry women and we're here to say,
> "Down with the army and the CIA!"

In honor of International Women's Day they carried puppets representing Army and CIA officials draped with signs "WANTED FOR WAR CRIMES" as well as large portraits of women freedom fighters. In a statement of solidarity with other International Women's Day actions, they protested the United States' acts of aggression against the people of Nicaragua, El Salvador, Mexico, the Philippines, Puerto Rico, and Cuba, as well as the colonization of Native American lands. Then they threw their own blood on the walls of the headquarters and began to chant:

> Built on blood, built on war,
> We know what this place is for!

The military police, armed with guns and riot gear, tried to block the women, and the commander demanded the protesters leave at once. The women shouted back, "We'll leave when you leave Central America, the Caribbean, and the Middle East!" But the women did leave the headquarters. They marched to the Army Museum on the base, where they threw more blood on the building and on the tanks stationed outside. Then they proceeded on to the Army Hospital where they protested the hospital's germ warfare research. One of the protesters shouting her denunciation of germ warfare research was arrested by two military policemen. The other demonstrators doused the police car with blood as it drove away.

The protesters inside the base eventually joined the picketers outside the main gate where the demonstration continued. Calling the base a place "where decisions are made with a shuffling of paper—decisions which shed blood from Central America to Watts," the demonstrators vowed to continue their protests until violence against women, including pornography and the forced sterilization of women of color, is stopped. "We are inspired by the women of Nicaragua and El Salvador who, in their fight to liberate their nations, are liberating themselves as women," they said.

INDIA: In 1986, women throughout India addressed a range of concerns on March 8. In Delhi, women carried posters through the streets demanding the withdrawal of the divorce bill that had been imposed on Muslim women. They also protested the lack of educational opportunities for women in India. That same day, women carrying cans of black paint went through the city of Patna defacing pornographic posters that they believed degraded or insulted women. In the town of

Gaya, five hundred women from the surrounding rural area gathered to celebrate International Women's Day. They presented a petition to the district commissioner demanding that land be given in women's names as well as in men's.

MAURITIUS: In 1987, women in this small island nation east of Madagascar in the Indian Ocean chose March 8 to make public a list of demands. The "Muvman Liberasyon Fam" (Women's Liberation Movement) outlined what it called a minimum women's program, that included the right of workers to strike and an amendment to the constitution of Mauritius making sex discrimination illegal. The women also demanded toilets for factory, agricultural, and domestic workers.

CANADA: Over two thousand people marched through Toronto on International Women's Day that, in 1989, had as its theme "Women Against Poverty: Fighting for Social Equality." The marchers stopped in front of the headquarters of an anti-abortion group and placed a black coffin filled with coat hangers on the sidewalk. The coat-hangers symbolized feminist fears that, if abortion rights are not protected, women will be forced to relive the horror of illegal abortion; in the past, women have died after desperate attempts to induce their own abortions by inserting coat-hangers into their uteruses. Elsewhere in Toronto that day, members of a group calling itself the "Broads of Bay Street" were arrested after they disrupted traffic in the business district. Across Canada, women chose a range of issues for the day's celebration. In Vancouver, women demonstrated in support of a women's health center; in Montreal, they focused on violence against women; in Prince Albert, they held a conference with speakers from South Africa, Iceland, and Nicaragua; in Edmonton, women marched against racism, and in Halifax, they marched for peace.

ISRAEL: In 1989, women from The Movement of Democratic Women (Tandi) organized a Peace Tent in Tel Aviv on March 8. The tent event attracted almost four hundred women, at least one third of them Palestinian. The participants included members of the Israeli Women's Alliance to End the Occupation (Shani) and Women in Black, a group which holds weekly peace vigils throughout Israel. Inside the tent, the women enjoyed a bazaar of West Bank women's products, performances, and group art projects, including the creation of a peace statue and the beginning of a new peace quilt. The organizers of the event designed the Peace Tent to suggest models for negotiations for peace; Jewish and Palestinian women were afforded the opportunity to dialogue.

As women's global connections to each other are strengthened and women's involvements in the great variety of struggles for justice are intensified, Mother's Day and March 8 celebrations are themselves becoming increasingly diverse in creativity, style, and focus.

SOURCES

Mother's Day

Andreas, Carol. *When Women Rebel: The Rise of Popular Feminism in Peru.* Westport, CT: Lawrence Hill & Co., 1985.

"Birth Strike Protests Nukes." *off our backs* (Jan. 1980).

"Mother's Day Declared Day of Mourning For U.S. Citizen Killed by Contras" (press release). *Clergy and Laity Concerned.* May 6, 1987.

Clifford, Deborah Pickman. *Mine Eyes Have Seen the Glory: A Biography of Julia Ward Howe.* Boston: Little, Brown and Company, 1978.

Hausen, Karin. "Mother's Day in the Weimar Republic." In *When Biology Became Destiny: Women in Weimar and Nazi Germany.* Renate Bridenthal, Atina Grossmann, and Marion Kaplan, eds.New York: Monthly Review Press, 1984.

Holderness, Mike. "Mother's Day Action: 740 Arrests." *Peace News.* May 15, 1987.

Mead, Edwin. *Julia Ward Howe's Peace Crusade.* Boston: World Peace Foundation pamphlet, serial 4, no. 7 (Mar. 1912).

"Mother's Day." *Out and About: the Seattle Lesbian Feminist Newsletter.* (Apr. 1978).

"Mother's Day Brigade." *Out and About: the Seattle Lesbian Feminist Newsletter.* (June 1978).

"Mother's Day Goes Political." *Nuclear Times,* vol. 11, no. 8 (Jul. 1984).

"A Mother's Day Pentagon March." *Whole Life Times.* (Sept./Oct. 1980).

"Mothers Protest Defense Spending Rise." *The Washington Star.* May 11, 1981.

Pegg, Bob. *Rites and Riots: Folk Customs of Britain and Europe.* Dorset, England: Blandford Press, 1981.

Richards, Laura and Maud Howe Elliott. *Julia Ward Howe, 1819-1910.* Boston: Houghton Mifflin, 1916.

Telitha Cumi. "Reflections on Mother's Day." In *Latin American Church Women Challenge Patriarchy In Church and Society.* New York: Women's International Peace Resource Exchange, 1987.

"Universal Peace: A Woman's Festival Held in This City." *The Boston Daily Globe.* June 3, 1873.

International Women's Day

Andors, Phyllis. *The Unfinished Liberation of Chinese Women, 1949-1980.* Bloomington, IN: Indiana University Press, 1983.

Bourget, Clémence. "Was the First International Women's Day Really March 8?" *Communiqu'Elles* (Mar. 1988).

Bouvier, Libby. "International Women's Day 1985." *Sojourner* (Mar. 1985).

"Canada: I.W.D. Marked." *off our backs* (May 1989).

Cole, Johnetta B. "Women in Cuba: The Revolution Within the Revolution." In *Comparative Perspectives of Third World Women: The Impact of Race, Sex, & Class.* Beverly Lindsay, ed. New York: Praeger Publishers, 1980.

Cook, Alice and Gwyn Kirk. *Greenham Women Everywhere: Dreams, Ideas and Actions From the Women's Peace Movement.* Boston: South End Press, 1983.

"Day Marks Working Women's Struggle." *Majority Report,* vol. 3, no. 11 (Mar. 1974).

Dunn, Erica & Judy Klein. "Women in the Russian Revolution." *Women: A Journal of Liberation* (Summer, 1970).

Ezkiel, Judith. "March 9 In Managua." *off our backs* (June 1980).

Flynn, Elizabeth Gurley. "International Women's Day, 1947." *Political Affairs* (Mar. 1947).

Harford, Barbara and Sarah Hopkins. *Greenham Common: Women at the Wire.* London: The Women's Press Ltd., 1984.

Henry, Alice. "Freedom's Dawn, No Freedom." *off our backs* (Apr. 1979).

"International Women's Day, March 8, 1982." *Workers' Tribune* (Mar./Apr. 1982).

The International Women's Day Research Project. "'Give Us Bread But Give Us Roses': A History of International Women's Day." *WIN Magazine* (Mar. 8, 1979).

"International Women's Day: Reports Received." *Manushi: A Journal About Women and Society* no. 33 (1986).

Jewish Women's Committee to End the Occupation of the West Bank and Gaza. *Jewish Women's Peace Bulletin* nos. 3 and 4 (June and Sept. 1989).

Kaplan, Temma. "On the Socialist Origins of International Women's Day." *off our backs* (Mar. 1986).

"Latin America: Our Feminism." *Connexions: An International Women's Quarterly* no. 19 (Winter 1986).

"Letter from Chile." *off our backs* (Apr. 1979).

Mandelbaum, Sara. "Women's History Week." *Ms.* (Mar. 1983).

"Mauritius: Women Organize." *off our backs* (Jul. 1987).

"Militant Women for Peace." *Connexions: An International Women's Quarterly* no. 1 (Summer 1981).

National Women's Commission, C.P. "Special Issue on International Women's Day." *Monthly Bulletin* (Feb. 1948).

"Newshorts." *Spare Rib: A Women's Liberation Magazine* no. 82 (May 1979).

New Women in New China. Peking: Foreign Languages Press, 1972.

Organization of Angolan Women. *Angolan Women Building the Future: From National Liberation to Women's Emancipation.* Marga Holness, trans. London: Zed Books Ltd., 1984.

Women Against Imperialism. "Women Deface Army Base." *Big Apple Dyke News*, vol. 4, no. 3 (Apr./May 1984).

Yuval-Davis, Nira. "Anti-Semitism/Zionism/Racism." *Connexions: An International Women's Quarterly* no. 19 (Winter 1986).

Zinn, Howard. *A People's History of the United States.* New York: Harper & Row, 1980.

5

Invasion of the Justice Seekers!

> Beware of the women when they are sickened by all that is around them and rise up against the old world. On that day, the new world will begin.
>
> —Louise Michel
> French revolutionary

IN THE MONTHS BEFORE JULY 4, 1776, as the male revolutionaries were busy preparing to declare independence from the British, Abigail Adams wrote her husband, John, urging the men to "remember the ladies." She cautioned them not to once again give unlimited power to men for, "all Men would be tyrants if they could," she wrote, restating one of her husband's own political maxims. And she added, "That your Sex are Naturally Tyrannical is a Truth so thoroughly established as to admit of no dispute."

In her letter, Adams warned that women of the future would not feel bound to obey laws in which they had had no voice and that someday they might even incite a rebellion of their own. But John Adams wrote back with an affectionate chuckle, "Depend upon it, we know better than to repeal our Masculine systems."

One hundred years later, men were still protecting their masculine systems and women were still fighting to be included. Plans for the July 4, 1876, Centennial Celebration excluded women from everything but the behind-the-scenes work. A Women's Centennial Committee raised over one hundred thousand dollars for the huge national exhibit in Philadelphia that boasted a display of everything from the unfinished Statue of Liberty to safety pins and false teeth. After raising the money, the women were told that there was no room for their own display or participation in the exhibition. But the women didn't give up. They raised more money and erected a separate Woman's Pavilion that featured machines operated by women, including a press that printed copies of a women's rights newspaper, *The New Century for Woman.*

Still, there were no plans to include women in the official government ceremony in Philadelphia's Independence Hall. Two months before the big event, at a meeting of the National Woman Suffrage Association in New York City, feminist historian Matilda Joslyn Gage stood to voice her discontent. "Let us take as our credo for the centennial year the words of Abigail Adams," she said. "'We are determined to foment a rebellion and will not hold ourselves bound by any laws in which we have no voice or representation.'" This sounded good to the activists. After all, a number of those present had petitioned the government for the right to vote, claiming that the authors of the Constitution had not meant to limit the interpretation of the word "man" to mean only male. Some of the women had even been arrested at the ballot box trying to cast votes. But every effort at claiming their rights as citizens had failed. Now they listened to the words of a woman who, one hundred years earlier, had warned of a woman's rebellion, and they liked what they heard.

Susan B. Anthony was at the meeting that day. She called on women to meet in Philadelphia on the Fourth of July "not to rejoice but to declare our freedom." What was needed, she said, was a women's Declaration of Independence! Convinced, the women at the meeting passed a resolution that women throughout the United States would meet in their own towns on July 4th "to declare themselves free and independent, no longer bound to obey laws in whose making they have had no voice, and in presence of the assembled nations of the world, gathered on this soil to celebrate our national Centennial, to demand justice for the women of this land."

It was no simple task to set up National Woman Suffrage Association Centennial headquarters in Philadelphia. The women signed a lease for property that was legally owned by a woman, but by law they were required to get her husband's consent as well. He refused, and the Association was forced to look elsewhere. Finally, headquarters were set up at 1431 Chestnut Street, and the work began. Letters were sent to various Republicans and Democrats urging them to "remember the Ladies" this time, albeit one hundred years too late, by endorsing a suffrage plank during the Centennial year. Visitors to the headquarters were educated about women's suffrage, loaded down with literature advocating votes for women, and sent on their way to spread the word. Almost every day, the beloved Quaker activist Lucretia Mott, now eighty-three years old, came to visit the headquarters, bringing gifts of eggs, cold chicken, and oolong tea.

As the July 4th celebration drew near, Elizabeth Cady Stanton, Susan Anthony, and Matilda Joslyn Gage concentrated their efforts on writing a Declaration of Rights for Women.

While the nation is buoyant with patriotism, and all hearts are attuned to praise, it is with sorrow we come to strike the one discordant note, on this one-hundredth anniversary of our country's birth....Our faith is firm and unwavering in the broad principles of human rights proclaimed in 1776, not only as abstract truths, but as the corner stones of a republic.

The women's Declaration went on to praise the progress that the nation had made with freedom of speech, of the press, and of religion as well as progress in the areas of the arts, education, and commerce. But, it continued, there had been abuses of power by men over women in direct opposition to the principles of just government. For these violations of principles, the women presented articles of impeachment protesting denial of suffrage, denial of a right to trial by a jury of one's peers, and taxation without representation. The document ended:

And now, at the close of a hundred years, as the hour-hand of the great clock that marks the centuries points to 1876, we declare our faith in the principles of self-government; our full equality with man in natural rights; that woman was made first for her own happiness, with the absolute right to herself—to all the opportunities and advantages life affords for her complete development; and we deny that dogma of the centuries, incorporated in the codes of all nations—that woman was made for man—her best interest, in all cases, to be sacrificed to his will. We ask of our rulers, at this hour, no special favors, no special privileges, no special legislation. We ask justice, we ask equality, we ask that all the civil and political rights that belong to citizens of the United States, be guaranteed to us and our daughters forever.

It was a good document, and the women were proud of it. But what should they do with it? After some discussion they agreed that it should be made a part of the July 4th celebration. Elizabeth Cady Stanton wrote later in her *Reminiscences*:

We thought it would be fitting for us to read our Declaration of Rights immediately after that of the Fathers was read, as an impeachment of them and their male descendants for their injustice and oppression. Ours contained as many counts, and quite as important, as those against King George in 1776.

Stanton wrote a letter to General Hawley, the chairman of the Centennial Commission. She asked for enough tickets to the celebration so that a female representative from each state could attend the grand affair. She also asked for permission to read the women's Declaration of Rights as a part of the official July 4th program. Hawley wrote back immediately, expressing regret that he could grant neither request. However, he did send five tickets for reserved seats.

Undaunted, the women decided to hold their own convention on the Fourth of July at the First Unitarian Church. They determined their own platform and program and invited their own speakers. Still, it was a shame to waste those five tickets!

The big day finally came. There were flags and people everywhere, and even the sun seemed to show extra enthusiasm as it rose hot and broiling into the summer sky. Inside the great hall, the men gathered to celebrate independence, but outside women activists were angry. Some of them would be taxed to pay for the celebration, and they felt they had a right to be a part of it. And they did have five tickets! Matilda Joslyn Gage, who held one of the tickets in her hand, later wrote of the impulse that guided the women that day:

> Five officers of the National Woman Suffrage Association, with that heroic spirit which has ever animated lovers of liberty in resistance to tyranny, determined, whatever the result, in defiance of whatever mandate to the contrary, to present Woman's Declaration of Rights at the chosen hour. They would not, they dared not sacrifice the golden opportunity to which they had so long looked forward; their work was not for them alone, nor alone for the present generation, but for all women of all time. The hopes of posterity were in their hands, and they determined to place on record for the daughters of 1976, the fact that their mothers of 1876 had thus asserted their equality of rights, and thus impeached the government of today for its injustice towards women.

Moments before the men's program was to begin, Anthony, Gage, and three other women—Sara Andrews Spencer, Lillie Devereux Blake, and Phoebe Couzins—tickets in hand, boldly made their way into the official celebration. Surrounded by hot and sweaty men, the women listened respectfully as Richard Henry Lee of Virginia read aloud the Declaration of 1776.

Scheduled next on the program was the official welcome of the Emperor of Brazil, the guest of honor. But just as the members of the band lifted their instruments to play the Brazilian national anthem, the five women rose suddenly and marched down the aisle. They expected to be stopped but in the confusion of the moment they were allowed to continue past the guests, past the military officers, past the gaping government officials until they actually reached the speaker's platform. There, Anthony stood face-to-face with the bewildered moderator and, bowing low, handed him a parchment on which the Women's Declaration had been handsomely copied. The document was received without a word.

At this, the women turned and headed for the exit. As they went, they scattered printed copies of the Declaration to the men on both sides of the aisle. Immediately the hall was thrown into chaos as men stood on their chairs, calling to the women and grabbing wildly for the papers, though no one seemed sure what it was the women were handing out. Back on stage, the program organizers were shouting, "Order! Order!" but no one listened.

With their dramatic gesture so successfully executed, the five women emerged grinning and triumphant into the oppressive heat of the day. They made their way through the crowds to a platform that had been erected in front of Independence Hall. Stanton later described what happened next:

> Here, under the shadow of Washington's statue, back of them the old bell that proclaimed "liberty to all the land and all the inhabitants thereof," they took their places, and, to a listening, applauding crowd, Miss Anthony read the Woman's Declaration. During the reading of the Declaration, Mrs. Gage stood beside Miss Anthony and held an umbrella over her head to shelter her friend from the intense heat of the noonday sun. And thus in the same hour, on opposite sides of old Independence Hall, did the men and women express their opinions on the great principles proclaimed on the natal day of the Republic.

After they had finally read their Declaration, the women hurried to the church where the alternate women's independence celebration was being held and told those assembled about what had happened at the men's celebration at Independence Hall. After a good laugh, everyone settled in to enjoy five hours of speeches presided over by Lucretia Mott. The afternoon also included entertainment by the Hutchinson Family Singers, who sang popular suffrage songs. The favorite was the one about the future that included this verse:

> Then woman, man's partner, man's equal shall stand,
>   While beauty and harmony govern the land;
> To think for oneself will be no offense,
>   The world will be thinking, a hundred years hence.

IN THEIR EFFORTS TO GAIN POLITICAL RECOGNITION, women worldwide have sometimes invaded government bodies, disrupted the men's proceedings, upstaged the legislators, and given voice to their grievances where their voices were not welcome.

In England, in the days before the militant suffragettes began throwing rocks and smashing windows to make their point, they developed a tactic of attending men's political rallies and sessions of Parliament and heckling the speakers. It was a tactic defended as English custom by suffrage leader Emmeline Pankhurst. As she explained in her autobiography:

> In almost every one of my American meetings I was asked the question, "What good do you expect to accomplish by interrupting meetings?" Is it possible that the time-honoured, almost sacred

English privilege of interrupting is unknown in America? I cannot imagine a political meeting from which "the Voice" was entirely absent. In England it is invariably present. It is considered the inalienable right of the opposition to heckle the speaker and to hurl questions at him which are calculated to spoil his arguments. For instance, when Liberals attend a Conservative gathering they go prepared to shatter by witticisms and pointed questions all the best effects of the Conservative orators. The next day you will read in Liberal newspapers headlines like these: "The Voice in Fine Form," "Short Shrift for Tory Twaddle."...In accordance with this custom we heckle Cabinet Ministers.

To be sure, it didn't take much to be considered a heckler if one was a suffrage activist in England in October of 1905. That's when the frail, young Annie Kenney, fresh from the harsh life of the mills, and Emmeline Pankhurst's privileged daughter Christabel attended a meeting at the Manchester Free Trade Hall the night Sir Edward Grey was the invited speaker. Hoping to secure a promise of support from the incoming Liberal government, the two women quietly seated themselves in the gallery. Christabel held tight to a neatly folded banner declaring "VOTES FOR WOMEN." As Christabel later remembered:

> The Free Trade Hall was crowded. The sky was clear for a Liberal victory—save for a little cloud no bigger than a woman's hand! Calm, but with beating hearts, Annie and I looked at the exultant throng we must soon anger by our challenge. Their cheers as the speakers entered gave us the note and pitch of their emotion. Speech followed speech.

At the end of the speeches, questions were invited. Several men rose, their questions recognized and politely answered. Then Annie stood and asked, "Will the Liberal Government give women the vote?"

One would not think such words would drive men to madness, but by all accounts they very nearly did just that. Outraged men began shouting. Sir Edward Grey refused to answer the question. Men near Annie forced her back into her chair, one man pressed his hat over her face. At that, Christabel jumped up and repeated Annie's question, "Will the Liberal Government give women the vote?" Again there were outraged shouts of "Be quiet!" though a few voices urged, "Let them speak!" As the meeting came to an end, Annie stood on her chair to shout the question one more time. According to Emmeline Pankhurst's account:

> Then the audience became a mob. They howled, they shouted and roared, shaking their fists fiercely at the woman who dared to intrude her question into a man's meeting. Hands were lifted to drag her out of her chair, but Christabel threw one arm about her as she stood, and with the other arm warded off the mob who struck and scratched at

her until her sleeve was red with blood. Still the girls held together and shouted over and over: "The question! The question! Answer the question!"

The two women were dragged from the Hall and arrested. Annie was sentenced to three days in jail when she refused to pay bail. Upper-class Christabel had to fight to get herself arrested with working-class Annie and finally resorted to making a halfhearted attempt to spit at an officer for which she was successfully sentenced to a week in jail.

This one small action served to put the Women's Suffrage Movement on the front pages of English newspapers, that had previously all but ignored the issue and spurred a sluggish movement into new life. Women throughout the country determined that they would use every opportunity to call for an answer to Annie's question.

Indeed, a few days before Christmas that year, at a public meeting in Royal Albert Hall in London, Sir Henry Campbell-Bannerman, the new Prime Minister, introduced his cabinet and gave a speech. When the speech contained no reference to the question of women's suffrage, Annie Kenney stood, held up a little white banner with the words "VOTES FOR WOMEN" and called out, "Will the Liberal Government give women the vote?" Just at that moment, from seats directly above the platform, another activist unfurled a banner with the words, "WILL THE LIBERAL GOVERNMENT GIVE JUSTICE TO WORKING-WOMEN?" The women were seized and expelled from the meeting.

From then on, when they'd least expect it, men attending public meetings would be thrown into chaos when women would stand with their white banners and ask "the question." A favorite target of the suffrage activists was Winston Churchill, who had foolishly vowed, "Nothing would induce me to vote for giving women the franchise; I am not going to be henpecked into a question of such importance."

In April 1906, a resolution on women's suffrage was presented in the House of Commons which stated, "That in the opinion of this House it is desirable that sex should cease to be a bar to the exercise of the Parliamentary franchise." The resolution did not hold any legislative power but was considered important by supporters of women's suffrage as a vehicle for presenting the arguments. Women flocked to Parliament that day in high excitement, though they were, as usual, allowed to attend the debates in Parliament only if they sat in a Ladies' Gallery, out of sight behind a brass grille, where they would not distract the men who were about the serious work of running the world. The grille that hid them became a symbol for the women of their oppression and their banishment from the decision-making process. (Men visiting Parliament sat in the Strangers' Gallery, that had no grille.) In great anticipation, suffrage activists waited throughout the afternoon and evening to hear the men grapple with the suffrage resolution. Instead, to their dismay and disgust, they heard speaker after speaker make condescending jokes that were greeted by roars of laughter from the men. Just before eleven, when the debate was scheduled to close, a line of police officers quietly formed along the back of the Ladies' Gallery. The women, desperate for serious consideration of their objectives, impatient and tense from a day of insults, suddenly began to shout, demanding that the legislators vote on the resolution before them. One activist pushed her white "VOTES FOR WOMEN" flag through the grille. The police, primed and waiting for such an outburst, rushed the women. To the men's horror, the women laughed in their faces. As Sylvia Pankhurst, Emmeline's radical pacifist, socialist daughter, remembered:

> We laughed as the police came rushing down over the tiers of seats to drag us out; it was fun to show our contempt for the "Talking Shop," the mace, the Speaker, and all the rest. Its Members had spent the evening laughing at us; and this was how little we thought of them!

In the next few years, women in England continued to invade men's meetings and heckle the speakers and laugh. Nor was this the last time they would have to be dragged from the Ladies' Gallery of Parliament. On October 28, 1908, Muriel Matters, an inventive member of the Women's Freedom League (who, three months later, would sail over the House of Commons in a dirigible balloon painted with the words "VOTES FOR WOMEN,") interrupted the proceedings of the House of Commons by delivering a speech from the Gallery. When the startled men rushed to evict her, they found that Muriel had chained and padlocked herself to the brass grille. As the men pondered how to get her out of the Gallery, one of the attendants put his hands over Muriel's mouth so that she couldn't continue her speech, at which a second woman began to deliver a suffrage speech from the Ladies' Gallery. She too, it was soon discovered, had attached herself to the brass grille with a heavy chain. On this day the women were not alone. As sounds of struggle came from behind the grille of the Ladies' Gallery, a man sitting in the men's Strangers' Gallery began to shout, "Why don't you do justice to women?" and another man dropped women's suffrage leaflets onto the heads of the government representatives below. And in the lobby of the building, suffrage activists attempted to hold a meeting. When they were ousted, several speakers climbed the pedestal of Richard I's statue and began to address the crowd of curious onlookers. Meanwhile, work continued to dislodge Muriel and her friend from the grille. Pieces of the grille itself had to be removed. The two women were carried into a committee room, still attached by their chains to pieces of the heavy brass grill, and a metal worker was called to free them so that they could be taken to prison and placed behind bars. The grille was eventually restored, but only for a time. Years later it was placed on display in the suffragette collection of the London Museum as a symbol of women's past exclusion from government.

SUFFRAGISTS IN FRANCE, like suffragists around the world, were watching their militant British sisters, but the tactics did not translate easily. Women in France had a long tradition of revolutionary involvement and active leadership in social causes. Theirs was the country of Joan of Arc, who had led an army in 1429; Marie de Gournay, who had written about the equality of men and women in 1622, and the eight hundred women who had marched to the National Assembly at Versailles in 1789 to demand bread. They had seen their first feminist magazine in 1791, the same year that Olympe de Gouges had written a "Declaration of the Rights of Woman and of the Citizen"; she was beheaded two years later for "having forgotten the virtues which belong to her sex."

But by 1900, such examples of revolutionary zeal were rare among women in France. Perhaps Napoleon's 1804 Civil Code, which institutionalized and legalized the subjugation of women to men, had put a damper on women's spirits, or perhaps the oppressive influence of the Roman Catholic Church had made them cautious.

Whatever the reason, French suffragists in the early twentieth century were generally modest in their demands and extravagant in their patience, and they were shocked by the boldness of their British sisters. Those who dared to suggest that French women demonstrate in the streets were considered militant. Stringent regulations effectively restricted public demonstrations so that when women did take to the streets they were frequently outnumbered by the police. In 1904, suffragists publicly protested the one hundredth anniversary of Napoleon's Civil Code by releasing golden balloons into the sky bearing the words "The Code Crushes Women." For this, they were jailed on a charge of "injurious disturbance."

To make matters worse, French activists were snubbed by the international suffrage movement in 1904. A meeting in Berlin for the creation of the International Woman Suffrage Alliance (IWSA) was rescheduled at the last minute and held before the arrival of Hubertine Auclert, the founder of the French suffrage movement. The alliance was established with representatives from Canada, the United States, the Netherlands, Norway, Great Britain, and Sweden, but not France. It is not clear whether suffragists from these countries snubbed the French women because they were impatient with French conservatism or because of a Northern European bias against "Latin" (Catholic, southern) Europe. Whatever the reason, this exclusion effectively isolated French feminists from international support.

On March 18, 1906, Parisian feminists focused their attention on parliamentary elections with a suffrage rally inside the Musée Social. Hundreds of women turned out to hear rousing suffrage speeches. But these same women flatly refused an invitation to leave the great hall and ride in a procession of banner-covered cars behind a horse-drawn truck of suffragists flinging women's rights literature at the crowd. Such public display appealed to only fifty of the women in attendance that day. As these fifty rode through the streets they were subjected to curses and calls of "Back to your darning! Back to the kitchen!"

Moderate suffragists focused some of their energy on creating posters demanding votes for women. To be safe, they often tacked on what they considered their most compelling and persuasive argument: that with the vote women could better work against the evils of alcohol. The poster-makers were careful to obey the law and obtain a male signature at the bottom of the poster. Still, the women who dared to hang posters sometimes attracted such large crowds that they were charged with the crime of disturbing the peace.

There were, as there always are, a few women who were not so modest and patient as the rest of their peers; two such women were Caroline Kauffmann and Madeleine Pelletier. Despite a troubled life full of illness, or maybe because of it, Kauffmann had three passions: women's rights, physical fitness, and socialism. In 1898, she was made the secretary-general of Solidarité des Femmes, a socialist suffrage organization.

Her colleague and eventual successor at Solidarité, Madeleine Pelletier, was born fighting for a better world. Pelletier's mother, a woman so devout and hardworking neighbors nicknamed her "the Jesuit," bore the scar of a government branding iron for the crime of bastardy. Her father sexually abused Madeleine and mocked his wife's religious devotion. They lived together in utter poverty at the back of a small store. When she was sent away to a convent school, Pelletier was cruelly treated as the dirty little poor girl; she ran away at the age of twelve. Pelletier had courage and intelligence and, despite overwhelming odds, she completed her education on her own, eventually became a physician, and won her fight for a hospital appointment. With her background, Pelletier cared little for society's acceptance nor did she expect it. She fought for everything she got and laughed at the world while she did it, dressing in men's clothes and cutting her hair short and slicked back. She became a tireless revolutionary, guided by the basic tenets of feminism and socialism, though she was often disappointed by their less-energetic adherents.

Frustrated with the limp timidity of the suffrage movement in France, Pelletier and Kauffmann banded together to create dramatic actions. Pelletier turned to her old friend, Adrien Meslier, a socialist deputy and a fellow physician. He willingly obtained tickets to the spectators' gallery at the Palais Bourbon for the opening of the new legislature. On June 3, 1906, Kauffmann and Pelletier presented their tickets. They were admitted to the gallery where they waited, looking down on the men below, men who were denying women the right to any voice in the government though they expected women to obey the laws. When they'd heard enough, Kauffman and Pelletier suddenly stood up and flung suffrage literature onto the heads of the men. In the confusion that followed, some of the men panicked, and, remembering a previous attack by terrorists, ran for the exits in fear that a bomb was about to explode. The two women were seized and interrogated, but the government eventually let them go without arresting them, not wanting to make suffrage martyrs of the women. For Pelletier, the action resulted in the loss of her friendship with Meslier, who never forgave her for using the tickets he'd provided for such a disruptive protest. Parisian feminists, too, were outraged.

Nevertheless, the radical women continued their agitation. In December of that year, Pelletier again went to the Palais Bourbon. This time she took one hundred women with her to the chamber where they surrounded socialist deputies and supporters of women's suffrage and urged them to push harder for concrete action. The men hurried to reassure the women that they would indeed see to it that the question of women's suffrage would be raised in the chamber and vigorously defended. "Yes, yes," they muttered, "the hour has come, the hour has come."

Six months later the socialist deputies had still not raised the question in parliament as they'd promised to do. Pelletier led another march to the chamber. This time the French activists were joined by a deputation of militant British suffragettes. Together they walked under a large white banner proclaiming their common cause. Little came of the action. For the time being, radical activists were destined to grow lonely and discouraged. As in most other countries, theirs would be a long struggle. Pelletier shrugged, concluding that she'd "never find grace among the bourgeoisie."

In THE TURMOIL OF CHINA'S 1911 REVOLUTION, Tang Junying, founder of the Chinese Suffragette Society in Beijing, led women in their invasion of the the newly formed National Assembly in Nanjing. Many of the women had helped to overthrow the Manchu dynasty and were committed to the new constitutionally-based government. At meetings of the Suffrage Society, the women had written their own constitution, that called for the education of women, the right to vote, abolition of footbinding, prohibition of child marriages, and a range of other reforms that they believed were basic to their lives. The women of the Society had also educated themselves about women's rights movements in other countries and had published this information. They had come too far to be tossed aside, once again, by an all-male legislative body.

Like the French radicals, Tang Junying freely confessed her own fascination with the militant English suffrage movement. She followed the news of their attempts to petition the government, and, when that had failed, their willingness to destroy private and public property to force the question. Tang Junying was a convincing public speaker and was known as a woman of action. It was said that, once, when a newspaper office in her home province of Hunan published slanderous rumors about her, she had sought revenge by single-handedly breaking up the office furniture.

Under her leadership, the members of the Suffragette Society stormed the new government body. On the first day, the women did their best to present their point of view, arguing for their right to vote, debating the logic of their demands, and loudly voicing the urgency they felt. Still, the men of the Assembly flatly refused to consider writing any assurance of women's equality or political rights into the new Constitution.

The women vowed to gain the attention of the President himself, and it is likely that they succeeded because of their actions the following day. Frustrated by the failure of words, the women, like their British counterparts, joined in the minority tradition of nonviolent activists willing to destroy property. They forced their entry into the legislature and began to break windows, desks and chairs. (Some of the women involved went beyond the destruction of property and, crossing the line from nonviolent action to violent action, floored several police officers.) On the third day, as women formed into marching order and approached the doors of the Assembly, the legislators sent for help, requesting the protection of government troops. The women's action was brought to an end, though it did inspire at least one other similar action by women in Canton.

SUFFRAGE ACTIVISTS IN THE UNITED STATES were less inclined to use tactics involving the destruction of property than their British and Chinese counterparts, but they too invaded the men's government meetings. On December 4, 1916, after months of lobbying and demonstrating, but a full year before the "Night of Terror," suffrage activists scrambled for seats in the first rows of the visitors' gallery to hear President Woodrow Wilson deliver his annual address in the House of Representatives. Wilson had long been the target of the women's protests because of his courteous apologies and meek explanations regarding his failure to promote women's suffrage. Time and again he graciously explained that other matters were too pressing and urgent to postpone in order to discuss women's suffrage and that the cause was really a matter to be left to state governments. Time and again women watched, voteless and voiceless still in the twentieth century, as men made decisions, rules, and laws governing their lives.

At dawn on that December morning in 1916, women lined up outside the doors of Congress. Members of the suffrage organization, the Congressional Union, had advance information that Wilson would not refer to the question of women's suffrage in his annual speech. What would it take, they wondered as they stood in line, for this president to say something? After a long wait, the doors to the gallery were opened, and the women rushed to claim seats directly facing the Speaker's desk, from which the President would read his message. Mabel Vernon, dressed in a large cape, was one of five women who managed to get several front row seats together. Once seated, Mabel reached inside her cape and unpinned a glossy yellow banner that the women discreetly arranged at their feet.

After the usual pomp and circumstance, the President began to deliver his speech. Halfway through the speech, at a prearranged cue from Mabel, the five women in the gallery stooped, lifted the banner, and, holding tight to its long cords, dropped it over the edge of the balcony. The startled President looked up from his speech to see the large lettering, "MR. PRESIDENT, WHAT WILL YOU DO FOR WOMAN SUFFRAGE?" Graciously, the President smiled slightly and then continued to read to his distracted audience. Spectators in the gallery began whispering. The legislators couldn't take their eyes off the banner or the silent women holding it. Policemen and guards raced to the gallery stairs but found them tightly packed with gleeful members of the women's Congressional Union, who blocked the way. While all this was happening, a messenger from the women's Congressional Union headquarters ran to the press gallery of the House with copies of a prepared statement about the banner and the women's demands.

It was left to a young page on the floor of the Congress to observe that the cords holding the banner had been made a little too long for the women's purposes, so the offending banner was within his reach. He began to jump up and down, reaching for the edge of the yellow cloth until, at last, he grabbed it and yanked it free. Later, Mabel Vernon was heard to groan, "If it hadn't been for those long tapes, they never could have got it until the President finished his speech."

It was all over in five minutes. The audience respectfully turned its attention back to the President. But as soon as the President finished his speech and was ushered out of the room, Congressmen jumped to their feet and stared at the balcony to get a better look at the outrageous women who had dared to disrupt their business. And that evening, people across the nation opened their newspapers to see headlines proclaiming the women's action overshadowing reports of the President's speech.

SHORTLY AFTER WORLD WAR II, as the United States slipped into the squeaky clean 1950s, the nation was gripped as never before by an atmosphere of fear and suspicion. Petty-minded bullies launched an all-out campaign to dig up anything they deemed "un-American." And "un-American" translated freely into "leftist" or "liberal," which in turn translated into "Communist." With the nation already steeped in hysteria, President Harry Truman's Attorney General gave the green light to a witch hunt when he said, "There are today many Communists in America. They are everywhere—in factories, offices, butcher shops, on street corners, in private business—and each carries in himself the germs of death for society." From the comic pages Captain America bellowed, "Beware, commies, spies, traitors, and foreign agents! Captain America, with all loyal, free men behind him, is looking for you...."

While teenaged girls donned bobby socks and poodle skirts and swooned over Elvis Presley, a mean spirit seeped into the bloodstream of the United States carried by a few simple, suddenly menacing words and phrases: "pinko," "dupe," "subversive," "are-you-now-or-have-you-ever-been," and "card-carrying." Neighbor spied on neighbor. Students, professors, factory workers, legislators, soldiers, and Hollywood filmmakers were expected to sign loyalty oaths and to name names of people who they suspected held liberal ideas. Immigrants holding leftist views or involved in progressive organizations were deported. FBI surveillance of political radicals turned every meeting into a circus of suspicion. People who refused to cooperate in the hysteria were blacklisted; they lost their reputations, their jobs, and their futures on the weight of malicious rumor. Though a recent entertainment-inspired revision of history has induced a nostalgia for the 1950s and rendered the era benign and wholesome,in truth, as historian David Caute has written, it was a time when "the wealthiest, most secure nation in the world was sweat-drenched in fear."

In December, 1962, shortly after the tense days of the Cuban missile crisis, the House on Un-American Activities Committee (HUAC), in the federal House of Representatives, summoned the new Women's Strike for Peace (WSP) to appear before the anticommunist proceedings led by Senator Joseph McCarthy.

But these women didn't seem to care whether peace was deemed American or un-American by the Committee. They were worried about the aboveground testing of atomic weapons, that left radioactive strontium 90 traces in their children's milk. They wanted an end to the school air raid drills, that left their children terrified and psychologically prepared for the inevitability of another world war. One woman told Barbara Deming that, during the Cuban missile crisis, her young daughter had brought home a best friend—so that they could die together.

When the Committee looked at Women Strike for Peace, it did not see women genuinely outraged by a war-ready world but a potentially sinister organization which was threatening the American way of life, unwittingly or not. The Committee issued subpoenaes to a number of women associated with WSP, including Dagmar Wilson, the founder—or rather, the one in whose livingroom the concept had been conceived.

Many WSP supporters sent telegrams of protest, asking the Committee to reconsider the subpoenaes. Telegrams came in from religious leaders, actors, legislators, professors, writers, and scientists. Lorraine Hansberry, the African-American playwright who authored *Raisin in the Sun* wrote:

> In these perilous times, when the fate of the world is in such delicate balance, the fullest debate of the issue of war and peace is vital to survival. Any attempt to intimidate mothers and housewives from participating in peace discussion and activity only serves to narrow the arena of debate and silence the voices of conscience and reason. Freedom of ideas has always been a national necessity. In the name of democracy and survival, we ask you to cancel the proposed investigation into the peace movement.

There is an ancient admonition that one should be careful of what one asks for because one might just get it. The House Un-American Activities Committee would have done well to remember this. After issuing subpoenaes demanding that certain women appear before the Committee, they began to receive telegrams from WSP women indignant at having been overlooked. The women turned the tables and called the bluff of the grand intimidators. They said to the Committee, in effect, "if you're going to call her, call me, too. If it's subversive to work for peace, then count me in!" The women pleaded guilty to the crime of agitating against nuclear war. In all, eighty-six women volunteered to testify.

Around the country, women activists used the occasion to full advantage in the media. Editorials appeared like the one by Los Angeles Women Strike for Peace titled "Gentlemen: What Are You Afraid Of?":

> The women's peace movement has struck fear into the hearts of the House Committee on Un-American Activities....
>
> Are they afraid that women will talk too much? Yes, very likely. Although the House Committee on Un-American Activities itself

spent $180,000 last year in printing costs and the women have no
budget except voluntary expenditures of their own limited resources;
and although other government agencies, like the Defense
Department, spend our own money to send to us the Fallout Shelter
booklet based on faulty reasoning about the nature of atomic warfare,
the Committee is afraid of the women and their mimeographing
machines!...

Free speech, although guaranteed by the Bill of Rights, (the 175th
anniversary of its adoption is the week of the Committee's hearing)
has always been challenged by the fearful...When a democracy
believes that freedom is only for popular ideas—it has decided on
suicide. We believe democracy works. We will continue to make
democracy work. We believe in life—for ourselves, our children and
our universe. In spite of the frightened men of the House
Un-American Activities Committee, our American traditions and our
love of life will prevail!

In another press release, a WSP group wrote, "We do not fear the
contamination of ideas; we fear the conspiracy of silence."

On the day of the hearing, bus-loads of women who had traveled all
night arrived at the House Office Building. Other women came in cars.
Five hundred women, some of them carrying their babies or toddlers,
filled the hearing room. It looked for all the world like an invasion.

For three days the Committee called before it the women they
intended to interrogate, the women they hoped to scare into silence.
But, as Mary McGrory, a staff writer for Washington's *Evening Star*
wrote, "The committee was trying to find out if the ladies' group is
subversive. All it found was that their conduct in the caucus room
certainly was."

As each witness was called to testify, all five hundred women stood
up as one body in solidarity. They gave bouquets of gardenias,
carnations, or roses to each witness as she took her place. The
Committeemen tried to get straight answers—while babies crawled in
the aisles.

When accused of being the organization's leader, Dagmar Wilson
corrected the misperception. "We're all leaders," she said. The women
behind her cheered and applauded.

One inquisitor demanded to know if it had been Mrs. Wilson's idea
to send delegates to a Moscow Peace conference. "I wish I had thought
of that," lamented Wilson.

"Where is the Women Strike for Peace headquarters?" the committeemen
demanded to know. "Alas," said Wilson, "we need one badly."

"Would you knowingly permit Communist Party members to take
leadership positions in WSP?" the men asked. "I hope everyone in the
whole world joins," Wilson answered. "Unless they do, then God help
us!"

The women cheered.

Iris Freed of Larchmont, New York, took the stand. She tried to explain to the baffled Committee that Women Strike for Peace was a movement of sorts, not an organization at all. At this, Committee Counsel Alfred Nittle whipped off his glasses and raised his eyebrows. "That's interesting," he growled. "If a group isn't an organization and has no members, how on earth does it function?!" The hearing room exploded into raucous laughter.

Barbara Deming was there that day. Later she wrote:

> We lived through together on those three days the experience of being treated like foolish or wicked children, and the chilling vision of that defeatism with which we have above all to contend. And we lived our common refusal to accept either—the role of those without a voice or the lesson of hopelessness. Our response was: you don't understand. This particular phrase sounded again and again throughout the hearings, springing irresistibly to nearly every witness's lips. Though none was allowed to make a formal statement, though each was cut off time and again in the middle of a sentence, each managed, by a phrase here and a phrase there, in patchwork fashion, to say that the committeemen understood neither the rights of Americans to act to influence the course of government, nor the new facts of the nuclear age which make our particular attempt to influence government a very plain necessity. Nor, each made clear, did they understand anything about women and how they go about getting things done. How little the committeemen understood— under any of these headings—became progressively so obvious that after awhile the most common response evoked by the questioning was uncontrollable laughter, circling the hearing room. Indeed some of the questions—some of the sinister charges—seemed lifted from a Marx Brothers comedy. Counsel takes off his glasses to point them at the witness, portentously demands: "Did you then...have you recently operated a mimeograph machine?"

Nor were the Committeemen spared humiliation in the press. Russell Baker wrote a devastating account in his syndicated column describing the women's irreverent behavior, though he relied on the condescending sexist humor of the era to do it. Baker claimed that, "by Wednesday morning the investigators looked less like dashing Red-Hunters than like men trapped in a bargain basement on sale day." He pointed out that "the three luckless politicians watched the procession of gardenias, carnations and roses with the resigned looks of men aware that they were already liable to charges of being against housewives, children and peace, and determined not to get caught coming out against flowers."

And newspapers across the country ran a political cartoon by *Washington Post* artist Herblock. The cartoon depicted one gray-suited congressman anxiously whispering to another, "I came in late. Which was it that was un-American—women or peace?"

SOURCES

Women Invade July 4th Celebration, 1876

Bacon, Margaret Hope. *Valiant Friend: The Life of Lucretia Mott.* New York: Walker and Company, 1980.

Butterfield, Friedlaender, Kline, eds. *The Book of Abigail and John: Selected letters of the Adams Family 1762-1784.* Cambridge, MA: Harvard University Press, 1975.

Flexner, Eleanor. *Century of Struggle: The Woman's Rights Movement in the United States.* New York: Atheneum, 1974.

Foner, Philip S., ed. *We, the Other People: Alternative Declarations of Independence by Labor Groups, Farmers, Woman's Rights Advocates, Socialists and Blacks, 1829-1975.* Chicago: University of Illinois Press, 1976.

Gage, Matilda Joslyn. *Woman, Church & State: The Original Exposé of Male Collaboration Against the Female Sex.* Watertown, MA: Persephone Press, 1980.

Griffith, Elisabeth. *In Her Own Right: The Life of Elizabeth Cady Stanton.* Oxford: Oxford University Press, 1984.

Stanton, Elizabeth Cady. *Eighty Years & More: Reminiscences 1815-1897.* New York: Schocken Books, 1971.

British Suffragists

Kramarae, Cheris and Paula A. Treichler, eds. *A Feminist Dictionary.* Boston: Pandora Press, 1985.

Mackenzie, Midge. *Shoulder to Shoulder.* New York: Alfred A. Knopf, 1975.

Pankhurst, Emmeline. *My Own Story.* London: Virago, 1979.

Pankhurst, Sylvia. *The Suffragette Movement.* London: Virago, 1977.

French Suffragists

Hause, Steven C. and Anne R. Kenney. *Women's Suffrage and Social Politics in the French Third Republic.* Princeton, NJ: Princeton University Press, 1984.

Chinese Suffragists

Croll, Elisabeth. *Feminism and Socialism in China.* Boston: Routledge & Kegan Paul, 1978.

U.S. Suffragists

Irwin, Inez Haynes. *The Story of Alice Paul and the National Women's Party.* Fairfax, VA: Denlinger's Publishers, 1964/1977.

Papachristou, Judith. *Women Together: A History in Documents of the Women's Movement in the United States.* New York: Alfred A. Knopf, 1976.

Women Strike for Peace at the HUAC Hearings

Baker, Russell. "U.S. Lysistratas Foil Red Hunt." *Boston Herald.* December 15, 1962.

Deming, Barbara. "Letter to WISP." *We Are All Part of One Another: A Barbara Deming Reader.* Jane Meyerding, ed. Philadelphia: New Society Publishers, 1984.

Hardman, Kay. "Gentlemen: What Are You Afraid Of?" Los Angeles Women Strike for Peace press release. December 4, 1962.

Harris, Sydney. "Peace is Everybody's Business." *Chicago Daily News.* December 18, 1962.

Jack, Homer. "The Will of the WISP versus the Humiliation of HUAC." WBAI Pacifica Radio broadcast. New York: December 28, 1962.

"HUAC Subpoenas Women for Peace." *The Christian Century.* (December 19, 1962).

McGrory, Mary. "Nobody Controls Anybody." *The Washington Evening Star.* December 14, 1962.

"Peace Movement Is Under Attack." Women Strike for Peace press release. New York: December 2, 1962.

Women Strike for Peace press release. New York: December 6, 1962.

Women Strike for Peace press release. Washington: December 11 and 12, 1962.

"Stifling Protest." *The Washington Post.* December 6, 1962.

von Blum, Paul. "Not So Happy Days: The Politics and Culture of the 1950's." In *The Rosenbergs: Collected Visions of Artists and Writers.* Rob A. Okun, ed. New York: Universe Books, 1988.

"Women Strike for Peace Statement on House Un-American Activities Committee Subpoenaes to WSP Participants In New York." *Women Strike for Peace Press Release.* New York. (not dated)

Zinn, Howard. *A People's History of the United States.* New York: Harper & Row, 1980.

6

Oh Sister, Shelter Me

We need to be looking above all for the greatness and sanity of ordinary women, and how these women have collectively waged resistance. In searching that territory we find something better than individual heroines: the astonishing continuity of women's imagination of survival, persisting through the great and little deaths of daily life.

—Adrienne Rich
"Resisting Amnesia"

KILL ALL THE JEWISH BOYS AT BIRTH! the Egyptian pharoah ordered the midwives. Today we would call such an action genocide, the deliberate destruction of a racial or cultural group. We do not know what the midwives called it, only that they refused to obey the pharoah's command.

In 1300 B.C.E., the Israelites were slaves in Egypt. Despite this, the Egyptian pharoahs feared them. According to a story told in the literature on which both the Jewish and Christian faiths are founded, one pharoah proposed genocide; he ordered midwives to murder the new-born Jewish boys. But the midwives conspired to disobey the pharoah.

According to the Bible, the pharoah then issued a new command: that every newborn Hebrew boy be thrown into the Nile River. We are left to imagine the sobs of weeping mothers and the sight of the bloated bodies of dead babies floating in the river. It is in this context that we find mention of a second conspiracy of women. Unlike the conspiracy of the midwives, the second conspiracy involved women from both the ruling Egyptian family as well as Hebrew slave women.

This story begins with the birth of a Jewish boy. He was, like all Hebrew boys, condemned to death, but his mother hid him for three months. When she could hide him no longer, she placed him in a waterproof basket of reeds and set the baby to float down the river.

Heartbroken and grieving, she instructed her daughter to hide near the river and watch what happened to the baby.

As the ancient story goes, the pharoah's own daughter was bathing in the river and discovered the baby crying in the basket. She understood at once that it was a Hebrew baby, abandoned by a desperate mother. The Hebrew daughter, watching from the river's edge as her mother had instructed her, boldly approached the princess and offered to find a Hebrew woman to nurse the baby. When the princess agreed, the girl ran home and brought back the mother. Breaking the law in her own house, the Egyptian princess made an agreement with the Hebrew slave mother. The mother would be paid to nurse and tend the baby who would be adopted by the princess and reared as her own son. The princess named him Moses. This baby, given sanctuary from the laws of his time by women who refused to be enemies, grew up to lead the Israelites out of Egypt, out of bondage and slavery.

Women's hands have reached through bulrushes to rescue babies from the pharoah's death orders. Women's voices have sung out directions to freedom, "Follow the north star!" Women have opened their doors to bewildered people fleeing persecution and have found them safe hiding places in a hostile world. When either church or state has ordained one group of people the "hunters" and another group the "hunted," some women always have refused to honor the yellow stars, the branded flesh, the auction block papers, and the emigration orders. They have seen instead only frightened neighbors in need of shelter, and so the shelter has been offered.

IN 1510, BEATRICE DE LUNA WAS BORN INTO HIDING. Her very name was a disguise. To be born a Jew in the days of the Holy Inquisition of the Catholic Church was to be born doomed.

Four hundred years of Crusades, chaos, famine, and plague had ushered in a brutal age of law and order. Priests linked forces with the rulers of Europe to appease their concept of a wrathful God with mass tortures and witch-burnings. The victims, who numbered in the millions, were Jews, women, healers, midwives, worshipers of the pagan religions, and anyone else those in power wished to exterminate.

In 1484, Pope Innocent VIII gave his official blessing to two Dominican monks, Heinrich Kramer and James Sprenger, both hard-working Inquisitors. He asked them to define witchcraft and standardize trial procedures to deal with suspected witches. Two years later, Kramer and Sprenger authored the *Malleus Maleficarum* (The

Hammer of Witches) that outlined the justification for the systematic slaughter of suspected witches. This text, which became the witch-hunter's manual and the law of the land, brought all women under suspicion with statements such as "All witchcraft comes from carnal lust, which is in women insatiable." "When a woman thinks alone, she thinks evil," and warnings such as "Woman is a wheedling and secret enemy. She is a liar by nature." According to the witch-hunters, women (especially spinsters, widows, and poor women) and Jews shared a propensity for worshiping the devil and desecrating Catholic religious symbols. With the help of the newly invented printing press, the *Malleus Maleficarum* was widely distributed, and Europe became a playground for sadists.

The merchants of death set up shop. New instruments of torture were invented and used: an iron machine called the "Spider" was designed to tear away women's breasts. In France one could be paid forty-eight francs for the work of boiling a "heretic" in oil. Witch-burning paid only twenty-eight. In England, boiling the condemned to death was worth a shilling but scrubbing the kettle after the execution was worth only two pence. Still, the shillings and francs could add up. In a single afternoon in Toulouse, France, four hundred women were burned to death in the public square. Then, too, there was the work of stacking the bodies of homosexual men onto the kindling as "faggots" to burn at the feet of the "witches."

In Spain, on the eve of Christopher Columbus's great adventure, Isabella the warrior queen was busy uniting her country. She valiantly battled the Moors and, with her husband Ferdinand, welcomed the Inquisitors. On March 31, 1492, when Catholic authorities in Spain signed the Edict of Expulsion that ordered all professing Jews to leave the country, Isabella gave the Jews four months to get out and personally supervised their departure.

Many of the Jews fled the country they had helped make great after almost fifteen centuries of life there. They left ancient cemeteries, libraries, synagogues, and great art. They took only the scrolls of their most treasured Torah as they fled to neighboring Portugal. Still, Ferdinand and Isabella were not satisfied. When Portugal's young King Manoel asked for their daughter's hand in a politically-designed marriage, they gave their consent on the condition that the entire Iberian penninsula be freed of Jews. Manoel agreed to their conditions, but he was reluctant to rid his country of such a hard-working and creative segment of the population. He proposed, instead, to baptize the Jews into the Catholic Church en masse. In the chaos that followed, Jews were rounded up by the thousands and holy water was flung at them. Many Jews protested, even to the extreme of killing their own children rather than have them baptized into an alien faith. But others chose to feign cooperation. These "New Christians" were commonly called "Marranos" ("pigs") or, sometimes, "Conversos" (converts).

(One modern writer, Rita Arditti, has refused to use the insulting term "Marranos" in her recounting of this history; however, others feel that such a refusal does less to restore dignity to our Jewish forebears than it does to whitewash or minimize the relentless malice of the medieval Christian church. The term is used here in condemnation of the Catholic oppressors, not in disrepect for their Jewish victims.)

Those called Marranos changed their names and tried to keep a low profile in religious matters, doing little more than attending Catholic mass. At home they would quietly fast on the Jewish Day of Atonement, join in the prayers of their ancestors and eat unleavened bread on Passover. But publicly they embraced the Christian faith. Still, there was no security. In 1506, a Marrano in Lisbon carelessly murmured a word of scepticism after hearing about a "miracle." With such small provocation, the Christians rioted, killing hundreds of Marranos that day.

It was into this atmosphere that Beatrice was born in 1510. Only at home was she secretly called by her Jewish name "Gracia Nasi." ("Gracia" was the equivalent of the Hebrew "Hannah" and "Nasi" was the name of the Jewish clan of her ancestors.) Despite the severe oppression, her family was extremely wealthy. She added to her wealth when she was eighteen by marrying Francisco Mendes, the son of another affluent Marrano family. Just eight years later, in 1536, her husband died. That same year, the Holy Office of the Inquisition was established in Lisbon.

Portugal was no longer safe. With all the resources at her disposal, Beatrice, her young daughter, and her sister fled to Antwerp in Flanders (an area now encompassed by Belgium and France). She sought the protection of her husband's brother, Diogo, who had lived in Antwerp for some time. Antwerp was better than Lisbon, but not much. The Inquisitors, jealous of the Mendes fortune, repeatedly harassed Diogo, arresting him for heresy or for harboring Jews who had not yet "converted." He endured trials and imprisonment and had to fight to keep his fortune. Antwerp was not a secure home for Beatrice but only the first stop in a long search for safety.

In Antwerp, Beatrice worked with Diogo, not only as a business partner, but also as a partner in an intricate covert operation to assist Jews trying to escape persecution. Together they acted as if to fulfill the mandate of the ancient scriptures:

> You shall not pervert the justice due to the sojourner or to the fatherless, or take a widow's garment in pledge, but you shall remember that you were a slave in Egypt and the Lord your God redeemed you from there; therefore I command you to do this.
> (Deuteronomy 24: 17-18)

Despite all his troubles with the Inquisitors, Diogo Mendes was the spice king of Europe, and he had a monopoly on the pepper trade. His business empire reached into Italy, France, Germany, England. Beatrice and Diogo used these connections to help the Jews fleeing from the Inquisitors. When spice ships docked at Southampton or Plymouth, for example, a Mendes employee from London would board the ship to assist any Marrano on board in the next leg of the journey.

But the Inquisition was closing in. For their own safety, Beatrice and Diogo made plans to leave Antwerp, but, before they were able to get out, Diogo died. Beatrice inherited the fortune, the business enterprises, and the underground railroad. Beatrice and her family abandoned their home and fled to Venice, and from Venice they fled to Ferrara, Italy.

It was in Ferrara that Beatrice dropped the Marrano facade and embraced her true religious heritage. From that time on she was known by her Jewish name, Gracia Nasi. And it was in Ferrara that Doña Gracia, as she was called, became fully involved in providing safe passage and sanctuary to the Jews fleeing the Inquisition in Portugal. Samuel Usque, who chronicled her efforts in the 1906 publication, *Consolation for the Tribulations of Israel*, wrote of her:

> Who has seen, as you have, the Divine mercy reveal itself in human guise, as He has shown and continues to show you for your succor? Who has seen revived the intrinsic piety of Miriam, offering her life to save her brethren? the great prudence of Deborah, in governing her people? that infinite virtue and great sanctity of Esther, in helping those who are persecuted? the much praised strength of the most chaste and magnanimous widow Judith, in delivering those hemmed in by travail? Such has the Lord sent to you in these days from the most supreme rank of His armies, embodying them in a soul of His which by high chance and your happy lot is installed in the most proper womanly body of the fortunate Jewess Nasci.

> She it is who at the beginning of their journey greatly helps your necessitous sons, who are prevented by penury from saving themselves from the pyre and undertaking so long a road, her hope giving them strength.

> As for those who have already left and have arrived in Flanders and elsewhere overcome by poverty, or who stand distressed by the sea in danger that they will not be able to fare further, she helps these her dependents with a most liberal hand, with money and many other aids and comforts.

> It is she who shows them favor in the asperity of the stormy Alps or Germany and in other lands, and in the extreme misery when the many horrors and misfortunes of the long voyage overtake them, helping them willingly with her succor....

In such wise, with her golden arm and heavenly grasp, she raised most of those of this people from the depths of this and other infinite travail in which they were kept enthralled in Europe by poverty and sin; she brings them to safe lands and does not cease to guide them, and gathers them to the obedience and precepts of their God of old.

Thus she has been your tried strength in your weakness; a bank where the weary rest; a fountain of clear water where the parched drink; a fruit-laden shady tree where the hungry eat and the desolate find rest; and for you, more particularly, she was part of that great succor, and remains at all times a tried relief in all the miseries of the Portuguese people....

In brief, the wide pinions and outspread wings of this eagle have saved a great part of your sons in their flight from the cruelty of the Portuguese, so that she thus imitated the Lord at the time of the Exodus from Egypt.

Shortly after Doña Gracia arrived in Ferrara, there was an outbreak of the plague. The Inquisitors used this disaster to stir up fear and hatred of the Jews. Marranos fleeing Portugal were blamed for infecting the whole population, and suddenly new rules were issued expelling the newly-arrived Portuguese Marranos from the city. Once again, the Jews were forced out of their homes, salvaging only what they could carry on their backs. No one, it seemed, would lend a hand to the suffering wanderers except Doña Gracia, who filled boats with food and other supplies for them as they fled in the night. Again, she used her business contacts to help fleeing people find new places to rest from their persecution.

Doña Gracia left Ferrara after only two years and took her energy, skill, and compassion to the Turkish Empire that was, at that time, a comparative Promised Land to the Jews fleeing Europe's Inquisition. Those who saw the forty-four-year-old businesswoman arrive in Constantinople remembered her four coaches filled with beautifully-dressed women, mostly servants, and the procession of forty horsemen.

In Constantinople, Gracia Nasi continued to prosper. She owned fleets of ships which carried wool, pepper, grain, and textiles to ports around the world. This woman, who was called "the heart of her people," continued to use her influence to work for change in both the personal and the larger political arenas. She was instrumental in promoting a boycott against the city of Ancona where unrepenting Jews had been massacred by order of the Pope. She also continued her philanthropy, feeding eighty of the most needy at her table every day as well as funding hospitals, synagogues, schools and scholars. She earned a reputation as a patroness of Jewish learning. And she continued to conduct an underground railroad, using her business agents in the world's great cities to provide sanctuary for those escaping persecution.

> The Underground Railroad didn't run on steam,
> The Underground Railroad didn't run on coal.
> The pounding you heard was a pulsing blood stream.
> What made the Road run was the strength of the soul.
>
> —Canadian folksong

A SANCTUARY MOVEMENT called the Underground Railroad emerged in the 1800s in the United States in resistance to the prosperous slave trade. White, African-American and Native Peoples in the Americas worked together to organize the series of codes, temporary places of refuge, and systems of transportation used to assist in the escapes of enslaved people. Successful escapes, however, depended primarily on the strength of the African-American community, both free and enslaved.

The cooperation and skills of a whole network of people were needed for each escape. Information about plants, roots, and herbs was needed to secure food and medicine on a long journey through swamps and woods. Knowledge of the night sky and weather patterns as well as a keen sense of direction were also skills that could mean the difference between survival and capture. Slaves were prohibited by law from learning to read and write, so obtaining these skills was subversive activity. With a little education, slaves forged passes and read public notices or newspapers for information vital to the resistance.

Harriet Tubman, the most famous of the conductors on the Underground Railroad, successfully led three hundred people out of slavery on nineteen trips into auction block territory. She used every skill her father had taught her, including how to walk through the woods without making a sound.

Secret codes were common among the enslaved people, and a network capable of passing secret information was vital to the sanctuary movement. In "Memories of a Contraband," written in 1893, Elizabeth Hyde Botume wrote about some of the ways information was shared among slaves:

> Without any knowledge of newspapers or books or telegraphy, the slaves had their own way of gathering news from the whole country. They had secret signs, an "Underground Telephone"....Intuitively they learned all the tricks of dramatic art. Their perceptions were

quickened. When seemingly absorbed in work, they saw and heard all that was going on around them. They memorized with wonderful ease and correctness....Not long ago I heard some Negro women talking of old times over their sewing. One said, "My father and the other boys used to crawl under the house an' lie on the ground to hear massa read the newspaper to missis when they first began to talk about the war."

The remarkable account of slavery and escape written by Harriet Jacobs (who wrote under the pseudonym Linda Brent) reveals how important the secret acts of resistance were in aiding those trying to escape. Her autobiography, *Incidents In the Life of a Slave Girl: Written By Herself*, was edited by the antislavery writer Lydia Maria Child and published in 1861. The author's claim to the work was largely disputed by scholars for one hundred and twenty years until 1981 when Jean Fagan Yellin, a persistent and now acclaimed researcher, verified the details of the story.

Jacobs was born into captivity in South Carolina in 1818. When she was twelve she, by the law of the land, became the legal property of the five-year-old daughter of a physician named Dr. Flint. Flint found the intelligent young mulatto woman attractive and spent the rest of his life in the pursuit of Harriet Jacobs' "voluntary submission" to his sexual desire.

> My master met me at every turn, reminding me that I belonged to him, and swearing by heaven and earth that he would compel me to submit to him. If I went out for a breath of fresh air, after a day of unwearied toil, his footsteps dogged me. If I knelt by my mother's grave, his dark shadow fell on me even there. The light heart which nature had given me became heavy with sad forebodings.

Repeatedly in her account, Jacobs wrote of the double bind of women who were considered favorite slaves. These women suffered crude sexual harassment and rape from the master as well as the misdirected jealousy and rage of the mistress. Jacobs endured every hated minute of a life that was not her own until her children were of the age to be put to work. She wrote:

> When I lay down beside my child I felt how much easier it would be to see her die than to see her master beat her about as I daily saw him beat other little ones. The spirit of the mothers was so crushed by the lash that they stood by without courage to remonstrate. How much more must I suffer before I should be "broke in" to that degree?

In 1839, being reasonably sure that she could secure a promise from a prominent white male friend that he would purchase her children and allow them to live with her grandmother, Jacobs began a seven-year-long process of escape. Many of the details were omitted from her account because, at the time of publication, the United States not only still had legalized slavery but had passed the Fugitive Slave Law, a law that made it possible to retrieve escaped slaves from free states. In her writing, Jacobs took great care not to implicate anyone still living in the slaveholding South nor those who had assisted her in the North. Still, the details in her account document that resistance among the slaves was part of their daily routine of survival in bondage. Jacobs recognized this:

> Who can blame slaves for being cunning? They are constantly compelled to resort to it. It is the only weapon of the weak and oppressed against the strength of their tyrants.

It took over seven years for Jacobs to reach the North and freedom. For those seven years she remained in hiding in her own community. One of the first to respond to a plea for help was a white woman who owned several slaves. According to Jacobs, "she treated them kindly and would never allow any of them to be sold. She was unlike the majority of slaveholders." Some in the African-American community trusted her, though not her husband who "held many slaves." The white woman agreed to be a part of the conspiracy. Word of her offer of asylum was sent to Jacobs who was hiding at the home of a friend.

> I received a message to leave my friend's house at such an hour and go to a certain place where a friend would be waiting for me. As a matter of prudence no names were mentioned. I had no means of conjecturing who I was to meet or where I was going. I did not like to move thus blindfolded, but I had no choice. It would not do for me to remain where I was. I disguised myself, summoned up courage to meet the worst, and went to the appointed place.

The person who met her was a black slave named Betty, the white woman's trusted cook. Together, the black slave and the white slaveholder hid Jacobs in the heart of a thriving plantation. Jacobs stayed in a locked storeroom for most of her time there, but on the few occasions when Dr. Flint and the slavecatchers ventured too near, Betty whisked Jacobs away to an even more secret hiding place; she lifted up a plank in the kitchen floor and hid the escaped woman in a narrow space prepared with a lining of buffalo skin and a quilt. The fact that this hiding place was furnished suggests that Jacobs was not the first person nor probably the last to be hidden in Betty's kitchen.

During the hours that Jacobs hid in the crawl space, Betty cleverly used her proximity to provide Jacobs with information:

> In my shallow bed I had but just room enough to bring my hands to my face to keep the dust out of my eyes; for Betty walked over me twenty times in an hour, passing from the dresser to the fireplace. When she was alone I could hear her pronouncing anathemas over Dr. Flint and all his tribe....When the housemaids were about, she

had sly ways of drawing them out that I might hear what they would say. She would repeat stories she had heard about my being in this or that or the other place. To which they would answer....

As she walked back and forth in the performance of her culinary duties, she talked apparently to herself but with the intention that I should hear what was going on....

When it became necessary for Jacobs to leave this plantation, Betty managed to find a disguise for her: a suit of sailor's clothes which included a jacket, trousers, and canvas hat. She accompanied Jacobs to the gate of the plantation, instructing her to "walk ricketty, like de sailors."

At the gate, Jacobs left behind the white-controlled plantation and gave her life over to the African-American community. Peter, a young slave whom Jacobs knew and trusted, accompanied her through the streets:

It was a long time since I had taken a walk out of doors and the fresh air revived me. It was also pleasant to hear a human voice speaking to me above a whisper.

They walked to the wharf where they were met by her uncle, a seaman. Here she learned that her friends and relatives were at a loss as to how to help her. Every vessel sailing North was being searched. Dr. Flint was following even the most remote leads in his efforts to find his female slave. Her escape was his humiliation, and he was turning the world upside down to find her.

For two days Peter and her uncle hid Jacobs in Snaky Swamp, a thirty-mile stretch of abandoned bamboo marsh populated only by mosquitos and snakes.

I dreaded to enter this hiding place. But I was in no situation to choose and I gratefully accepted the best that my poor, persecuted friends could do for me....

Peter landed first and with a large knife cut a path through bamboos and briers of all descriptions. He came back, took me in his arms, and carried me to a seat made among the bamboos. Before we reached it, we were covered with hundreds of mosquitos....As the light increased, I saw snake after snake crawling round us....I passed a wretched night for the heat of the swamp, the mosquitos, and the constant terror of snakes had brought on a burning fever....But even those large, venomous snakes were less dreadful to my imagination than the white men in that community called civilized.

As there were no ships available on which to conceal Jacobs, she was led back through the streets in her sailor's disguise and, with her face darkened with charcoal, to her grandmother's house. Her uncle had prepared a trap-door entrance to a garret in a shed behind the house.

The space was three feet high, nine feet long, and seven feet wide. There were no windows, only a one-inch hole for light and air. This was to be Jacobs' universe for the next seven years.

For seven summers the heat was intense, and the air in the closed space was stifling. For seven winters the chilly, wet air left her feet and hands numb. For seven years she looked out of the one-inch peephole at her children who were living in her grandmother's home. They were not told that their mother was hiding there because it was believed that the secret would have tormented and endangered them. Only later, on the night before she finally departed for the North, did Jacobs learn that her young son had heard her cough just once and had thereafter suspected that she was hiding in the ceiling of the shed. He had actually tried to protect her by leading playmates and visitors away from the place near the shed where he had once heard his mother cough. He was so cautious and protective of his secret that he didn't mention his suspicion to anyone, including his grandmother or sister.

And for seven years she peered through the one-inch hole, watching enslaved people and free walk past her hiding place. What she observed from her narrow vantage point often left her feeling thankful for her terrible refuge.

> I saw a woman rush wildly by, pursued by two men. She was a slave, the wet nurse of her mistress's children. For some trifling offence her mistress ordered her to be stripped and whipped. To escape the degredation [sic] and the torture, she rushed to the river, jumped in, and ended her wrongs in death.

Night after night for seven years, the old grandmother and a few other relatives managed to keep Jacobs alive with food, medicine, news, and words of encouragement. And still the slavehunters searched for her, offering a reward for her capture. Finally, the day came when a message was sent from her uncle, still employed at the wharf, that arrangements had been made for her escape by sea. Jacobs crawled out of the three-by-seven-by-nine-foot space that had been her refuge and knelt to pray beside the old woman who had faithfully sheltered her through seven years of danger. Jacobs recounts that:

> I never could tell how we reached the wharf. My brain was all of a whirl, and my limbs tottered under me. At an appointed place we met my uncle Phillip who had started before us on a different route that he might reach the wharf first and give us timely warning if there was any danger. A rowboat was in readiness....

"WHOSOEVER SAVES A SINGLE SOUL SAVES A WORLD." This truth, gleaned from the religious literature of the Jews, holds within it whatever magic and goodness there is to be found in the world's experience of the Nazi reign of terror. In Nazi Europe, the courts, the police, the schools, the hospitals, and all of the institutions a person might rely on to be just or fair turned into institutions of persecution and mass torture almost overnight.

Under Nazi rule, it was a crime punishable by death to give a Jew a loaf of bread. People who offered bread were hanged in the center of town as a warning to others. And still there were the few who offered bread until the last.

Under Nazi rule it was a crime not to greet another with the words "Heil Hitler." Those who chose instead to call out a traditional "hello" were reported to authorities as "suspicious" and inevitably lost their jobs. And still there were the few who said "hello" until the last.

It was a crime to own or listen to a radio. To be found listening to a radio could mean immediate deportation to a death camp. And still there were the few who hid radios and listened to Allied news reports and spread information until the last.

It was a crime to write, distribute or read opinions that differed from Nazi propaganda. To be found with illegally mimeographed leaflets could mean torture and death. And still there were the few who wrote and distributed outlawed opinions, hiding bundles of such flyers beneath maternity dresses or in baby carriages or sliding pieces of paper with the words "Hitler is a butcher" in between the pages of library books.

It was, of course, a crime to hide people marked for extermination: Jews, socialists, gay men, lesbians, gypsies, intellectuals, people who were mentally retarded, or anyone the Nazis found objectionable or uncooperative.

It was a crime to help people escape to safety. Most good citizens looked the other way. They did not want to see the injustice, the starvation, the deportations, the death. They did not want to hear the screams or the weeping. And still there were those who offered sanctuary until the last.

Rachel Auerbach, a Jewish survivor of the Warsaw ghetto, wrote about those who helped Jews:

> They were university professors, railroad workers, bus drivers, priests, wives of high officers of the army, peddlers, merchants, peasants, particularly peasants who, for a single act of charity, giving of a loaf of bread to a Jew, a pint of milk or a night's accommodation in the barn, were cruelly punished, often killed, and their homes set on fire by the Germans.

In considering why such people risked so much when they could not possibly have known the scope of the horror, and when they were faced with such severe consequences for the sake of only the few lives immediately before them, historian Claudia Koonz wrote:

> People who said No to Hitler did not begin to be brave in 1933; the habit of perceiving injustice and defending one's principles had developed in childhood. In interviews I have noticed that, whereas ex- (and not-so-ex-) Nazis routinely justify their participation in the Third Reich in terms of "higher" ideals, like patriotism and admiration for Hitler's authoritarianism, the resisters minimize the decision-making process altogether. They state simply that they saw no alternative; they do not recall suffering agonies of doubt. Looking back, they see their choices as personal and moral rather than ideological. Phrases like "my belief in Marxism" or "my Christian principles" occur only rarely in their memoirs. Instead, people recall that events in daily life—friends and neighbors in trouble—led them to resist.

The details of the Holocaust are always numbing, as are the details of any institutionalized and overt persecution, torture, and extermination directed toward one group of people by another. Who can comprehend the numbers: 25,000 Jews murdered per day at Treblinka, 34,000 at Auschwitz? But in the heart of the most massive horror are stories of courage, and at the core of each story of courage is the truth: "Whosoever saves a single soul, saves a world."

Ellen Nielsen and Elise Petersen were two Danish women who saved a number of "worlds" by offering sanctuary. They were neighbors in Dragør, and both were naïve about world affairs. Neither had paid much attention to Hitler or even to German occupation of Denmark. They simply went on with the business of their lives.

The business of Ellen Nielsen's life was fish. She was a widow with six children to support which she did as a fishmonger. Every morning she went to the docks and bought fresh fish to sell. Her neighbor, Elise Petersen, was a schoolteacher.

One day in October 1943, as Nielsen hawked her fish along the docks, two brothers who worked the docks as flower vendors approached her with a question. They wanted to know if she would speak to her friends, the fishermen, on their behalf and ask if any would be willing to sail them to Sweden. But why did the flower vendors want to go to Sweden? Nielsen wanted to know. The brothers were amazed. Hadn't the fishmonger heard that the German Nazis had started rounding up Danish Jews and deporting them to concentration camps? No. And hadn't the good fishmonger realized that the brothers were Jews? No. Nielsen hadn't known any of this, but, now that she did know, she was stunned by Nazi savagery and was determined to help. She spoke to the fishermen and found several willing to help her friends get to Sweden. The brothers made it to safety.

Word of Nielsen's bold action reached the underground resistance movement, and soon she was asked to aid more Jews fleeing for their lives. Nielsen never hesitated. She became the liaison between the underground conductors and the fishermen who sailed to Sweden through the moonlit waters with their human cargo. Often Nielsen and her children hid Jews in their tiny house as they waited for nightfall. Her oldest sons helped lead the frightened people from the house to the boats.

It was about this same time that Nielsen's neighbor, Elise Petersen, received a telephone call from her old friend Kaj Holbeck, a newspaper editor. She had once worked for him as a housemaid and had often hoped he would visit her in Dragør now that she was a teacher, but Holbeck had always been too busy. She was surprised at his phone call. She was even more surprised when she invited him to dinner, and he not only accepted but asked if he might bring seven guests with him. Petersen suspected at once that his guests were people in trouble with the German Nazis who now patrolled the streets of Denmark. Without hesitating, she said yes.

Holbeck showed up that evening with a six-month-old girl, two boys of eight and ten years, and four trembling adults. Petersen looked at the baby. How could this little person be anyone's enemy? It was perverse. The tension of the evening was overwhelming, and no one ate the food Petersen had prepared. At midnight a doctor arrived to medicate the three children so that they wouldn't make any sounds during the escape. The schoolteacher's heart almost broke as she watched the children drift into unconsciousness. What sort of world had made this escape necessary? she wondered. Again there was a quiet knock at her door. It was a Danish policeman who quickly reassured the schoolteacher that he was a member of the resistance and had come to lead the people to the boat. As the little party stumbled into the darkness, Petersen whispered to Holbeck, "You can use my house for this type of thing any time you wish."

Soon the neighbors were working side by side, sharing the work of hiding refugees in their tiny homes. Sometimes Petersen would take the overflow from Nielsen's house, hiding people for anywhere from a few hours to a few days. The fishmonger and the schoolteacher found the Nazi attitude toward women an advantage in their resistance work. The Nazis regarded women as stupid. Who would ever guess that the fishmonger's daily conversations with fishermen and flower vendors were subversive or that the schoolteacher sometimes had fifty people hiding in her three rooms?

In August 1944, Petersen's underground sanctuary work was discovered by the Nazis. She spent the duration of the war on the run, changing identity papers and hiding with friends. Nielsen was caught by the Gestapo in December 1944. When she refused to reveal the names of her contacts in the resistance, she was sent to Ravensbruck, the notorious women's concentration camp, and was ordered to carry babies to and from the gas chambers.

"ONE OF THESE DAYS—POW! RIGHT IN THE KISSER!" Ralph Kramden shouted at Alice night after night on the 1950s television sitcom, "The Honeymooners." Jackie Gleason's character, Ralph, would roll his big eyes and threaten Alice with his bunched-up fist. And Alice would roll her eyes and feign boredom with a sarcastic smirk, perhaps because she knew that "one of these days" would never come in the context of a television comedy, that the scriptwriters would protect her from Ralph's fist "right in the kisser." The line was meant to be funny.

In real life, however, there are no scriptwriters to protect women from the fists of their husbands or lovers. On the contrary, the scriptwriters of life have penned laws, scriptures, scholarly texts, and proverbs sanctioning male violence.

> "A woman, a horse and a hickory tree,
> the more you beat them the better they be."
> —English proverb

> "A wife may love a husband who never beats her,
> but she does not respect him."
> —Russian proverb

> "The man who is not master of his wife
> is not worthy of being a man."
> —18th century French saying

> "Women should be struck regularly, like gongs."
> —Chinese saying

In male-dominant cultures, the cries and occasional protests of individual women have been taken for granted; the beating, sexual abuse, and even murder of wives have been deemed domestic, private matters. In the twentieth century, however, women riding the waves of mass movements for social change have managed, at times, to challenge the silence shrouding male violence and have organized to resist it. One form of women's organized resistance to male domestic violence has been the establishment of networks providing sanctuary where women could hide from batterers, heal, and consider new options.

IN THE YEARS FOLLOWING THE RUSSIAN REVOLUTION, women in villages near the Caspian Sea, in an area known as Soviet Central Asia, were encouraged to come out of their brutally-imposed isolation. Special community centers called *shenotdyel* were set up to provide assistance to women, and these soon became places of refuge for those escaping tyrannical husbands. Women began to learn about each other's lives and discovered that the brutality they had experienced as individuals was a shared experience.

The *shenotdyel* became places of refuge. They also became places where stories of women's pain and survival were shared and recorded, stories like the following.

One day in the mid-1920s, a woman escaped from her home to a *shenotdyel* in Turkmenia. She appeared to be an elderly woman, frail and frightened, with matted hair and skin covered with deep dark bruises and crawling with lice. At the *shenotdyel*, she soaked in a hot bath for more than an hour, and, when she emerged, the other women were stunned to see that she was not the elderly woman they had supposed, but a girl of seventeen. As the girl regained her strength and confidence, she told her story. In exchange for a few camels and some silver ornaments, her uncle had sold the young woman to an old man to be his second wife. In her new home she was starved, beaten by the man and his other wife, and forced to sleep in ashes in a dark corner of the hut. One day this real-life Cinderella was hung upside down from the roof, beaten, and tortured with hot irons.

In the shelter, the young woman met others who had stories as horrifying as her own. She learned that she was not the only one, that the way she had been treated was common but wrong, and that it was against the ideals of sexual equality being espoused by the new Soviet government.

In China later that same decade, a ten-year-old slave, Yu Whei, escaped from her home and found refuge in a women's sheter in Hupeh province. The refuge was provided by one of the many women's unions set up during the Nationalist Revolution, a revolution that was, that year, being brutally squelched. But the child did not know this as she and the other escaped slave girls and battered women in the shelter told their stories to a sympathetic visitor from the West, Anna Louise Strong, a pro-communist journalist. Strong and the others listened as Yu Whei told how she had been sold for a large sum of money at the age of four to the mayor of a small town and how the man had routinely beaten her with iron tongs two or three times a day. Now, she said, she was happy at the women's shelter because she was safe and learning to read.

Strong learned that the Chinese women's unions also assisted those who sought to leave their abusive husbands through divorce. The unions facilitated divorce proceedings during the revolution and occasionally punished batterers by forcing them to walk through village streets wearing dunce caps until they vowed to stop beating women.

The women's unions were up against three thousand years of custom, and the organizers knew it. They traveled from district to district, entering homes and marketplaces to talk with women, encouraging them to tell their stories. They brought a new message to the women of China:

> We tell them we come to save them from oppression and to bring a new way of thinking. We explain that men and women are now equal. Even though you are a woman you are still a person. We say they have a duty to society and not only to husbands.

WORLDWIDE, WOMEN STOPPED HIDING the violence in their lives and started hiding each other during the 1970s, fifty years after the early women's centers were organized in Soviet Central Asia and in China. The new sanctuary movement for battered women was the direct result of the global feminist movement that called into question traditional assumptions about gender, including the age-old violence against women, inside the home and out. But even more than providing a new framework within which to examine the phenomenon of male power and privilege, women everywhere began to tell their stories. Breaking the walls of isolation and shame, they heard in each other's stories variations of the same experience. What had felt like a personal matter—a husband's fist, "pow, right in the kisser"—*was* personal. It was also repeated in household after household, on street after street, in nation after nation and as such could be understood as a statement of power. The women concluded that "the personal is political."

In London in 1971, Erin Pizzey got tired of talking about the violence in women's lives. She asked her local city council for a house that could be a women's "advice center." The council gave her a rat-infested four-room shack with an outhouse in the middle of a London slum. Before Pizzey could finish painting the cracked walls of her Chiswick Women's Aid, women began to crowd into the tiny shelter, seeking escape from their violent partners and a safe place for their children.

In St. Paul, Minnesota, in March 1972, members of the Women's Advocates Collective, who started a legal information phone service, were surprised when most of the calls were from battered women desperate for escape. Day after day the calls came in—from pregnant women who feared miscarriages after being beaten directly in the belly, from women whose ankles or wrists had been broken, from women who hid the butcher knives every evening when their husbands came home, from women who lived in pain and fear day in and day out. They got calls from women who had repeatedly called the police but had been refused help for what was deemed "only a family matter." They got calls from women whose lives were in danger. The Advocates were stunned to learn that none of the public welfare or social services in the city provided emergency shelter for battered women. These women were literally trapped in their own homes. The Advocates decided to provide sanctuary in their own homes and apartments, and for two years they had women and children sleeping on their living room floors. Finally, in April 1974, they obtained a house, and, in October of that year, women began to move in.

That same year, six women in Amsterdam got fed up with waiting for social services to aid battered women in the Netherlands. In September 1974, they occupied an abandoned house and established it as a sanctuary for women and children who needed refuge from violent men. They called their shelter "Bliff van m'n Liff" ("Hands Off My Body"). As is always the case with shelters for battered women, regardless of the country, within ten days the house was filled to capacity with women sporting black eyes and loosened front teeth, women with cigarette burns on their bellies and welts on their backs.

Also in 1974, feminists in Sydney, Australia, took over two abandoned houses and refused to move out. These houses became Elsie, a shelter for battered women. Halfway around the world feminists in Glasgow, Scotland converted a three-bedroom apartment into Interval House, a haven for women escaping violent homes. And across the Atlantic Ocean, Transition House was opened in Vancouver, British Columbia.

On November 2, 1979, Danish feminists stormed the huge, old, dilapidated Danner House, scheduled to be turned into offices and shops for Copenhagen's business class. The women demanded that the nineteenth-century palace be used for its original purpose: to house desperate working-class women in need of help. It had been built by Louise Rasmussen, Countess of Danner, whose life was the stuff of fairy tales. She had been born out of wedlock in 1815 to an impoverished maid, but she escaped her mother's fate to become a dancer in the Royal Danish Ballet, through which she met the King of Denmark, Frederick VII. She fascinated the king and became his mistress. He granted her the title of countess and left her a large sum of money upon his death. Rasmussen never forgot her origins. When she inherited the king's money, she built the little palace in the middle of Copenhagen with the intent that it house the city's homeless and poor women. The twentieth-century feminists who occupied the house reminded the city fathers of this bit of history. Nevertheless, the government claimed the building, demanding that the women either vacate or purchase it. The women refused to give in. They launched a fierce media campaign and in five months had raised enough money to rescue Rasmussen's palace. Even before renovations began, battered women and their frightened children were streaming through the doors of Danner House seeking refuge from violent men.

By the beginning of the 1980s, feminists the world over were forcing men's private violence into the public spotlight, and women were protecting each other. In every city where women began to speak the truth of what happened in private behind the walls of their homes, they discovered oceans of pain. Crisis centers opened in Berlin and Barcelona, in Bogota and Tokyo. Battered women sought the help of their sisters in New Delhi, and in war-torn Jerusalem. In 1981 in Thailand, Kanitha Wichiencharoen, an active member of the Women Lawyers' Association, founded that country's first shelter for battered women when she turned her own home into a refuge. In 1989, the southern African country of Zimbabwe opened its first counseling service for survivors of rape and battery in the city of Harare. It was called Musasa which, in the Shona language, means temporary shelter.

"WHAT IS IT TO LOSE ONE'S CHILD?" asked author E. M. Broner of the four hundred women attending the conference on The Politics of Child Custody in New York City in March of 1986. "What is it to lose the person to whom you were the first syllable?...It is to lose the greatest part of our world....It makes craters in our soul like the moon. It hollows us." The women listened in grim silence. "Despite our bringing the child to our breast and covering the soft spot on its head, we cannot ultimately protect our child."

This desire, to protect the children, had prompted the development of a new Underground Railroad in the second half of the 1980s. This time the focus of the sanctuary movement was sexually abused children. In courtroom after courtroom, judges were awarding custody to economically-secure fathers, even when those fathers had been accused of being physically violent or sexual with their own children. As a result, some of the mothers had taken their children into hiding. This was not the first time women had helped each other challenge the laws which have traditionally granted men ownership of children.

In 1860, the wife of a Massachusetts state senator and mother of three discovered that her husband had committed adultery. When she confronted him, he kicked her down a flight of stairs, beat her, and then had her committed to an insane asylum. Over a year later, upon her release, she abducted her own daughter and fled. She sought the help of Lydia Mott in Albany, New York, and Susan B. Anthony who was visiting Mott at the time. The two activists listened to the story told by the disheveled, frantic woman and decided to help her. For a year they hid her with various friends, most of them Quakers and abolitionists. But many women's rights leaders and antislavery activists (including William Lloyd Garrison) felt that Anthony's interference would endanger their causes and urged her to have the child returned to the father. But Anthony responded:

> Don't you break the law every time you help a slave to Canada? Well, the law which gives the father the sole ownership of the children is just as wicked and I'll break it just as quickly. You would die before you would deliver a slave to his master and I will die before I will give up the child to its father.

The daughter was eventually kidnapped on her way to Sunday School and returned to the father.

At the Politics of Child Custody conference in 1986, women once again told horror stories of violence and celebrated the networks of women willing to help each other. During the speakout, one woman who called herself Bridgette stood nervous and thin, disguised beneath a dramatic black veil. She had been beaten early in her marriage and had eventually left the marriage with her infant daughter. During custody proceedings, the courts had awarded her husband weekend visits with the child.

> When my daughter was about nine months old, she came home from a visit with her father bleeding vaginally. I took it to court. All I asked for was protection for my daughter, nothing more, nothing less.

What she got was a lot less. The judge decided Bridgette was overreacting, and he awarded the father full custody.

> Fourteen weeks later, I found my daughter on the floor holding her genitals and crying. I brought her to the hospital. There was medical evidence of abuse. There was an emergency hearing and custody was reversed.

But the nightmare was not over. The judge awarded the father supervised weekend visitations. During the conference's roundtable discussion, "Incest, Battery and Custody," Louise Armstrong, the author of *Kiss Daddy Goodnight: A Speakout on Incest* said, "It is almost inconceivable to believe what it feels like on a Friday night to send your kid to his [sic] weekend molestation." And she commented on the notion of supervised visitations:

> It is a silly thing to have babysitting for grownup men! I don't know where this idea comes from that you're supposed to have his mother watching when he plays with his kid.

When questions and comments were invited from the floor, a woman passed around a drawing her five-year-old son had made after his last visit with his father. A stick-figure daddy with a huge penis held a stick-figure child by the ankle. The child's mouth was open, red and screaming.

Faced with the failure of the courts to protect their children, a number of women formed the new Underground Railroad, helping each other's children "disappear." Mothers and children became fugitives on the run, hiding behind secret identities in safe houses. Some women, like Dr. Elizabeth Morgan and Karen Newsom, went to prison rather than disclose the whereabouts of their children. By 1989, there were an estimated one thousand safe house sanctuaries in the United States alone, hiding children from sexually abusive parents. Those who hide the children are primarily from feminist, children's rights, and religious organizations.

The most public personality behind the Atlanta-based Underground Railroad is Faye Yager. She has dedicated her life to helping in the rescue of other mothers' children, perhaps because she was unable to rescue her own. In 1973, she walked into her kitchen in time to see Roger, her husband, sexually abusing her daughter, Michelle, who was in a high chair. Roger told her she had imagined the whole thing and had her hospitalized, saying that she had attempted suicide. Months later, when Yager was released from the hospital, she obtained temporary custody of Michelle, but Roger was allowed unsupervised contact. When a medical checkup revealed that Michelle had gonorrhea, Yager thought the judge would now protect her child. He did not; instead he awarded Roger full custody. Yager gave up. Years later, in 1986, Roger was arrested after police found videotapes showing him engaged in sex with two girls, one only ten years old. By then, Michelle had a drug habit. In 1987, when Yager read a newspaper report of another mother trying to rescue her children from what she perceived to be court-protected sexual assault, she finally understood that she was not the only one who had experienced this nightmare. "I saw this as my chance to change things, to make some sense out of what I had lived through," Yager said. And she vowed not to spend another dime on the legal system that had failed her and her daughter. She would spend her dimes instead on hotels where fugitive mothers and their children could hide.

This chapter began with the retelling of the story of a Jewish slave mother and an Egyptian princess who conspired together to provide sanctuary. It is a story that, 3,290 years later, still has the power to inspire.

SISTER DARLENE NICGORSKI WAS FOUND GUILTY on May 1, 1986, of transporting, aiding, and abetting the harboring of illegal aliens. Nicgorski was a nun of the Milwaukee-based School Sisters of

St. Francis. In 1980, she went to Guatemala to help set up a preschool program and began to train farm women to teach:

> We helped them learn to read by giving them bibles which, in their hands, became very radical books. They learned God is on the side of the poor and oppressed. Helping them understand the reality of their own lives became a very subversive act.

Six months later she was on the run, fleeing the death squads that had assassinated the priest, Father Tullio Maruzzo, with whom she had been working:

> Poor Tullio, his only crime was visiting the people in their village. I remember how the word "communist" was tossed around so freely when I was there; how we were labeled as such because we were working with the poor *campesinos* [small farmers]—helping them to serve their people and villages in areas of health, spiritual leadership and community development.

Nicgorski and the rest of the group of sisters went next to Chiapas, Mexico, to work with the 45,000 Guatemalan refugees living along the border of Mexico. There she heard the stories: stories of kidnapping, torture, terror, and death—stories that linked United States aid to the violence in the lives of the people of Central America. In 1982, Nicgorski returned to the United States, but she had been changed by her experiences in Central America. "At times I wished I was like I used to be—before I ever went to Guatemala," she has said. "When you come back, you don't fit here anymore. Not with your family, not with the social values. You feel only anger and a great sense of guilt at leaving so many who need help. I saw that I could move from guilt to responsibility by involving myself in the movement."

By "the movement," Nicgorski means the sanctuary movement, begun in 1980 to help Central American refugees find safety and new lives in the United States and Canada. Nicgorski found herself at odds with the laws of the United States. She served in immigration court as an expert witness for the refugees who were pleading for asylum, testifying to the repression in Guatemala. She watched a judge in Phoenix deny every application. She learned about the human rights violations suffered by the Central Americans hunted by the Immigration and Naturalization Service (INS) and detained in Phoenix. She was already discouraged with a legal system that sent refugees back to terror and death when she was told about the sanctuary movement. She knew that she had no choice but to be a part of it. She would side with those who had eluded border guards and ten-foot-high barriers and barbed-wire fences in search of safe havens. She found inspiration in ancient scripture:

When the question is one of life or death for a people, there is no room for equivocation or reasonable doubt. We must always side with life. Moses' Mother and Pharaoh's daughter did not waiver in the face of death....When the law supports death, it is separate from God.

Her own special hope was that she would be able to make it possible for some of the Guatemalans to tell their stories, albeit with masks and bandanas covering their faces. She became an outlaw for assisting people fleeing war and helping them speak the truth.

Probably the most important challenge of sanctuary is to ourselves. When we encounter masked refugees telling stories of persecution, we are invited to remove our own masks of security and power that often keep us from one another. The message of terrorism and hostages and guns soon becomes clear: until no one needs to ask for refuge, wear a mask, or watch their children starve, none of us is free.

Nicgorski herself chose to be a listener. For her, the refugees from Guatemala had become teachers bringing to life the word of God who sides with the poor and with those who seek justice:

Instead of us—the powerful, the educated, the wealthy—bringing the word to others, ironically our opportunity to hear the word of God comes from the refugees. But, it is real hard for us to be listeners and receivers in North America. We've got it all. We think we know it all....The refugees are the real missionaries....The church in Central America is a persecuted church: in Guatemala and El Salvador thousands of Christians have been massacred....Churches have been bombed, assaulted or burned....The church in Central America is alive and growing. It is the church of the prophets and martyrs today.

In her work for the sanctuary movement, Nicgorski helped connect hundreds of frightened and weary refugees to a network of activists in more than three hundred churches, synagogues, and universities throughout the United States and Canada that were willing to provide sanctuary until contacts could be made with relatives of the refugees. She also helped facilitate forums for discussion of INS involvement in the crisis of the Central American peoples. But in January 1985, she and ten colleagues were indicted by a federal grand jury for conspiracy and for transporting and harboring illegal aliens. After a trial lasting six months, Nicgorski and seven others were found guilty; she was given a suspended sentence and five years probation.

In Nicgorski's experience, it is primarily women who lead their neighbors to safety, though men continue to be publicly identified as the spokespersons for the movement. After their indictment, many priests and clergymen surfaced to speak for the defendants to give them "credibility." Nicgorski was not surprised; though men dominate the media spotlight, it is women who do the work.

> The underground railroad that transported Central American refugees from the desert of Arizona to the sisters' house of prayer in Kansas was sustained primarily by women. It was and to my knowledge still is women and many over forty who are doing the feeding, transporting, housing, and clothing of the Central Americans.

She has also noted that it is mostly low-paid, overworked female attorneys who spend twelve to fifteen hours a day defending refugees and handling their appeals for asylum in the courts.

Since her involvement in the sanctuary movement, Nicgorski has often reflected on the story of Moses' mother and Pharaoh's daughter, finding in it a message that reinforces her own courage and commitment.

> I realized that they were the first co-conspirators. These two women, one inside the system and one outside the destructive system conspired together to save a life....These women defied every law and order by the male paternalistic system to follow the truth they knew within themselves as women—life is valuable.

SOURCES

Gracia Nasi

Arditti, Rita. "To Be A Hanu." In *The Tribe of Dina: A Jewish Women's Anthology.* Melanie Kaye/Kantrowitz and Irena Klepfisz, eds. Montpelier, VT: Sinister Wisdom Books, 1986.

Daly, Mary. *Gyn/Ecology: The Metaethics of Radical Feminism.* Boston: Beacon Press, 1978.

Dworkin, Andrea. *Woman Hating.* New York: E.P. Dutton, 1974.

Gage, Matilda Joslyn. *Woman, Church and State: The Original Exposé of Male Collaboration Against the Female Sex.* Watertown, MA: Persephone Press, 1980.

Grahn, Judy. *Another Mother Tongue: Gay Words, Gay Worlds.* Boston: Beacon Press, 1984.

Henry, Sondra and Emily Taitz. *Written Out of History: Our Jewish Foremothers.* Fresh Meadows, NY: Biblio Press, 1983.

Roth, Cecil. *Doña Gracia of the House of Nasi.* Philadelphia: Jewish Publication Society of America, 1948/1977.

Harriet Jacobs

Brent, Linda. *Incidents in the Life of a Slave Girl.* New York: Harcourt Brace Jovanovich, 1973. Also see *Incidents in the Life of a Slave Girl.* Harriet A. Jacobs, Jean Fagan Yellin, ed. Cambridge, MA: Harvard University Press, 1987.

Davis, Angela Y. *Women, Race and Class.* New York: Random House, 1981.

Ford, Karen, Janet MacLean and Barry Wansbrough, eds. *Great Canadian Lives: Portraits in Heroism to 1867*. Scarborough, Ontario: Nelson Canada, 1985.

Gates, Henry Louis, Jr. "To Be Raped, Bred or Abused." *The New York Times Review of Books*. November 22, 1987.

Giddings, Paula. *When and Where I Enter: The Impact of Black Women on Race and Sex In America*. New York: Bantam Books, 1984.

Lerner, Gerda, ed. *Black Women in White America: A Documentary History*. New York: Random House, 1972.

Global Battered Women's Sanctuary Movement

Croll, Elisabeth. *Feminism and Socialism in China*. Boston: Routledge & Kegan Paul, 1978.

"Dirty Laundry." *Wives' Tales: A Newsletter About Ending Violence Against Women in the Home*. Park Slope Safe Homes Project, Brooklyn, NY (Spring 1984).

"A Fairy Tale Comes True: Copenhagen's Refuge for Battered Women." *Connexions: An International Women's Quarterly* no. 1 (Summer 1981).

Halle, Fannina W. *Women In the Soviet East*. Margaret M. Green, trans. New York: E.P. Dutton, 1938.

Martin, Del. *Battered Wives*. New York: Pocket Books, 1976.

Morgan, Robin, ed. *Sisterhood Is Global: The International Women's Movement Anthology*. Garden City, NY: Doubleday, 1984.

Schechter, Susan. *Women and Male Violence: The Visions and Struggles of the Battered Women's Movement*. Boston: South End Press, 1982.

Search, Gay. "London: Battered Wives." *Ms.* (June 1974).

Strong, Anna Louise. *China's Millions*. New York: Coward-McCann, Inc., 1928.

Women in the Custody Underground Railroad

Bader, Eleanor. "Court Gives Kids to Abusive Dads." *New Directions for Women* (Mar./Apr. 1988).

Chesler, Phyllis. *Mothers On Trial: The Battle for Children and Custody*. New York: McGraw-Hill, 1985.

Laurino, Maria. "Special Report: Custody Wars—Moms Held Hostage." *Ms.*, (Dec. 1988).

McAllister, Pam. "A Her-Story of Resistance." *Wives Tales: A Newsletter About Ending Violence Against Women in the Home*. Park Slope Safe Homes Project, Brooklyn, NY (Fall/Winter 1984-85).

McAllister, Pam. "Mothers Speak Out on Child Custody." *off our backs* (June 1986).

Podesta, Jane Sims and David Van Biema. "Running for Their Lives." *People Weekly* (Jan. 23, 1989).

Women in Resistance to the Nazis

Eliach, Yaffa. *Hasidic Tales of the Holocaust*. New York: Avon Books, 1982.

Flender, Harold. *Rescue in Denmark*. New York: Holocaust Library, 1980.

Friedman, Philip. *Their Brothers' Keepers: The Christian Heroes and Heroines Who Helped the Oppressed Escape the Nazi Terror*. New York: Holocaust Library, 1957/1978.

Koonz, Claudia. *Mothers in the Fatherland: Women, the Family and Nazi Politics*. New York: St. Martin's Press, 1987.

Laska, Vera, ed. *Women in the Resistance and in the Holocaust: The Voices of Eyewitnesses*. Westport, CT: Greenwood Press, 1983.

Rittner, Carol and Sondra Myers, eds. *The Courage to Care: Rescuers of Jews During the Holocaust*. New York: New York University Press, 1986.

Wyman, David. *The Abandonment of the Jews: America and the Holocaust 1941-1945*. New York: Pantheon Books, 1984.

Sister Darlene Nicgorski and the Sanctuary Movement

Brown, Rusty. "Sister Darlene Nicgorski." *Ms.* (Jan. 1987).

Gelbspan, Ross. "An Activist Recalls the Roots of Her Effort." *The Boston Globe*. January 10, 1987.

Hersh, Kathy Barber. "A Refuge for Refugees." *Mother Jones* (Jan. 1984).

Nicgorski, Darlene, SSSF. "Coming Together for Action." An address made to the Conference for All Arizona Women, Phoenix, Arizona, January, 1987.

Nicgorski, Darlene, SSSF. "Women, Church, Conspiracy and Truth Telling." An address made to the Harvard Divinity School Forum, 1987.

7

Hair Faces Bodies Feet
Bondage, Beauty, Being

Ladies, unhook your dresses and let everything hang loosely
about you.

—Elizabeth Cady Stanton
editorial in *The Lily*, 1851

Standing in line at the movies, I look around me at the women in
t-shirts and jeans who wait in relatively comfortable outfits today
because some nineteenth-century radical activists waged a very
serious struggle for the right of women to move freely. Bending to tie
my running shoes, it is easy to forget that women's bodies have
sometimes been the battlefields on which gender-specific restrictions
have been challenged and fought.

IN VICTORIAN ERA LITERATURE, on page after page, we find
delicate middle- and upper-class white women in the United States
and England fainting, languishing, and dropping like flies with
dizziness or headaches. Little wonder that they fainted—they couldn't
breathe. Fashion for these women had become increasingly restrictive.
By the mid-1800s, they were buried under yards of heavy material.
They were molded into tightly laced corsets, a combination bra and
girdle, with whalebone stays that dug severely into the soft flesh of
their bodies. Autopsies performed on women of the day often revealed
long, narrow grooves in their livers, caused, it is now believed, by the
stays that dug into them day after day as women tried to attain
sixteen-inch waists. Today's cultural ideal of western women is of
boyishly flat, adolescent bodies, but in the mid-1800s, girls in finishing
schools sometimes slept in their corsets to shape their developing
bodies into the hourglass figure or wasp waists that were in vogue. The

143

cost was great. By pinching their ribs and bellies into the vise grip of corsets, they actually displaced some of their internal organs. Doctors did a brisk business with pale women who were constantly ill with gallstones, ulcers, anemia, extreme menstrual problems, liver damage, lung diseases, and spine and rib injuries.

Only women of privilege could afford to so damage their bodies that they could not bend, walk, sit without great effort, or get dressed without assistance. As historian Janet Horowitz Murray has noted, fashionable women in restrictive clothes were "employed as billboards of their fathers' or husbands' wealth." Their clothes "simultaneously announced their importance and their lack of activity." To be feminine, one had to be fragile and as idle as possible. This, said women's rights advocate Elizabeth Cady Stanton, was the "poetry of dependence."

Outside of the urban areas and among the poor and working classes, women continued to wear loose-fitting gingham, wool, or calico dresses, and aprons. Some, like the mining women or the women who lived along the coasts and caught shrimp or fish, wore knee breeches or trousers under their dresses or pulled their skirts up between their legs and pinned the hems to their waistlines. But even these women were impeded in their work by the bulk and heaviness of the clothes. Both urban and rural women in the United States and in Europe continued to drag their long skirts in the mud. Dresses were dangerous, especially when they got caught on factory and farm machinery or brushed too near fireplaces.

Sarah Grimke, the feminist-abolitionist orator, was one of the first to identify the significance of the physical restrictions inherent in women's fashions of that period. As early as 1838 she had written to her sister Angelina:

> [Men] know that so long as we submit to be dressed like dolls, we never can rise to the stations of duty and usefulness from which they desire to exclude us.

A challenge was in the air by 1849. That year, actress Fanny Kemble caused a slight stir with her mountain climbing outfit of baggy trousers under a shortened skirt. The idea of practical but modest clothes was made tangible by her bold gesture.

That same year, Lydia Sayer, a twenty-two-year-old graduate of Central College in Elmira, New York, designed and wore a knee-length skirt over pantaloons merely to fulfill her desire for practical, comfortable clothes. Dress reform eventually became a matter of principle to Lydia after she was refused admission to the Seward Seminary because of her clothes, but it was not Lydia's fate to have her name remembered for the cause of dress reform. Perhaps it was an accident of geography that left her abandoned by the history books.

Seneca Falls, a farm and factory town in upstate, western New York State, was, at that time, a hotbed of radical reform. Like planets and stars that align in some cosmic mystery of astrological significance, women invited to tea parties in Seneca Falls could find themselves fomenting revolution the next week, as had happened in 1848 when Elizabeth Stanton, Lucretia Mott, and three other Quaker women casually sat down to tea and decided it was time to host a meeting to discuss women's rights. Six days later, over two hundred women and about forty men, including the great abolitionist leader Frederick Douglass, gathered in a Seneca Falls chapel for the historic Woman's Rights Convention and passed a Declaration of Sentiments calling for an end to the oppression of women.

Three years later, in February 1851, a mysterious constellation of feminists again aligned in Seneca Falls. This time, it was twenty-nine-year-old Libby Smith Miller who came to visit her cousin Elizabeth Stanton. Libby was the privileged daughter of Gerrit Smith, a liberal politician who frequently made it his business to tell women how to be better feminists. His conviction that women should not be crippled by the clothes they wear had inspired his daughter to dress comfortably. Disgusted with current fashions, Libby had designed an outfit for herself consisting of black Turkish trousers which ballooned around her legs beneath a knee-length skirt. Of her experiment with dress, she wrote:

> It was in the fall of 1850 that I adopted the short skirt after years of annoyance in wearing the long, heavy skirt, and of dissatisfaction with myself for submitting to such bondage. Working in my garden—weeding and transplanting in bedraggled skirts that clung in fettering folds about my feet and ankles, I became desperate and resolved on immediate release.

> With the short skirt I wore Turkish trousers, but these soon gave place to the straight pantaloon which was much better adapted to walking through the snow-drifted roads of my country home. My father and husband fully approved of this change of costume, but with scarcely an exception, my relatives and friends were sadly grieved.

When Elizabeth Stanton saw her young cousin's practical outfit and the freedom of movement it allowed, she immediately understood the significance of challenging the current fashion that kept women in literal bondage. She later recalled her reaction:

> To see my cousin, with a lamp in one hand and a baby in the other, walk upstairs with ease and grace, while, with flowing robes, I pulled myself up with difficulty, lamp and baby out of the question, readily convinced me that there was sore need of reform in woman's dress, and I promptly donned a similar attire. What incredible freedom I enjoyed for two years! Like a captive set free from his ball and chain,

I was always ready for a brisk walk through sleet and snow and rain, to climb a mountain, jump over a fence, work in the garden, and, in fact, for any necessary locomotion.

A few days later the two cousins strolled down the main street of Seneca Falls, both wearing the trouser outfit. They stopped at the post office where the energetic Amelia Bloomer was employed as deputy postmaster. Bloomer, too, was impressed with the outfit. As soon as she was able, she created a trouser outfit for herself and began wearing it. But more than that, she publicized the new dress in the newsletter she edited, the *Lily*. People began to read her editorials about the joys of wearing short skirts and Turkish trousers, and, though she repeatedly acknowledged Libby Miller as the originator of the design, her own name stuck to the new outfit. Amelia Bloomer was stunned by the public reaction which greeted her editorials.

> At the outset, I had no idea of fully adopting the style; no thought of setting a fashion; no thought that my action would create an excitement throughout the civilized world, and give to the style my name and the credit due Mrs. Miller. This was all the work of the Press. I stood amazed at the furore [sic] I had unwittingly caused.

Now, suddenly, people began to call the trouser dress the "Bloomer Costume" or simply "Bloomers." Letters poured in to the Seneca Falls post office from all over the country. Women wrote to ask for the pattern and details of the design. Rather than answer each letter, Amelia began to use more and more columns in the *Lily* to discuss the design of Bloomers and the rationale for dress reform.

Elizabeth Stanton also began to write pro-Bloomer articles for the *Lily*. In one passage she wrote:

> We say to you, at your fireside, ladies, unhook your dresses, and let everything hang loosely about you. Now, take a long breath, swell out as far as you can, and at that point fasten your clothes. Now please cut off those flowing skirts to your knees, and put on a pair of loose trousers buttoned about your ankle. Let us correct our garments, until they assume their proper place; all standing out of the way of the full and perfect development of the woman!

For a brief period it seemed that the comfortable Bloomer outfit was to become the fashion without a struggle. From all over the country reports came in that women were dressing in comfortable Turkish trousers. At the July 4th ball in Akron, Ohio, that year, sixty women came wearing Bloomers, and in Cleveland two hundred women were reported dancing in the outfit. The factory girls at Lowell, Massachusetts, organized a Bloomer Institute for emancipation from the "goddess Fashion," the "enforcement of the right and duty to dress according to the demands of Nature," and for the women's "mutual improvement in literature, science and morals." In September of that year, the *Advertiser* of Apalachicola, Florida went into fine detail about the outfits worn by three wealthy young visitors from Alabama who were wearing the "new costume":

> Miss Julia Mortimer, who attracted most of our attention, was richly dressed in a scarlet bodice and costly blue barege skirt, with fine white linen cambric pettiloons, tipped with lace and fastened around her small ankles with fancy ribands which gave her little feet an exquisite appearance.

Feminists, too, began to wear the variations on the Bloomer outfit including Lucretia Mott, Susan B. Anthony, Sarah and Angelina Grimke, and Lucy Stone. In England, women formed the "Association of Bloomers" to experiment with the new dress.

In 1856, Lydia Sayer, still dedicated to dress reform, wore a white Bloomer outfit when she married publisher John Hasbrouck, and, with his help, she became the editor of a feminist newspaper called *Sibyl: a Review of the Tastes, Errors, and Fashions of Society.* In her editorials, she lamented the ways women had deformed their own faces and bodies. "If only a woman would study the laws governing her physical being," she wrote, "instead of the fashion laws to adorn her outward seeming, we would hear less of the catalogue of fearful consequences resulting from civilization." The paper was published for eight years and promoted dress reform and suffrage as well as issues of women's health. From 1863 to 1864, Sayer was president of the National Dress Reform Association. Dedication like Sayer's to the cause of dress reform was rare.

Despite indications of early acceptance, the goal to dress reform in the western world was not to be so easily won. Crowds of boys followed women who wore the new outfit and harassed them, chanting,

> Heigh ho! in rain and snow,
> The Bloomer now is all the go.
> Twenty tailors take the stitches.
> Twenty women wear the breeches.
> Heigh ho! in rain or snow,
> The Bloomer now is all the go.

Men laughed and women jeered. In London, playwrights had a field day writing farces about the Bloomer outfit. In newspapers, political cartoonists drew unflattering sketches, and reporters wrote satires poking fun at the experiment in dress. Albert Smith and John Leech wrote a clever parody:

> Trousers or no trousers, that is the question;
> Whether it is better on the legs to suffer
> The dirt and scrapings of the bespatter'd crossings,
> Or to take arms against the present Fashion,
> And with new dresses change it? to fix, to change,
> No more; and by this change to say we stop
> Mud splashing, and the thousand natural woes
> The legs are heir to, 'tis an emendation
> Devoutly to be wished.

Public ridicule was bad enough, but then the clergy got hold of the issue. In Syracuse, New York, when Amelia Bloomer and Susan Anthony arrived at the State Temperance Society convention in the Bloomer outfit, the clergy asked them to leave town. When the women refused, they were subjected to a lengthy speech by Rev. Dr. Mandeville of Albany who denounced them as "a hybrid species, half man and half woman, belonging to neither sex." Other clergymen from Lockport and Buffalo all began talking at the same time, and Rev. Mandeville made a grand and outraged exit. The men took a vote and decided against allowing the Bloomer-wearing women to participate.

Again in Syracuse, another minister published a sermon in pamphlet form and distributed it to local churches. He quoted Moses from the Old Testament as an authority forbidding women to wear men's clothes. In response, Amelia Bloomer wrote an article in the *Lily*, suggesting that the minister should have taken his argument back to the days of Adam and Eve and their aprons of fig leaves.

Despite the opportunity for wit, the endless debate about the Bloomers took energy away from other issues women activists cared about. They cared about suffrage. They cared about the right to higher education. They cared about the right to be paid fairly and about decent work hours and conditions. They cared about the questions of slavery and temperance. And they got tired of being laughed at.

People's lives are brutally limited or distorted by systems of oppressive cultural traditions as often and as effectively as by oppressive or restrictive laws. Breaking these traditions can have serious consequences. Though they were generally less likely to inspire violent responses than actions challenging racist, anti-Semitic, or homophobic traditions, these challenges to the restrictive and unhealthy style of dress in the mid-1800s nevertheless met with intense public ridicule and, as we have seen, occasionally resulted in women being denied access to public places or, as in Hasbrouck's case, to further education.

Elizabeth Stanton gave up the battle for dress reform and stopped wearing the Bloomer outfit after two years. She wrote:

While the few realized its advantages, the many laughed it to scorn and heaped such ridicule on its wearers that they soon found that the physical freedom enjoyed did not compensate for the persistent persecution and petty annoyances suffered at every turn. To be rudely gazed at in public and private, to be the conscious subjects of criticism, and to be followed by crowds of boys in the streets, were all, to the very last degree, exasperating.

One by one, the feminist leaders abandoned the new outfit and put on their long skirts again. The world was not ready for Bloomers. Lucy Stone experienced a "vast deal of annoyance" in the dress reform experiment. Susan Anthony, sensitive about her awkward, angular figure to begin with, could not endure the emotional anguish of the harassment. Stanton wrote to her, "It is not wise, Susan, to use up so much energy and feeling that way. You can put them to better use. I speak from experience."

It was left to the women in the 1880s to push once again for dress reform and for outfits called, not Bloomers, but bifurcated (divided) skirts. In England, dress reform was promoted most effectively by Lady Harberton who founded the Rational Dress Society and used a riding whip to punctuate her lectures. But it was the popularity of the bicycle in the 1890s that gave women's dress reform in the West the boost it needed and ushered in new styles of the trouser outfit.

SHOPPING IN DOWNTOWN BROOKLYN, I pass sidewalk salesmen whose tables are laden with Islamic paraphernalia (incense, perfumes and oils, wall plaques, jewelry), pamphlets about the prophets, writings on the Islamic faith. Now and then I see the Muslim women in groups of two or three. They are stately and graceful in their long veils as they walk past the garish store windows, the Big Ed's Discounts, and the Burger Kings. I feel frumpy beside them, ordinary, white bread American. But I imagine I somehow have more freedom than they and feel lucky to roam in my jeans and boots. I glance away, confused.

The veil, to western, non-Islamic eyes, seems at first both alien and oppressive, an obvious target in the battle for women's rights. But such an oversimplified assumption is false. More than anything else, women's campaigns regarding the veil have been campaigns for the freedom of choice. Women of Islam—in Africa, the Middle East, Central Asia, and Asia—have at times fought fiercely to free themselves from the stifling shrouds, to walk with their bared faces turned to the sun. But these same women have sometimes fought just as fiercely for the right to wear the veils, often in defiance of what they perceive to be Western imperialism or for the love and preservation of their people's traditions. In both extremes of battle, women have lost their lives for the freedom to wear the veil or the choice to remove it.

> The first sight of them was terrible. Like black birds, like death, like fate, like everything alien. Foreign, dangerous, unfriendly. There were hundreds of them, specters crowding the barrier, waiting their own. A sea of *chadori*, the long terrible veil, the full length of it, like a dress descending to the floor, ancient, powerful, annihilating us.

This is how feminist author-artist Kate Millett described her first reactions to seeing women swathed in the full length veil called the *chador* when she arrived in Iran in those turbulent few days between the Shah's fall and the full impact of Khomeini's power. Millett observed:

> There is a mana of antiquity in the sight of their *chador*, the length, the ferocity of that fall of black cloth, the masses of them like the chorus in Greek tragedy. You would never be close to it; these women seem utterly closed to women. Here in this public place defended by their robes, the fabric held tightly under the chin, much of the face hidden by the fold of cloth....

> Yet the *chador* is theater, some theater of women so old I no longer know it. Before this garment was forced upon us for our shame, it must have been our pride; before it was compelled upon us, we must have worn it out of self love, vanity, grace, thoroughly conscious how glamorous it could be in evening, how seductive. A glance thrown from it, the way it frames the face, reveals the bones, accentuates, turns every face into mystery, eyes, eyebrows speaking. Effective.

The veil is part of the Islamic custom of *purdah*, a complex system of rules meant to define the segregation of the sexes, rules that dictate how and when women are to be covered and proscribe circumstances of contact with men. *Purdah* may include, for example, veiling only the face; concealing the entire body beneath heavy cloth but not the face; concealing face and body; relegation to secluded quarters; or the denial of all association with men who are not kin. According to Elizabeth Fernea and Basima Qattan Bezirgan in the introduction to their book *Middle Eastern Muslim Women Speak*, the insistence that women be veiled is not based on the teachings of the Koran that originally did much to improve the status of women; the prophet Muhammad merely decreed that women be modestly covered. It is, rather, a practice grounded in ancient tribal and patriarchal custom, reinforced by the Koran's decree that "Men are in charge of women because Allah hath made one of them to excel the other" (Surah IV, verse 34).

The requirements of *purdah* vary widely, not only from region to region but also from class to class within a community. So too, women's fight for the freedom of choice regarding the uses and expressions of *purdah* have varied, as we will see in this chapter, from the examples of Muslim women's experiences in four countries: (1)

turn-of-the-century Bengal, (2) Central Asia following the Russian Revolution of 1917, (3) twentieth-century Iran, and (4) West Germany in 1985.

Freedom of choice, as it relates to *purdah*, is evident in the reform efforts of Rokeya Sakhawat Hossain. Rokeya was born in 1880 into a privileged Muslim family in Bengal (today's Bangladesh). Her mother observed strict *purdah*, while her father acquired land, wealth, and knowledge, mastered seven languages, and provided his sons with an extravagant education. Rokeya and her older sister Karimunnessa had to be very devious to secure their education. After Karimunnessa persuaded her younger brother to teach her the Bangla alphabet, she spent hours squatting in the courtyard, drawing the letters on the ground with a stick. But one afternoon she was discovered reading a book and was soon after sent to live in close confinement on the estate of her maternal grandparents until she was married off at the age of fifteen. Rokeya had better luck than her sister. She turned to her older brother, Ibrahim Saber, who had been exposed to Western thought at St. Xavier's College in Calcutta. He was in favor of women's education and secretly taught Rokeya both Bangla and English late at night after their father was asleep.

Rokeya's luck continued to hold when she was married, at the age of sixteen, to a man of liberal ideas. Like her brother, Rokeya's husband also believed that women should be educated, and he encouraged Rokeya to make friends with educated Hindu and Christian women. Gradually, Rokeya became aware that there were women in the world who did not live by the laws which confined her mother and sister.

After only thirteen years of this happy marriage, Rokeya's diabetic husband died, but he left his wife enough money to live on as well as money specifically designated for the opening of a school for girls. Before the end of that year, Rokeya opened the school in Bhagalpur but closed it soon after because of the severe harassment she encountered from her relatives. Rokeya moved to Calcutta and, in 1911, she opened the Sakhawat Memorial Girls' School there. This time she was successful beyond her wildest dreams. Within a few years, the school grew from eight students to eighty-four. As the school thrived, Rokeya began to see women's needs for other services as well. In 1916, she organized the Muslim Women's Association that offered assistance to widows, shelter to battered wives, and literacy training for poor women in Calcutta's slums. Teams of women from the Association went from house to house teaching women personal hygiene and child care as well as basic reading and writing.

Western readers may assume from all of this radical activity that Rokeya also worked to end the custom of *purdah*. She did not. She endorsed a moderate system of *purdah*, challenging primarily what she considered to be its extreme limitations. This meant she was always treading a fine line as far as her contemporaries were concerned; she was criticized by nearly everyone. When she transported her students to school in a bus, for example, she was careful to observe the laws of purdah by covering all the windows with airtight shutters. On their first day inside the dark, hot bus, the girls and their chaperones became sick from the lack of air, fainting and vomiting in the aisles. On each successive day more and more shutters were replaced by colorful curtains, but still the students and their parents complained of the confinement. A Hindu friend teased Rokeya about it and reported that her nephew, upon seeing the bus, had shouted, "Oh, aunty! Look! The moving black hole of Calcutta is passing by."

But while she was enduring the jeers and criticism of progressive parents, Rokeya was receiving criticism from the other extreme as well. Conservative Muslims notified her that they had seen the curtains of the bus move in the breeze which, in their watchful eyes, made the bus *"purdah*less." It was to be a lifelong dilemma that had no end. Rokeya and her staff faced daily harassment, receiving repeated threats from the fundamentalists that they would take action if violations of *purdah* were not remedied and receiving demands from the parents that the restrictions of *purdah* be eased.

Rokeya, the educator and activist, was perhaps best known as an essayist. Her observations on Bengali society were published as early as 1903. With her pen, she advocated women's rights and waged war against the strict observance of *purdah*. She documented the suffering of women under the absurd extremes of *purdah*, raised her voice against crimes against women, and specifically challenged notions of male superiority. In one essay, Rokeya wrote about a woman whose house had caught on fire but, seeing men in the courtyard who had rushed in to fight the flames, the woman had stayed in her room and burned to death rather than break *purdah*.

In another example, Rokeya wrote about a woman who had stumbled under the weight of her voluminous *burqa* (a tentlike cloak) and had fallen onto the railway tracks. Porters had rushed to her aid but her maid had advised them that they were not allowed to touch her. The train conductor waited for half an hour but then was given orders to move. Rokeya wrote, "A whole stationful of men witnessed this horrible accident, yet none of them was permitted to assist her. Finally her mangled body was taken to a luggage shed."

Rokeya understood the economic nature of women's oppression; she wrote, "Some say that women tolerate oppression from men because they depend on men's earning. They are right." And she saw that religion was used to manipulate women's obedience. "Men are using religion as an excuse to dominate us at present," she wrote. "We should not submit quietly to such oppression in the name of religion." Nor did Rokeya believe oppression was reserved only for women who observed *purdah*. She understood that *purdah* was merely a tool of male domination and that other tools were used in other societies.

In 1905, Rokeya experimented with both form and language when she wrote a utopian fiction in English. *Sultana's Dream* described a place called Ladyland where reverse *purdah* was observed: women were permitted to walk freely in public while men were secluded and confined. In her fantasy, the result of this reversal was that women had rid the world of war and had made remarkable scientific advancements with the inventions of solar power and travel by "air cars."

Rokeya tirelessly advocated women's rights and protested what she considered to be the extremes of the *purdah*, but she always wore the *burqa* in public and observed "open faced *purdah*." Even when she was among friends and relatives, she covered her head with the end of her sari, arguing, "Veiling is not natural, it is ethical." Nor was she necessarily impressed by the liberation of women who were unveiled. She saw that they, too, were oppressed by men and that such women were sometimes used as political pawns, even in the question of the veil. She observed this among the Parsi, a South Asian community descended from Persian Zoroastrians who were among the first to work with the British during colonial times.

> Recently we see the Parsi women moving about unveiled, but are they truly free from mental slavery? Certainly not! Their unveiling is not a result of their own decision. The Parsi men have dragged their women out of *purdah* in a blind imitation of the Europeans. It does not show any initiative of their women. They are as lifeless as they were before. When their men kept them in seclusion they stayed there. When the men dragged them out by their "nose rings" they came out.

For Rokeya, then, the veil was a matter of freedom of choice. In other parts of the world, the battle has been one of life or death.

> The shameful laws
> Of the dead past
> For aeons cast
> A net o'er you.
> Ye brown skinned women
> Haste to work;
> Unveiled, ye weave
> The dawn's red glow.

The poet who composed these lines anonymously was inspired by the Russian Revolution of 1917 and its impact on the veiled women of

Soviet Central Asia. In the lands just north of Turkey and Afghanistan, women in Islamic families were subjected to a range of restrictions that were particularly brutal. When teams of women revolutionaries arrived in the early 1920's, bearing slogans and pamphlets outlining the new order, they found women, hidden under heavy black cloth since infancy, who had never seen the sunlight. Most were married as children or sold and forced into hard labor. In the cold, mountainous region of the Caucasus, north of Turkey, women were deprived of any outer garments. And in the Kalmuck region, it was the custom to sew eleven-year-old girls into leather bodices called *kamsols* in order to inhibit the growth of their breasts. The girls would be released from the *kamsols* only on their wedding nights.

The Soviet educators pointed out that these customs were unhealthy. Young women who had been sewn into *kamsols* contracted lung diseases and were unable to nurse their babies. Those who had lived their whole lives under thick, black cloth were subject to eye diseases, and they suffered from rickets. Those who were exposed to the cold and deprived of all cloaks died young.

The Soviet women sponsored a variety of campaigns to encourage reform. On behalf of the mountain women deprived of coats, they solicited clothes by using the slogan "CLOAKS FOR THE MOUNTAINEER WOMEN." At the same time, they educated the local men with a manifesto that read:

> Comrades, workers, set a good example, dress your wives, daughters, and sisters warmly and urge mountaineer workers to combat the out-of-date custom of wearing no cloak with all their might. Call upon the mountaineer women to break away vigorously from the custom. May the warm cloak stand for the first decisive step in the struggle on behalf of mountaineer women against ancient prejudices, the first step towards their liberation.

If some women were urged to cover up, others were encouraged to uncover, to remove their veils and restrictive garments. In 1921, in the region where girls were sewn into *kamsols*, a Commission to Combat the *Kamsol* was established. The Commission designed and manufactured a new outfit. It then sponsored mass meetings throughout the region. At the close of each meeting the men were asked to leave while the girls were cut out of the *kamsols* and given the new outfits to wear. The *kamsols* were then taken outdoors and publicly burned while musicians played the "Internationale," the rousing anthem of the Russian Revolution.

In the city of Bukhara, the heart of Islam in Central Asia, poor women responded enthusiastically to the call for liberation. They threw off their stiff dark veils called *paranjas* and then proceeded to tear them off rich women. They forced their way into weddings and other festivals and collected ornate *paranjas*. Sometimes they set fire to the veils in the inner courtyards. Other times they took them to sewing rooms set up for the purpose of altering the veils into more practical clothing.

In Bukhara, on March 8, 1927, at a celebration of International Women's Day, observers wrote about the frenzy of the women as they caught the revolutionary spirit and removed their veils.

> On that day, preparations for which had begun months before, tens of thousands of women huddled in *paranjas* and *chachvans*, poured like a menacing avalanche through the narrow, crooked streets, squares, and bazaars....But above this silent, gloomy, approaching mass, still without faces or eyes, a sea of red flags floated high in the air....And like a blossoming red flower bed in the midst of a barren, weedy field, a group of women with uncovered faces and red kerchiefs on their heads contrasted with the strange procession.... These were the few who had previously had the courage to break with their past and no longer to look upon the blue sky through a black grating.

> Amidst strains of music the vast multitude, including a number of men and children, gathered round the Lenin monument....Then the great meeting began. Thundering, stinging words, but words, too that were new, unaccustomed, and inspiriting, that moved the hearers' hearts so deeply that they called forth a real frenzy of enthusiasm and unceasing shouts of exultation. And when the storm continued unabated, and all the bands struck up the "Internationale," and the cries of Hurrah! rang across the ancient, tottering city walls and out into the desert, then the real proceedings began.

> They were flung aloft into the quivering air, timidly at first, but then with ever wilder and more frenzied speed, these symbols of slavery that the women cast off, *paranjas* and *chadras*. They were piled in rapidly growing heaps, drenched with paraffin, and soon the dark clouds of smoke from the burning common abjuration of a thousand year old convention, now become unbearable, flared up into the bright sky of the spring day. But at the sight of this unique pyre the women's souls flamed aloft; they were ready to drop for shame, fear, and joy, for here they were daring, for the first time since their childhood, to show their faces openly, to break the prison bars.

The papers reported that in Bukhara and the surrounding district, ten thousand women had cast off their veils. The March 8 celebration and casting off of the veils was repeated the next year. But both years most of the women who took off their veils put them back on the next day. Some explained that they had assumed they were meant to unveil only for the festive day.

There was another reason why the women returned to the veil: they paid dearly for every minute their faces were not covered. Most who participated in the revolutionary experiments with the removal of the veils were forced to endure increased harassment by their relatives. Some were raped by angry neighbors or even, it was reported, by Communist men who regarded unveiled women as "fair game." Wherever women threw off the veils, some were murdered; perhaps, it is estimated, as many as four hundred women lost their lives, many in the region of Turkmenia. Religious leaders in the various regions did their part to repress the women's actions. They said that the Soviets would steal their babies and send them to China, where they would be boiled down to soap. They warned of earthquakes, famines, and plagues if the women disobeyed Allah by removing their veils. When an earthquake devastated the Ferghana Valley in Uzbekistan in 1927, the unveiled women were blamed. And when the women did put the veils on again, the men rejoiced at public festivals.

Why the fuss? Men are God's servants and women are too.
What have women done wrong to feel shame before men?
What are these unbecoming, uncouth, cloaks and veils?
They are winding sheets meant for the dead, not the living.
I say, "Death to the men who bury women alive
in the name of religion!" That is enough to say here.

If two or three poets add their voices to mine,
the people will soon start humming this song.
Their hums will uncover the women's fair faces,
the women will proudly throw off their vile masks,
the people will then have some joy in their lives.
But otherwise, what will become of Iran?
With the women in shrouds, half the nation is dead.

These words, from the struggle in Iran, were written by a male activist and poet, Mirzadeh Eshqi. He had witnessed the strength of Iranian women. He had seen the women of the royal harem who, in 1905, had launched a nationwide boycott of British tobacco to protest foreign economic domination. When the Constitutional Revolution erupted in 1906, masses of veiled women had taken to the streets alongside the men to demand a written constitution limiting the monarch's power. That same year, a crowd of women had surrounded the Shah's carriage and handed him a petition and a hostile letter which read, "Fear the time when we shall finally take away the crown off your head and the royal cane off your hand." In August 1906, Mozzafar al Din Shah gave in to the demands, and a National Assembly was established to write a constitution for Iran. The new Constitution, however, did little to change the status of women, depriving them of suffrage as it denied "minors, fraudulent bankrupts, beggars, murderers, thieves and other criminals." The Shah died days after signing the constitution. When Mohammad Ali Shah was crowned in January of the next year, he immediately resumed the battle against the constitutionalists, and the revolution became an armed struggle.

Again, women participated in the struggle. They organized new boycotts, including one against imported sugar. They formed secret societies and, in 1908, launched a literacy campaign for women. In 1910, a secret society published a weekly newspaper, *Knowledge*, written by and for women. Female orators addressed mass meetings of women crowded into the mosques. Some urged women to take up the gun for the struggle. After the Russian invasion of northern Iran, Morgan Shuster, the United States Treasurer General of Iran in 1911, reported seeing three hundred women march out from their walled courtyards and harems, clad in black robes with white veils over their faces. The women had heard a rumor that the men in the National Assembly were about to concede to various demands of the Russians. The women demanded to be heard. Shuster wrote:

> Many held pistols under their skirts or in the folds of their sleeves....The President consented to receive a delegation of them. In his reception hall they confronted him, and lest he and his colleagues should doubt their meaning, these cloistered Persian mothers, wives and daughters exhibited threateningly their revolvers, tore aside their veils, and confessed their decision to kill their own husbands and sons, and leave behind their own dead bodies, if the deputies wavered in their duty to uphold the liberty and dignity of the Persian people and nation.

On another occasion, women removed their veils and marched through the streets of Tehran. They chanted, "Long live the Constitution, long live freedom! We must free ourselves from religious obligations to live the way we want!" For daring to focus on their own rights, the women were denounced as prostitutes.

When Sediqeh Dovlatabady criticized the veil in her newspaper *Women's Voice*, founded in 1919, her life was threatened. Danger in the pursuit of justice was not new to her. As a child in Isfahan, she had dressed as a boy to attend school with her brother and had established a girls' school at the age of fourteen. The woman who agreed to become headmistress was imprisoned when the school was discovered and closed after only three months. Dovlatabady was forcibly married at the age of sixteen, but this didn't stop her. Her long life was devoted to political activism for the cause of women's rights and Iranian nationalism.

Throughout the 1920s, women in Iran established organizations and schools, published magazines with such names as *The Messenger of Happiness*, *Patriotic Women*, and *Women's World*. These magazines published anti-veil editorials and encouraged public debate on the issue. In 1923, women in Iran read about an Egyptian feminist, Huda Sharawi, who, upon returning from a women's conference in Rome, dramatically threw her veil into the Mediterranean. They too, occasionally, continued to demonstrate against the veil. One source cited an undated occasion on which hundreds of women sought sanctuary in a Tehran mosque to dramatize their demand that women be allowed to unveil. Their demand was denied.

It was during this period that Shah Reza Khan, brought to power in a military coup, established a dictatorial regime to maintain order by crushing dissent, banning labor unions, imposing strict censorship of the media, establishing military police and the draft, forcibly settling nomadic tribes, and banning the Communist Party. Oddly, he was just as brutal in his insistence that Iran be modernized. Part of his enforced modernization was the advocacy of women's education, women's inclusion in the work force, and women's dress reform. In 1934, he ordered all women teachers and students to be unveiled in public, and, in 1936, he prohibited all wearing of the *chador*. After this ruling, even government officials, if the wives accompanying them wore the *chador*, could be denied access to public places, and bus drivers were fined for accepting veiled women as passengers. Employees of government ministries were instructed that their paychecks would be handed to their wives and this only if the women were wearing European-style hats instead of veils. European-dress shops did a booming business in the wake of this decree.

The Shah had been inspired by the anti-veil campaign in Turkey, but in Turkey the veil was never outlawed. Instead, General Kemal Ataturk launched a propaganda campaign with the slogan, "Show your faces to the world and look the world in the face." Turkish women were free to choose the veil or free to remove it. But in Iran, the Shah's iron rule dictated women's fashion. In the streets, there was chaos as women were forced to abandon ancient customs almost overnight. Some zealous followers of the Shah took it upon themselves to rip the veils off women. One witness wrote, "I was in time to see police tearing silken scarves from the women's heads and handing them back in ribbons to their owners, for anything even remotely resembling a veil was forbidden." Men opposed to the new ruling, on the other hand, spit at the unveiled women or threw stones at them, calling them whores.

Some women appreciated the new law, especially privileged women who had previously advocated unveiling and rural women who preferred to work in the fields without the burden of the full *chador*. Other women, including many social activists, protested that veiling should be a matter of personal choice. They pointed out that the urban poor and religious fundamentalists bore the full impact of the Shah's decree and were deprived of their personal choice. Compulsory unveiling isolated a number of orthodox or elderly women in their homes for whom appearing without the *chador* was tantamount to appearing naked. Reze Baraheni, a child during this period, later remembered seeing his father carry his mother to the public baths in a large sack. Once, when his father was stopped and questioned by a police officer, he said he was carrying a bag of pistachio nuts. The officer prodded the sack a couple of times and, discovering a woman there, promptly arrested his father.

In 1941, the Shah abdicated in favor of his son, Mohammad Reza Pahlavi. Throughout the next decade, radical women formed organizations increasingly critical of both religious authorities and the new Shah's dictatorial regime. Both institutions, the women said, were exploiting women. Women began to demand labor reforms such as equal pay for equal work and day-care centers for the children of working mothers. There was little cohesiveness among the women's organizations during this period, but, in 1952, women secured one hundred thousand signatures on a petition demanding equal rights with men. Despite such efforts, women did not win the right to vote until 1963.

As the Shah enjoyed popularity among the ruling and social elite in the West, the Iranian people suffered under his rule. He boasted of spending $100 million for the 125th celebration of the Persian monarchy, though at the time the four million people living in Tehran had no sewage system. People who protested against the Shah's rule were severely harassed, and, by 1975, there were estimated to be between 25,000 to 100,000 political prisoners, many of whom later reported that they had been tortured.

Throughout the 1970s, women who participated in anti-Shah demonstrations returned to wearing the veil. The *chador* became their symbol of opposition to the Shah's courting of the Western world and what they perceived to be his betrayal of the Iranian people and their traditions. Women on college campuses who had once gone unveiled returned to the *chador*. It became their flag of independence from Western domination, their way of reclaiming Islam and asserting pride in their heritage. The veil was also useful as a disguise, hiding the identities of those women who opposed the Shah as they participated in the resistance to his regime.

And then, suddenly, the tables were turned again. The Shah was out and, in February 1979, the Ayatollah Khomeini became the recognized ruler. Women everywhere in Iran were optimistic. Khomeini's rhetoric had been reassuring. He had said, "As for women, Islam has never been against their freedom. It is, to the contrary, opposed to the idea of woman as object and it gives her back her dignity. A woman is man's equal; she and he are both free to choose their lives and their occupations." Didn't such statements imply that he would support the advancement of women within the traditions of the Iranian culture? In early March of 1979, 100,000 women flooded the campus of the University of Tehran to celebrate the end of the Shah's regime.

Within days of his return to Iran, however, Khomeini began to change the laws regarding women's rights, eliminating anything that seemed to contradict the teachings of Islam. The night before a planned celebration of International Women's Day on March 8, 1979, Khomeini issued a new ruling: that all female employees of government agencies must wear the Islamic *hejab* (a term for covering that could refer to anything from a scarf to a *chador*). The next day, six thousand women took to the streets of Tehran chanting, "In the dawn of freedom, there is no freedom." Five days later, fifteen thousand women again demonstrated, seizing the Palace of Justice and demanding that their rights not be dismissed. The women chanted, "With the veil and without the veil, we opposed the Shah. With the veil and without the veil, we will march to uphold freedom 'til the day of our liberation."

Now suddenly, the women who had worn the veil in opposition to the Shah removed it in opposition to Khomeini. Immediately, the newly-empowered religious fundamentalists labeled the unveiled women "whores," "American agents," and "anti-revolutionaries"; some shouted, "Death to the foreign dolls." This last chant was prophetic, for indeed the women who rejected the veil were now to face death. By December, 1979, there was no doubt that Khomeini's rule meant new forms of repression for women. Several pro-women's rights groups tried to meet at the Conference of the Unity of Women to strategize their resistance to the new social order. They met in candlelight after Islamic fundamentalists cut off the electricity to the building.

That same month, Farrokhrou Parsa, the first woman to have served in the Iranian cabinet, was dragged into court and charged by a panel of hooded judges with "expansion of prostitution, corruption on earth, and warring against God." Her crimes had included establishing a commission for revising textbooks to include nonsexist images of women and authoring a directive to excuse schoolgirls from wearing the veil. Within hours of being found guilty, she was wrapped in a dark sack and machine-gunned.

> What will become of Iran? With the women in shrouds, half the nation is dead.

The words of the poet, Eshqui, are haunting today after the slaughter of so many women in Iran, some of whom were killed, after being condemned as prostitutes, merely for removing their veils.

As the world grows smaller and smaller and cultures mingle, women are asserting their freedom of choice regarding the veil outside the confines of Muslim society. The London Iranian Women's Liberation

Group published a strongly negative statement about veiling in the book *3rd World/ 2nd Sex*. They wrote:

> The question of the veil is the most important issue of women's liberation in Muslim countries. The veil, a long engulfing black robe, is the extension of the four walls of the home where women belong. The veil is the historical symbol of women's oppression, seclusion, denial of her social participation and equal rights with men. It is a cover which defaces and objectifies women. To wear or not to wear the veil, for Muslim women, is the "right to choose."

In 1985, twenty-five-year-old Serife Sahin, a Turkish woman living in West Germany, fought for her freedom to wear the veil. She refused to remove her veil when she applied for a job in a government day-care center. The Department of Youth informed her that she was free to wear her veil off the job, but not during work hours because it considered the veil a symbol of women's oppression. For Sahin, however, the veil was a matter of both cultural and religious tradition. She asked, "Why will I suddenly be a good teacher if I take off the veil at the center's door? What's important is how I get along with the children. If I were an oppressed woman then I wouldn't be defending my beliefs. The moment I allow the City Council to force me to take off the veil, I will be an oppressed woman." Sahin applied for a job in a "less progressive" district and was given the job. The West German children were curious about her veil. They wondered what Sahin's hair looked like. "I took off my veil to show them my hair," said Sahin. "After that they were satisfied."

MY MOTHER TOLD ME that most of the older women she interviewed for an extensive oral history project in my hometown could not remember the first time they voted, but they could remember getting their hair bobbed in the days following World War I. At first this seemed to be a disappointing bit of information, but then I remembered that hair has been a cultural battlefield for both women and men. Hair is inexorably linked, rightly or wrongly, to self-perception. There is power in a haircut and personal devastation in a shaved head—devastation made legendary by Samson's Delilah, boot camp instructors, and Nazi officers controlling the population of the concentration camps.

This is not merely an ancient battle. As recently as the 1980s in the United States, African-American women have had to fight for the right to wear cornrow braids to work. In January, 1981, Dorothy Reed, a television news reporter in San Francisco, was suspended from her job after she refused to give up her new hairdo of cornrows and multicolored beads. The news director told Reed the hairstyle was "inappropriate," but the local NAACP (National Association for the Advancement of Colored People) thought the issue was racism. Reed herself claimed, "This hairstyle gives me a tremendous amount of pride and reflects my heritage." A number of television viewers agreed and picketed the station for several days. After two weeks, Reed was reinstated at the station—with the cornrows but minus the decorative beads.

Tarigonda Venkamma was another woman who refused to give up her hair. She lived in India in the mid-1800s and is now revered as a Hindu holy woman. According to popular legend, after Venkamma was widowed, she refused to shave her head as local custom demanded. The villagers protested to her father, but Venkamma said,

> Dear father, heed not the opinions or the prattle of the wordly minded. Whom are we going to please? What is the good of removing this God-given hair, and what is the infamy in retaining it? So long as our inclinations are pure, the merciful Lord will not be offended with us even when we set aside wordly customs and manners. And if our inclinations are impure, though we may pay all homage to customs and manners, the Lord will not spare us. So please leave me alone.

But Venkamma was not to be left alone. She was called before a local *swamiji* (religious leader) before whom she again articulated her protest against meaningless custom. She said,

> Revered Swamiji, you are a Jagad Guru (world teacher). I am less informed than Your Holiness. Please tell me in which Veda it is enjoined that a widow should not keep her hair? Why should a woman be disfigured by shaving her head? Do not our scriptures maintain that where women are not honored, there all works and efforts come to naught? When a widow's inclinations are pure, what is wrong in her keeping her hair or even wearing ornaments? This hair, which is the gift of the merciful God right from birth, will it not grow again after it is once shaven? If Your Holiness has the power to prevent it from growing again, you can have it shaven right now. I deem it wrong to abuse the gifts of God.

The *swamiji* could not answer her questions, nor did he understand the nature of her protest; he saw only a woman who questioned authority and defied tradition. He ordered in a barber who forcibly shaved Venkamma's head. Then, according to the legend, the holy woman, widow with the shaved head, went to a river, offered prayers to a Hindu deity, and walked into the water. When she came out of the water her head was covered with long, beautiful hair.

Women in Japan and China were less fortunate. In the early 1870s, Japanese men were encouraged to adopt Western haircuts. Short hair was linked with progressive politics. When the Emperor cut his hair, the samurais followed suit. Progressive women decided to join in the new look and began bobbing their hair. In 1871, Japanese women formed an association for the purpose of advocating practical, short hairstyles. But they had misread the men's political intentions. In 1872, the Meiji government outlawed short haircuts for women and required any woman who needed to have her hair cut to obtain a license from a government office. The government did approve of an end to shaved eyebrows and blackened teeth for married women, but insisted the traditional, elaborate hairstyles remain. According to Sharon Sievers, Professor of History at California State University and author of a book about feminist consciousness in modern Japan, the government's policy regarding women's hairstyles reflected its resistance to women's participation in the changing society:

> The banning of short hair for women—however superficial the issue may seem—is one of the most important and revealing policies on women in the early Meiji period. To the extent that women cutting their hair can be viewed as a real, if spontaneous, attempt to join the progressive forces trying to create a new Japan, the government's denial of their right to do so was also a denial of their right to participate and contribute actively to that change. In fact, it can be seen as a symbolic message to Japan's women to become repositories of the past, rather than pioneers, with men, of some unknown future.

Many progressive women refused to obey the government's interference with their personal appearance and continued to experiment with breaking the traditional requirement for long hair.

In China, too, short hair became a symbol for progressive politics. For Chinese women, the body as battlefield for ideology stretched, literally, from head to toe. Since the mid-1800s, missionaries and progressive men had led various campaigns against the thousand-year-old custom of footbinding. After the Taiping Rebellion in 1851, footbinding had officially been outlawed for a while, but the practice continued. In 1892, the first Unbound Feet Society had formed and eventually grew to ten thousand members. By 1903, one could hear male reformers preaching against the custom on street corners, banging gongs to call attention to their cause.

Little girls, too, sometimes resisted the custom by which their feet were slowly crushed into three inches of bloody pulp. Wei Yu-hsiu, born in 1896, told about her youthful rebellion in her autobiography, *My Revolutionary Years*:

> When the bandages were first put on my feet, I submitted not only because it was being done to all little girls of the house, but because I knew if I rebelled it would bring fresh humiliation on my mother. But I simply could not stand it....My final rebellion was supported by the fact that I felt Mother did not want my feet to be bound. She

deeply regretted that her own had been so crippled....[One morning] I suddenly started screaming, without tears, but in great volume. I lay on my back, kicking and yelling. I kept up this bedlam for the greater part of the morning, disturbing the entire household. [In the end, Grandmother], whose final word was necessary to make any decision, looked down at me with great distaste and said, "Very well, then. Take the bandages off. Her feet will grow the size of an elephant's. No one will ever marry her, but so be it. I wash my hands of the whole business."

The masses of Chinese women resisted taking the leadership against footbinding, though they participated in the struggle against Japanese imperialism, in labor struggles in textile factories, and the fight for the right to vote. It was not until the formation of women's unions in the nationalist revolutionary movement of the mid-1920s that Chinese women, themselves, took the initiative in proclaiming the right to choose what was done to own bodies. Between three and four hundred female students formed their "propagandist teams" and traveled with the Nationalist armies. These young women bobbed their hair, unbound their feet, and wore trousers. In 1927, Anna Louise Strong, the American journalist sympathetic to experiments with Communism around the world, interviewed some of the women. They told her:

> We travel behind the army but we take no part in fighting.... Our work is to organize the women. For this we go into the homes and markets, wherever women are to be found, and talk with them. When we have talked enough, we organize a local women's union and leave it to handle affairs in that district. Then we move to another district.... We tell [the women] that we come to save them from oppression and to bring a new way of thinking. We explain that men and women are now equal....We explain the new doctrine of free choice in marriage, that young folks have the right to select their own life partners. We also explain that, by the new law, women may inherit property, and we say that the feet of young girls must not be bound.

When the propagandists left, the newly-formed women's unions took over the work of reshaping ancient traditions. In Hankow, the women of one union told Strong about the consequences of women's enthusiasm for the new ways:

> We started our work against footbinding in the cotton mills. These women stand all day on their feet; they realize that they did wrong to bind them. For many of them it is too late to change, but they are willing to save their daughters. Formerly a daughter was more profitable if she had "golden lilies" [bound feet] for they could get a better marriage price for her. But now she is more profitable for work in cotton mills if she has normal feet. Economic pressure is against footbinding. Nevertheless it took the sudden blast of Revolution to destroy established custom.

Once the drive starts against footbinding, thousands of women join. There was such enthusiasm against footbinding in one cotton mill in the British Concession that the streets were littered with bandages which the women tore off. Those who were convinced tore off first their own bandages and then compelled the others to do likewise. But the women's union does not urge such sudden action for it is very painful. It is better to make the bandages shorter each day and at last remove them altogether without too sudden pain. Also it is no use to unbind the feet of older women, for they can never be normal.

In addition to removing the pus-soaked bandages from their feet, the women cut their hair short. And in this tradition too, some women were forced to change against their will. When Wang Suzhen, a peasant's daughter, arrived home from the American Mission School she attended, she brought with her the Nationalist fervor. She became president of the local women's union and expanded its membership to the hundreds. According to one of her friends, "she was happy, she was drunk with being happy as she swept more and more women, even old women, into her women's union." The union, too, seemed almost drunk with happiness.

They went into the streets with scissors, speaking to strangers, telling women to cut their hair off. They cut their hair off right there in the streets. They say that once or twice women who were over-persuaded or maybe compelled to cut their hair off went home and strangled themselves. The women's unions go into the houses, searching for bound feet women. If they find a bound foot woman under thirty, they give her a little time to get her feet unbound so that it will not hurt too much. After this they fine her.

Many activists were dismayed by these forced changes. The Dean of the Women's Training School in Hupeh discussed the problem with journalist Strong:

We have sent word again and again to all the local women's unions that the question of cutting hair is purely a personal matter and that no one has the right to cut another's hair by force. We have explained that the work of preventing footbinding is far more important and that this must really be enforced by fines against women who bind their daughters' feet.

And then, suddenly, midway through 1927, the wind shifted again. The Nationalist revolutionary movement was split in two. Chiang Kai Shek and the right wing of the Guomindang took the offensive, splitting off from Mao Zedong and the Communist Party, and China was suddenly at the mercy of the anti-Red forces. Now, women's bobbed hair and unbound feet were assumed to reflect Communist sympathies. According to the newspaper *Ta Kung pao*, women suspected of being Communists in Canton were wrapped in cotton-padded blankets, soaked in gasoline, and burned alive. Some were publicly stripped first to provide proof that these short-haired women dressed in trousers were actually women. Short-haired Wang Suzhen, once "drunk with happiness," was handed over to Chiang Kai Shek's soldiers who "cut her to pieces with knives and bayonets. They began with her breasts then they cut off her arms, they cut off many pieces."

In the following months, thousands of short-haired women were shot down in the streets of China. Secret underground networks of women were formed to smuggle short-haired friends away from the anti-Red soldiers. Strong interviewed four young women who had been smuggled into Hankow:

> Two of them had been forced to parade the streets between jeering soldiers, expecting every moment to be torn in pieces. They had hidden for weeks in friends' houses, and had been smuggled out of town with wigs over their bobbed hair. "The nearest guard at the gate looked at us suspiciously," they said, "and touched his hand to his hair and smiled. But he was a good fellow and did not tell his officers...."They had lain concealed for many weeks under the deck of a Chinese junk, as it slowly made its way downriver to Hankow. The junks could only travel in large companies, for fear of bandits or soldiers....The girls did not dare go out, lest their large feet and wigs be noticed and bring suspicion.

THE FREEDOM TO CHOOSE what is done to or put on one's own body for the sake of adornment, identity, tradition, physical comfort, or modesty has been a struggle in which women from all parts of the globe have engaged. But there are some women who have also challenged the common assumptions and prejudices of a world full of sighted, hearing, and able-bodied people, prejudices that render whole segments of the human community invisible, useless, and excludable. Marj Schneider, director of Womyn's Braille Press, a Minneapolis-based organization, has made it a point to challenge assumptions that perpetuate the association of physical limitations with negative attitudes.

> I have been aware for many years at how I flinch at hearing disabilities used as metaphors for human behaviors or characteristics. It seems I can't go a day without hearing about how "blind we are to what's happening with our environment," or how someone is "emotionally crippled." Sometimes I try to explain how this language is detrimental to disabled people and other times I don't because it would mean interrupting the flow of a conversation or sitting down to write yet another letter.

But she does write letters, like the one she wrote to two of her favorite folk singers after a concert. During the concert, one of the singers had joked that "love is really blind. In fact, love is sometimes blind, deaf, dumb and just plain stupid." Schneider wrote a letter in which she began with appreciation for the music, but then explained:

> I realize that you may not have thought about this before because words like blind and deaf are so commonly used as metaphors by writers and in everyday speech. But the connotation of these words, when they are used this way, is always negative, and people don't realize that these metaphors do reflect on how those of us with disabilities are perceived and treated in this society. Just think about how frequently blind, deaf, crippled, lame, etc. are used to mean ignorant, stubborn, thoughtless, inadequate or stupid. This transfer of language and meaning is not right. The lives of intelligent, thoughtful, gentle people who have disabilities are invaded and trashed daily by these stereotypes and the attitudes they perpetuate.

Schneider explained that, when she was young, she had been made to feel "shame about a part of who I was" and would never use the word "blind." It was not until she met other blind people who led happy and successful lives that she could accept and feel good about an identity that included being blind. Negative metaphors, she said, brought back the old feelings of shame and inadequacy. Schneider also included in her letter a positive suggestion: that the folksinger use the word "blankly" instead of "blindly" in his monologue. "There are un-offensive ways to say what we want to say," she concluded.

Another woman, Lisa Larges, blind from birth, explained the power of language to perpetuate systems of oppression and her efforts to challenge the assumptions.

> I have been on a small private campaign recently to cut back on my use of sight/blind based metaphors. A good deal of our culture's metaphors are drawn from darkness/light, black/white, blind/sighted analogies, so that if you are blind or have a dark skin color, you wind up on the wrong side of the symbolic tracks. Being conscious at least of the prevalence of such metaphors in our language makes me a bit more aware of how little of my own experience is ever validated or named—even by me.

Disabled women—so often defined by their physical limitations, by what they can't do—have persisted in the fight against the invisibility and isolation imposed on them. They have promoted accessibility to public buildings and public transportion, sign language interpretation for the hearing-impaired, and tape and braille services for the blind.

The Seneca Peace Encampment in upstate New York, in the summer of 1983, was intended as a place for all women who wished to participate to join in advocating for a peaceful, justice-inspired planet and to protest the nuclear arms race. The camp bordered the Seneca Army Depot and was located on a farm purchased by women. A system of boardwalks was built to make the camp more easily accessible to women with disabilities. Barbara Deming, then 66-years-old and in fragile health, was given a tent in a section of the camp reserved for disabled women. Observing the great variety of the women around her, Barbara marveled at what she perceived to be evidence of women's changing relationship to their own bodies.

> [The women at the peace camp] seemed to me to move with a lovely independence of spirit—or at least motion toward independence. The sturdy among them touching in one way. (In earlier days, I mused, I had rarely seen women so at ease in their bodies.) The frailer ones, or the disabled, touching in still another way. But no—not in another way, in just the same way: each seeming to have learned, or to be learning, not to despise her body—as we have all been taught to—but to discover in it new capabilities.

Barbara also observed the impact that physically-challenged activists had on their able-bodied colleagues. As a symbolic act of civil disobedience, many women had planned to climb over the fence at the depot on August 1. When several of the disabled (or "differently-abled") women joined the action as full participants, others got alarmed. It was an example of how people who are physically challenged are sometimes dis-abled—not by their own difficulties with mobility, but by the prejudices and fears of those around them whose caution serves to limit rather than support. Deming wrote:

> On August first, the day of the mass civil disobedience actions at the Depot, one woman on crutches and two blind women went over the fence....I was told that one of the military guards cried out in panic to Marianne, the woman on crutches: "Lady, why are you doing this?" And unhappily several of the demonstrators themselves cried out to the blind women, Sara and Diane, "You can't do that! You're blind!" But they could. And they did. This was the prevailing spirit at the camp, I'd say: We can and we will.

W HEN HER RIGHT BREAST WAS REMOVED, Audre Lorde, who has been called the Mother of Black Feminism, fought not to adorn her healthy body but to accept and love her healing one. But like the women before her who fought for the freedom of choice regarding long skirts, veils, comfortable shoes and hair styles, Lorde had to fight for the freedom of choice regarding the use of a prosthesis.

While she was still in the hospital recovering from her mastectomy, a kind and sincere volunteer with the American Cancer Society's Reach for Recovery Program handed Lorde a pale, pink breast-shaped pad stuffed with lambswool. This, the volunteer explained, was to be stuffed into Lorde's bra until she could later be fitted for a good prosthesis. Then the volunteer held open her own jacket so that Lorde could appreciate the symetrical figure beneath the tight blue sweater. "Now, can you tell which is which?" asked the volunteer. Lorde wrote:

> I admitted that I could not. In her tight foundation garment and stiff, up lifting bra, both breasts looked equally unreal to me.

Later, Lorde stood before the mirror and tried on the lambswool padding.

> I came around the bed and stood in front of the mirror in my room, and stuffed the thing into the wrinkled folds of the right side of my bra where my right breast should have been. It perched on my chest askew, awkwardly inert and lifeless, and having nothing to do with any me I could possibly conceive of. Besides, it was the wrong color and looked grotesquely pale through the cloth of my bra.

After a few moments of reflection, Lorde came to the conclusion that no prosthesis could ever undo the reality of her lost breast and that it was left to her to learn to love her one-breasted body or to remain forever alien to herself.

But in the following months, Lorde understood the struggle to be far greater than the struggle to live her life in her own body. As a forty-four-year-old African-American woman, as a lesbian, and as a feminist writer and poet, Lorde understood the adage of the women's movement that "the personal is political." Now this truth seemed imbedded into her very cells as she understood the lie she and other one-breasted women were being asked to make with their bodies in the United States in 1978. Unlike other prostheses—dentures, for example, or artificial limbs—false breasts are designed for appearance only. Women, Lorde found, are pressured to use this prosthesis before they have had a chance to adjust to their new body shape.

> To imply to a woman that yes, she can be the "same" as before surgery, with the skillful application of a little puff of lambswool, and/or silicone gel, is to place an emphasis upon prosthesis which encourages her not to deal with herself as physically and emotionally real, even though altered and traumatized. This emphasis upon the cosmetic after surgery reinforces this society's stereotype of women, that we are only what we look or appear, so this is the only aspect of our existence we need to address. Any woman who has had a breast removed because of cancer knows she does not feel the same....

> Women with breast cancer are warriors....I have been to war, and still am. So has every woman who has had one or both breasts amputated because of the cancer that is becoming the primary physical scourge of our time. For me, my scars are an honorable reminder that I may be a casualty in the cosmic war against radiation, animal fat, air pollution, McDonald's hamburgers and Red Dye No. 2 but the fight is still going on, and I am still part of it. I refuse to have my scars hidden or trivialized behind lambswool or silicone gel.

Ten days after she was discharged from the hospital, Lorde was eager for her first outing, a trip to the doctor's office to have her stitches removed. She had regained some strength and was in high spirits. With clean hair and new boots, wearing a tunic of African kente cloth, she felt beautiful and brave. She added a final touch to her ensemble, "I wore the most opalescent of my moonstones, and a single floating bird dangling from my right ear in the name of grand asymmetry."

But Lorde's "grand asymmetry" was not only not appreciated, it was taken as an affront to the medical establishment. The nurse at the surgeon's office coolly explained, "We really like you to wear something, at least when you come in. Otherwise it's bad for the morale of the office."

This explanation seemed to crystallize the argument for Lorde. Woman had to reclaim their own bodies and use the very fact of the changed landscape of their one-breasted bodies to speak the truth of their strength: a one-breasted woman could feel good about herself. Women would speak another truth as well:

> Prosthesis offers the empty comfort of "Nobody will know the difference." But it is that very difference which I wish to affirm, because I have lived it, and survived it, and wish to share that strength with other women. If we are to translate the silence surrounding breast cancer into language and action against this scourge, then the first step is that women with mastectomies must become visible to each other. For silence and invisibility go hand in hand with powerlessness. By accepting the mask of prosthesis, one breasted women proclaim ourselves as insufficients dependent upon pretense. We reinforce our own isolation and invisibility from each other, as well as the false complacency of a society which would rather not face the results of its own insanities. In addition, we withhold that visibility and support from one another which is such an aid to perspective and self acceptance. Surrounded by other women day by day, all of whom appear to have two breasts, it is very difficult sometimes to remember that I AM NOT ALONE. Yet once I face death as a life process, what is there possibly left for me to fear? Who can ever really have power over me again?

As freedom of choice regarding appearance, physical comfort, and well-being is claimed as a birthright, women are breaking the silences which have made us strangers to our own bodies. One by one, we stand in front of our mirrors, rehearsing the gestures of courage, designing new strategies of resistance, changing the world.

SOURCES

19th Century Dress Reform Movement in the U.S.

"Corsets Cramp Liver's Style." *Science Digest* (Jan/Feb. 1981).

De Marly, Diana. *Working Dress: A History of Occupational Clothing.* New York: Holmes & Meier Publishers, 1986.

Flexner, Eleanor. *Century of Struggle: The Woman's Rights Movement in the United States.* New York: Atheneum Publishers, 1974.

Gattey, Charles Neilson. *The Bloomer Girls.* New York: Coward-McCann, Inc. 1967/1968.

Kraditor, Aileen S., ed. *Up From the Pedestal: Selected Writings In the History of American Feminism.* New York: Quadrangle/The New York Times Book Co., 1968/1975.

McHenry, Robert, ed. *Famous American Women: A Biographical Dictionary from Colonial Times to the Present.* New York: Dover Publications, 1980.

Murray, Janet Horowitz. *Strong-Minded Women: And Other Lost Voices from Nineteenth-Century England.* New York: Pantheon Books, 1981.

Papachristou, Judith. *Women Together: A History in Documents of the Women's Movement in the United States.* New York: Alfred A. Knopf, 1976.

Sinclair, Andrew. *The Emancipation of the American Woman.* New York: Harper Colophon Books, 1965.

Spender, Dale. *Women of Ideas (And What Men Have Done to Them): From Aphra Behn to Adrienne Rich.* London: ARK Paperbacks/ Routledge & Kegan Paul, 1982/1983.

Stanton, Elizabeth Cady. *Eighty Years & More: Reminiscences 1815 - 1897.* New York: Schocken Books, 1898/1971.

Tucker, Linda Schechet. "Amelia's Bloomers: Stories for Free Children." *Ms.* (Dec. 1979).

Whitman, Alden, ed. *American Reformers: An H.W. Wilson Biographical Dictionary.* New York: The H.W. Wilson Co., 1985.

The Veil

Afkhami, Mahnaz. "Iran: A Future in the Past." In *Sisterhood Is Global.* Robin Morgan, ed. Garden City, NY: Doubleday, 1984.

Chafetz, Janet Saltzman and Anthony Gary Dworkin. *Female Revolt: Women's Movements In World and Historical Perspective.* Totowa, NJ: Rowman and Allanheld, 1986.

"Dress Code Decoded: West Germany." *Connexions: An International Women's Quarterly* no. 22 (Fall 1986).

Fernea, Elizabeth Warnock and Basima Qattan Bezirgan, eds. *Middle Eastern Muslim Women Speak.* Austin, TX: University of Texas Press, 1977.

Flanders, Laura. "Hard Line Oppresses Women." *New Directions for Women* (Jul./Aug. 1989).

Haberman, Clyde. "Turkey Feels the Pull of the Islamic." *The New York Times*. March 26, 1989.

Halle, Fannina W. *Women In the Soviet East*. Margaret M. Green, trans. New York: E.P. Dutton, 1938.

Hossain, Rokeya Sakhawat. *Sultana's Dream and Selections from The Secluded Ones*. Roushan Jahan, ed., trans. New York: The Feminist Press, 1988.

"Iranian Women Protest." *off our backs* (Aug./Sept. 1980).

Jayawardena, Kumari. *Feminism and Nationalism in the Third World*. London: Zed Books, 1986.

London Iranian Women's Liberation Group. "Iranian Women: The Struggle Since the Revolution." *Third World/Second Sex: Women's Struggles and National Liberation, Third World Women Speak Out*. Miranda Davies, comp. London: Zed Books, 1983.

Millett, Kate. *Going To Iran*. New York: Coward, McCann & Geoghegan, 1982.

Sanasarian, Eliz. *The Women's Rights Movement In Iran: Mutiny, Appeasement, and Repression from 1900 to Khomeini*. New York: Praeger Publishers, 1983.

Smith, Hazel. "Veil as Anti-Western Protest." *New Directions for Women* (Jul./Aug. 1989).

Hair and Feet

Croll, Elisabeth. *Feminism and Socialism in China*. Boston: Routledge & Kegan Paul, 1978.

"Dress Code Decoded." *Connexions: An International Women's Quarterly* no. 22 (Fall/Winter 1986-87).

Dworkin, Andrea. *Woman Hating*. New York: E.P. Dutton, 1974.

"Female Guards Face Firings Over Cornrows." *National NOW Times* (Apr. 1988).

"Hair-raising News." *Columbia Journalism Review* (May/June 1981).

Jayawardena, Kumari. *Feminism and Nationalism in the Third World*. London: Zed Books, 1986.

McElderry, Andrea. "Historical Background on Chinese Women." In *Lives: Chinese Working Women*. Mary Sheridan and Janet Salaff, eds. Bloomington, IN: Indiana University Press, 1984.

Ramakrishna Vedanta Centre (London). *Women Saints East and West*. Hollywood, CA: Vedanta Press, 1979.

Sievers, Sharon. *Flowers In Salt: The Beginnings of Feminist Consciousness in Modern Japan*. Stanford, CA: Stanford University Press, 1983.

Strong, Anna Louise. *China's Millions*. New York: Coward McCann, 1928.

Walker, Alice. "Oppressed Hair Puts a Ceiling on the Brain." *Ms.* (June 1988).

Challenging Notions of Disability

Corbett, K.J. "Invisible Women." *off our backs* (May 1981).
Deming, Barbara. *Prisons That Could Not Hold: Prison Notes 1964 - Seneca 1984.* San Francisco: Spinsters Ink, 1985.
Larges, Lisa. "Reflections on 'Reflections on Success'." *Womyn's Braille Press Newsletter* (Fall 1989).
Lorde, Audre. *The Cancer Journals.* Argyle, NY: Spinsters Ink, 1980.
Schneider, Marj. "Challenging Ableist Language." *Womyn's Braille Press Newsletter* (Summer 1989).

8

We Shall Not Be Moved

> One day I was driving home after a class, and I saw a huge
> rainbow over Oakland. I realized that women could survive if
> we decided that we have as much right and as much purpose for
> being here as the air and mountains do.
>
> —Ntozake Shange
> *for colored girls who have*
> *considered suicide/when the rainbow is enuf,*
> Original Broadway Cast recording, jacket notes.

PROSTITUTES IN LYON, FRANCE, in 1975, decided they needed to do something dramatic to call attention to their plight. The demonstrations they'd staged in 1973 had only inspired ridicule from the press, and the situation had seriously deteriorated since then.

The country's ten thousand prostitutes were being increasingly denied the most basic rights. Prostitutes couldn't live together because the apartment would be considered a brothel. They couldn't walk in certain neighborhoods under any circumstances. They couldn't date or get married or live with a man because any man who frequently socialized with a prostitute could be arrested as a pimp. And, ironically, while prostitution wasn't illegal in France, soliciting customers was! The women were constantly harassed by the police, arrested, fined, and imprisoned. There had been a recent increase in fines averaging $45 each. Some of the prostitutes, fined three or four times a night, had reason to believe that the police officers were pocketing the money.

Most alarming, however, prostitutes were being murdered with increasing frequency, and no one seemed to care.

In April, eighty prostitutes met for the first time to listen to each other and to strategize an action that would generate serious attention. They decided to go on strike and occupy one of Lyon's largest churches, St. Nizier.

On Monday, June 2, they were ready. Entering the church in inconspicuous small groups, their numbers soon reached close to one hundred and fifty, and the occupation was on. Outside, allies handed out leaflets to curious passersby and to the press explaining the prostitutes' grievances. Their "Letter to the Public" began:

> We are mothers who are talking to you, women who are trying to raise our children alone in the best possible way, and who today are afraid of losing them. Yes, we are prostitutes, but if we are prostitutes it is not because we are corrupt; it is the way that we have found to deal with life's problems.

The letter outlined the reasons the prostitutes had taken refuge in the church and reassured the public that the women intended to remain peaceful. The letter concluded:

> We are the victims of a political injustice. We are not asking you to defend prostitution, but to understand that they do not have the right to do what they're doing to us now. No one has ever been able to change their life while being hit with a bludgeon. Join us against this injustice which is crushing us. Afterwards we can discuss whether society needs prostitution....

The prostitutes occupying St. Nizier's had primarily sought a dialogue, one that soon developed with the use of a video camera installed by some feminist allies to enable the prostitutes to speak to the crowd in front of the church. The prostitutes demanded that police harassment stop, and they condemned proposals to create government-sponsored brothels that would make the women "civil servants of sex." The state, they said, was the biggest pimp of all. They urged that prostitutes be officially recognized as workers and be made eligible for pensions. And they insisted that those outside the church begin to see the real women behind the label "whore."

Word of the Lyon strike and church occupation spread, and soon prostitutes in other French cities joined in the revolt. In Paris, the prostitutes took over a chapel. Parisian feminists, lesbians, gay men, and New Left radicals stopped to offer moral support, as did Simone de Beauvoir, author of *The Second Sex*, who lived nearby. The government eventually called upon the police to intervene and to remove the women; as they left the sanctuaries, the women declared their action a victory.

It was soon evident that they were right. The murders stopped. Prostitutes and non-prostitutes strengthened the ties they had made during the strike to form the National Association of Action for the Defense of Prostitute Women to assist prostitutes, counsel them on their rights and options, and inform the public on the unique problems these women were facing. The Association also began publishing a newspaper, *Echo from the Pavement*, and in 1979 the prostitutes and their allies helped defeat a government proposal that would have created state brothels.

The Lyon prostitutes' nonviolent direct action was additionally effective because it reached beyond national boundaries. The story, though not always treated seriously, was reported around the world. In the United States, for example, *Newsweek* covered the story but trivialized it with the headline, "Filles Sans Joie."

News of the action encouraged prostitutes around the world to organize. London prostitutes were inspired by the Lyon action to organize the English Collective of Prostitutes (ECP). As in France, prostitution was legal in England, but a prostitute's individual civil liberties were severely limited, and police harassment was a number one problem. The ECP's goals were to abolish the laws against prostitutes and to fight the injustice of an economic system that forced poor women to turn to prostitution for money. They built a wide network of prostitutes and allies and in April 1982, set up a legal services center in the King's Cross red-light district, where half of the prostitutes were black women. When they immediately faced increased police harassment in that district, they followed the Lyon example. On November 17, they walked into Holy Cross Church with their children and informed the vicar they'd be staying.

The London occupation lasted twelve days, generating press coverage and support from working women, black and immigrant women's groups, and lesbian and gay groups as well as telegrams from all over the world. Women in Italy and the United States staged demonstrations in solidarity with the King's Cross prostitutes. The ECP sent a letter to the Greenham Common Peace Camp stating, "If prostitutes had a military budget, we wouldn't go into prostitution." This message prompted some Peace Camp women to join the occupation. They arrived at the church with their sleeping bags.

After the 1982 London occupation, ECP organized an international network, researched the history of prostitutes who have fought for human rights, and protested the military-industrial complex that perpetuates the economic and sexual subjection of women everywhere. At London's International Day for Peace demonstration in March, 1983, ECP carried a banner and distributed buttons which read "WHORES AGAINST WARS."

Prostitutes in Italy were also inspired by the Lyon action. In the northeastern city of Pordenone, prostitutes met on October 13, 1982, and decided to form a committee for the protection of their civil rights. Shortly after this first meeting, Italian prostitutes picketed the English Consulate in Venice in a solidarity action with the English prostitutes who were occupying Holy Cross Church in London. As a result of discussions among the prostitutes and the non-prostitute supporters who joined the committee, they began publishing a newspaper to give Italian prostitutes a voice. They called their newspaper *Lucciola* (firefly), the slang word for Italian prostitutes who build bonfires in the streets at night for warmth.

IN PERU IN 1978, WOMEN WORKERS at the LOLAS underwear factory in Lima arrived for work one day to find that the company had declared bankruptcy and established a "new" company in one wing of the building; in other parts of the building, the equipment had been removed. This was an old trick that had worked in the past to nullify women workers' right to collective bargaining whenever they began to organize. The women wasted no time. That same day over three hundred of them agreed to reconstitute a union and occupy the building to claim cooperative ownership.

After two weeks of occupying the building, the women were attacked one night by several hundred thugs hired by the management. The attackers were armed with knives, acid, and heavy metal chains. The police who arrived on the scene aided the attackers by shouting insults at the women and throwing tear gas into the buildings. Even when fifty-two women were badly injured in the attack, many of the women stayed on, continuing the occupation. There were more hardships to come. Some of the women were abandoned by their husbands or were literally dragged home. Still, the women managed to occupy the factory for over a year until they met with final defeat and were evicted by government troops.

The courage of the women who occupied the LOLAS factory inspired the women workers at Consorcio Electronico (CONEL) to occupy their factory the next year, 1979, when the management tried to replace workers with cheap, temporary help. Women who had worked at CONEL for over six years assembling radio and television parts returned from a "forced vacation" to find their jobs gone. They immediately began to occupy the factory and sent a petition to the government to form a workers' cooperative.

One week before Christmas, 1979, fifty men hired by the company stormed the factory and attacked the women, but the attack did not deter the women's fight. They joined with women workers fighting for a union at the LUCY children's clothing factory. Together, the women publicized the plight of factory workers in Peru. General public support grew as did the support of the Peruvian feminist movement that became actively involved in gaining both union and international support for the women. Women workers throughout the country were inspired by the women's factory occupation to demand changes at their own work places: maternity leave, child care, equal pay, and an end to sexual harassment. Women in male-dominated unions were inspired to take on more leadership roles. After two years of ongoing struggle, the workers' cooperative at CONEL gained the legal right to assume control of production.

The women who occupied the factories in Peru, regardless of the outcomes of their efforts, discovered a personal sense of empowerment. Each one had to summon vast amounts of courage to stand up to family pressures or to face company-hired thugs or to go to jail for the struggle. Courage was required, too, for the less dramatic support actions. One worker described the challenge faced by women who leafletted on the city buses:

> I remember one Saturday when we organized to do propaganda in the buses, entering them to distribute leaflets. Everybody knew who had taken on this responsibility. When the time came for them to give a report there was a long silence, no one said anything. Finally, at the insistence of the woman who directed the assembly, someone spoke. The compañeras had arrived at the bus stops, but were too embarrassed to get in. That made everyone think. The struggle we had begun was so hard for us, we had so many problems, problems that male workers don't have when they decide to wage a struggle. Then we said, "Why were we so embarrassed?" Because women were fighting? Because women were talking about a strike? Because women were distributing leaflets? The decision to sleep in the factory five months ago had created a hard life for us and we had been courageous. Why were we ashamed to enter the bus?

> With this conversation, we decided once again to enter the buses. The next Saturday the compañeras reported at the meeting that they had talked to people, given them leaflets, and collected money in the buses.

WOMEN HAVE DEFENDED THEIR HOMES AND HOMELANDS using the tactic of nonviolent occupation, as in the cases of the Native American women, whose peoples are being relocated from their traditional homes by the United States government and the women at the Crossroads Squatter settlement in South Africa, who are denied any home at all.

For centuries the Navajo (Dineh) and Hopi peoples peacefully shared the land around Big Mountain in relative peace. Big Mountain, in northeastern Arizona, is a sacred site for both peoples. Even after 1882, when the United States government established a separate Hopi reservation, the people shared the mountain, drawn there for religious ceremonies, for healing, and for spiritual nourishment. The people call the mountain "Mother."

The earth around the mountain is sacred, too. For centuries, Navajo mothers have buried the umbilical cords of their children in the land by their hogans, have passed on stories of the rocks and trees, have honored the passages of youth into adulthood by singing songs of the ancestors, and have collected soil from the earth for the medicine bundles that must never be taken outside the sacred circles. The land is steeped in legends about Changing Woman, who grows old and young again with the seasons, and, about Be'gochici, the "One Who Created People," and the Anasai, "Those Who Were Here Before Us."

But now the people are afraid that the land of their great-great-grandmothers and grandfathers will be dynamited, that everything will be destroyed. It has been a long season of worry. In 1921, Standard Oil Company found oil on Navajo land and proposed that land be leased to the company for its use. When the Navajo elders voted 75-0 against the proposition, the government, through the Bureau of Indian Affairs (BIA), set up a handpicked "tribal council" of three men who were easily persuaded to sign a lease. Another tribal council was also set up for the Hopis. Then coal and oil companies discovered minerals and oil buried in the earth. A Mormon lawyer, John Boyden, was appointed to represent the Hopi people. Conveniently, he also represented the Peabody Coal Company that, in 1966, was granted a lease to mine the land.

As corporations helped themselves to the minerals and the oil buried on the disputed lands, the earth was ripped open in huge, gaping wounds from coal and uranium strip mines, power plants, and uranium mills; the air became thick with pollution. A power plant located not far from Big Mountain was deemed the worst single industrial polluter in the world, emitting three hundred and fifty tons of sulfur compounds every day. In 1966, Gemini astronauts orbiting the earth reported seeing only two human-made creations—the Great Wall of China and the smoke from the power plant near Big Mountain. And while the multinational corporations tore about the earth for its energy sources and profits, the majority of Navajo hogans had dirt floors and no electricity.

The heartache of the destruction of the native homeland and sacred site has been compounded by the forced relocation of the Navajo and Hopi people. In 1974, the United States government passed Public Law no. 93-531 that ordered the relocation of the people; in 1977, the United States government decided that a three-hundred-mile barbed-wire fence should divide the land and that eight thousand people must move from their land.

The women have taken the leadership in resisting the relocation, usually with nonviolent ingenuity but sometimes with the threat of rifles. In September 1979, several days after Katherine Smith, a respected elder of the Navajo people and a leader of the resistance against relocation, fired a warning shot into the air when she found a government crew building a barbed-wire fence, women tore the new fence out of the earth. "We had reached the end of our wits," Smith explained, "and had to take the situation into our hands the day the fence was being put up, taking the land out from under us. We are not represented and are not informed of the decisions affecting our lives. The truth is kept from us. Because of this, we are in a state of melancholy; we will never move off this land....If we just stand by and watch, they will keep on putting up fence after fence after fence."

The women refused to stand by and watch. In September 1980, when a crew of workers tried to continue building the long barbed-wire fence, women elders took the keys from two of the crew's trucks while younger women pulled up the fence posts from the ground. Shortly after the confrontation, the Washington, D.C., headquarters of the BIA sent a representative to hear the people's complaints and announced that the construction of the fence would be temporarily suspended. In 1985, four grandmothers from Big Mountain toured the West Coast with an interpreter, telling stories of the struggle. The storytelling itself was an act of resistance to injustice and oppression.

"We are Navajo traditionals," Katherine Smith has said. "We do not change our prayer. But if we don't do something, I think pretty soon there's going to be no more Navajo prayer, Navajo singing.... Lightning, rainbow, earth, and night—that's where we came from. Now thousands of white people come, trying to take it, this land, away from us, trying to kill us."

"WE ARE NOT MOVING! WE ARE NOT MOVING!" This was the rallying cry of the women at Crossroads, outside of Cape Town, South Africa, in 1977 and 1978. They had formed the Crossroads Women's Committee to fight for the right to stay near the area where their husbands lived and worked rather than be moved to Transkei, an "'independent' Bantustan" with a population of over two million. The white South African government, enforcing the rules of apartheid, considered the community a "squatter camp," though it had a population of twenty thousand residents with schools and basic service organizations, and a majority of heads of households had lived there an average of eighteen years—hardly a transient community. Still, in 1977, the government decided it was time to relocate the people to the Transkei. They came with bulldozers and billy clubs. Regina Ntongana, a resident of Crossroads and one of the leaders of the resistance, told about the harassment:

> They used to come at all hours of the night and raid us. We women would warn each other and grab a blanket and sit together in the open field. There would be hundreds of us. They coudn't arrest all of us, and it was some protection. The babies and the men would stay in the

shacks, except for the very little babies on their mother's backs. And sometimes, you would go to the well for water during the day and when you got back home your shack was demolished.

The women of Crossroads organized demonstrations. In June 1978, over two hundred women demonstrated in front of the Bantu Affairs Administration Board. Seven women were elected to speak to the officials on behalf of the Crossroads community, articulating the grievances. All were called in for interrogation by the police ten days later, and the police raids on the community continued. In July, a multiracial crowd of over four thousand people held a two-and-a-half-hour prayer service for Crossroads, but still the police continued their raids. In September, over eight hundred people were arrested, three were shot, and one died.

When the bulldozers came, women sat in front of them. Three people were killed, but the protest began to generate international outrage and support. One member of the Women's Committee, Alexandre Luke, spoke of the spirit of the resistance:

> And when they come to demolish Crossroads, what will the women do? We are not going to move here in Crossroads. We are going to stay. And build our houses again.

On September 15, the Crossroads Women's Committee issued a statement:

> We are hurt. Three-month-old babies and eleven-year-old children are in jail—pregnant women and sick people. In jail, little babies are being fed on nothing but water all day long. Babies are crying.

Still, the women did not give up the fight. They sat in front of the bulldozers with the whole world as witness until, finally, in December, the white South African government—with all its jails and all its bulldozers and all its weapons—was forced to announce that the people at Crossroads would not be forced to move.

SOMETIMES THE "HOME" for which women struggle is far smaller than a homeland. Sometimes it is a fight for a decent place to live, a room of one's own. A homeless woman in Toronto shamed city officials and dramatized her frustration with the housing bureaucracy by occupying a plastic doll house that she set up in the middle of a city square. Her house, erected during the summer of 1987, measured only a meter (thirty-nine inches) high, but it succeeded in grabbing a mountain of media attention. Embarrassed city officials scurried to arrange a free room at the Carlton Inn while the woman waited for permanent housing.

A month later, in August, Amber Cooke, a thirty-four-year-old single mother, followed suit and pitched a little orange tent that she called home in front of Toronto's City Hall to draw attention to her plight. Her unemployment insurance had just run out, and both she and her thirteen-year-old daughter were homeless, tired, and discouraged. She had added her name to the waiting list for subsidized housing but was told by the Metro Toronto Housing Authority that the wait might be two years. But after she was arrested for trespassing on City Hall property with her tent, she was immediately granted a two-bedroom apartment from the limited low-income stock. Though Metro officials denied that Cooke's protest had anything to do with it, Cooke believed otherwise. "They don't want people to know that civil disobedience is the way to get what you want," she told reporters.

SOURCES

Prostitutes' Action

Brown, Wilmette. "Organising Together." In *Black Women and the Peace Movement*. Bristol, England: Falling Wall Press Ltd., 1983.

"England: Hands Off." *Connexions: An International Women's Quarterly* no. 12 (Spring 1984).

"France: Like Other Women." *Connexions: An International Women's Quarterly* no. 12 (Spring 1984).

"Filles Sans Joie." *Newsweek* (June 23, 1975).

"Italy: Firefly." *Connexions: An International Women's Quarterly* no. 12 (Spring 1984).

Peruvian Women Occupy Factories

Andreas, Carol. *When Women Rebel: The Rise of Popular Feminism in Peru.* Westport, CT: Lawrence Hill & Co., 1985.

Navajo and Hopi women

Big Mountain Support Committee. *Resistance at Big Mountain: 8000 Navajos to be Forcibly Uprooted.* Albuquerque, NM: Big Mountain Support Committee, 1982.

Matthiessen, Peter. "Battle for Big Mountain." *The New York Mobilizer* (Jan./Feb. 1981).

McDaniel, Judith. *Sanctuary: A Journey.* Ithaca, NY: Firebrand Books, 1987.

Seggerman, Victoria. "Navajo Women and the Resistance to Relocation." *off our backs* (Mar. 1986).

Sovereign Hotevilla Nation. An open letter to the governors of Arizona and New Mexico. March 4, 1985.

Women for Big Mountain. "Navajos Resist Forced Relocation" (a fact sheet).

Women at Crossroads

Lapchick, Richard E. and Stephanie Urdang. *Oppression and Resistance: The Struggle of Women in Southern Africa.* Westport, CT: Greenwood Press, 1982.

Homeless Women in Toronto

Taylor, Paul. "Put Up Tent, Woman Gets Apartment." *The Toronto Globe and Mail.* September 19, 1987.

9

Alone In The Wilderness

> To truly learn who we are, we have to turn to one another again.
> We do not belong to others, but our lives are linked; we belong
> in a circle of others. We learn best to listen to our own voices if
> we are listening at the same time to other women—whose stories,
> for all our differences, turn out, if we listen well, to be our stories
> too. Their anger, which they begin to acknowledge, we recognize
> as our anger; the strength which they have doubted, but which
> that very anger hints at, is our strength too.
>
> —Barbara Deming
> "Remembering Who We Are"

THE "NIGHT OF TERROR" is what suffragists in the United States, arrested for picketing in front of the White House, later called November 14, 1917.

Already that year they had endured harassment, mob attacks, arrests, and long prison sentences at the Occoquan Workhouse in Virginia. In prison, they had been ridiculed, called heretics and worse, been made to strip in front of each other, been denied toilet articles, pencils, and paper. They had shared prison cells with rats and had found worms floating in their soup. That night their leader, Alice Paul, was absent. The government, in an attempt to undermine Paul's credibility, had transferred the suffrage leader—who had been arrested several months earlier for picketing the White House—from prison to a psychiatric ward and had denied her legal counsel. The women's campaign of picketing and petitioning for the right to vote in the United States demanded a great deal of courage and fortitude. Still, nothing compared to the terror of that November night.

The thirty-one picketers arrested that day waited stubbornly to see the superintendent of the prison to demand that they be acknowledged as the political prisoners they were. As they waited, the room slowly filled with male security guards. Suddenly everything erupted into a

185

nightmare of violence. The furniture was overturned. Women were grabbed and shoved as one by one they were pulled out of the room.

Mary Nolan, a woman in her seventies, was dragged down some steps, across the prison yard, down a long corridor and shoved into a cell. Dorothy Day, described at the time as a very slight, delicate girl, was thrown hard against an iron bench in a cell. Later, in her autobiography she wrote:

> When another prisoner tried to come to my rescue, we found ourselves in the midst of a milling crowd of guards being pummeled and pushed and kicked and dragged, so that we were scarcely conscious, in the shock of what was taking place.

One woman was punished by being placed in the men's wing of the prison where she was subjected to jeers and taunts throughout the long, sleepless night. Another woman collapsed in her cell with severe chest pains but the guards refused to respond to her cellmates' calls for a doctor.

In the midst of this chaos, Lucy Burns, the fearless redhead from Brooklyn and the first to take charge whenever Alice Paul was absent, began to call the roll. Her voice was strong, clear, and calming to the others as she began to bring some sense of order. The guards warned Burns after each name that she had better stop of her own will or they'd be sure she did, but Burns kept calling the names.

"Where's Mrs. Lewis?" she called out, and down the row of cells a frightened voice called back, "They've just thrown her in here." "Shut up!" the guards demanded over and over, but Lucy Burns kept calling out the names of the arrested women, determining who was safe, who was missing, who was in need of aid. She forged ahead. Suddenly, the guards stormed into her cell. They grabbed her arms, roughly handcuffed her wrists and then fastened the cuffs above her head to the bars of the cell door. They threatened that, if she made another sound, they would return with a buckle gag.

What happened next is a story within a story, the story of a gesture of solidarity, a story that will never make it into our school history books. (Indeed, the entire account of the "Night of Terror" is omitted, let alone this story of one solitary gesture.) A young activist, Julia Emory, had been locked into the cell directly across from Lucy Burns. When she saw Burns' lonely punishment, Emory stood up and faced the cell where Burns was being forced to stand with her hands cuffed over her head. Then, Emory mirrored Burns' tortured posture by raising her own arms. She stood with her arms raised over her head, bearing silent witness in her own personal vigil of suffering, until the handcuffs were unlocked from the bars of Burns' cell several hours later. Then both women lowered their arms.

WHAT IS THE SHAPE OF COURAGE? Where is it fashioned? Often, courage is fashioned in crowds where hearts are collectively beating hard, where many voices are raised in unison to hide the lone trembling alto. Damp palms grasp other damp palms. Courage takes the shape of bodies en masse blocking the highway, ten thousand individual signatures on one petition, a chorus of stomach growls as hunger strikers huddle together in their cells.

But sometimes the gestures of courage are fashioned on a street where one stands alone, exposed, or in a lonely room where the heartbeats echo a deafening solo. And sometimes, indeed, we are alone. There is no great chorus of others, there are no others' arms linked side by side, there are no other footsteps. Then the course is even more bewildering, the night stretching moment by moment into an eternity. Julia Emory stood with her arms over her head in a gesture of solidarity and her action must have heartened Lucy Burns through the long hours of discomfort. But sometimes there is no one to witness, no one to breathe with, no one who will later tell the story.

Ralph Waldo Emerson wrote, "Do the thing and you shall have the power." It must often work that way—that the courageous action is taken before the power to take it is felt, the courageous action taking the doer herself by surprise. What makes it possible for anyone to stand alone? What creates the moment when an ordinary, frightened woman finds the courage she needs to hold fast and to act—alone—from the strength of her conviction?

Where did Fanny Lou Hamer, a poor African-American sharecropper, find the courage to fight for voter registration during the civil rights movement of the 1960s in Ruleville, Mississippi, when doing so meant having to endure severe beatings and imprisonment, the loss of her livelihood and her home, as well as threats on her life and the lives of her family?

Where did Elizabeth Eckford, a fifteen-year-old African-American girl in Little Rock, Arkansas, in 1957, find the courage to face the mob of angry white people who surrounded her, screaming threats and jeers, and the armed men in the National Guard who blocked her way when she tried to enter the segregated Central High School? And where did the lone white woman find the courage to step from that hostile crowd and comfort Elizabeth, telling the hecklers, "Leave her alone. She's scared. She's only a little girl"?

Where did Lois Gibbs, a shy twenty-six-year-old with sick kids, find the courage in 1978 to go up against city, state, and federal authorities armed only with her own kitchen-table research? Her research, dismissed at first by the state health department as "useless housewife data," proved that the entire Love Canal, New York, area had been contaminated with dangerous chemicals from the same chemical company in which Gibbs' husband was employed.

And what of Kathy Russell, the twenty-three-year-old director of the Washington County Public Library in southwest Virginia? In 1981, she endured months of public humiliation—denunciations from church pulpits, by radio commentators, in newspapers, and on television news—for her defense of the First Amendment of the United States Consitution which guarantees the freedom of expression. She refused to remove from the library the books several prominent citizens had found objectionable, nor would she hand over the names of the borrowers who had signed out those books. She stood alone, defending the right of American readers to have access to a range of ideas, until twenty-five hundred citizens signed a petition supporting her and denouncing the would-be censors. Russell said only, "It was hard, you know, during those times when you're by yourself, and you really do wonder what's going to happen. But I did what I had to do. As a librarian, I had no choice."

Where did Frances Baard, a black South African born in 1901, find the courage to sustain her commitment to union organizing among women in the food and canning trade? She repeatedly endured prison and banishment under the racist system of apartheid. After one long period of imprisonment, she was asked to renounce her membership in the African National Congress (ANC). She refused. The officials asked, "Don't you know the ANC is banned?" "Yes," she answered, "but you forgot to ban my spirit. I still want freedom in my lifetime."

Where did Marta Alicia Rivera find the courage to be a teacher in El Salvador in 1972 at a time when teachers were targets for the government security forces? Though it meant risking death, Rivera joined the National Association of Salvadoran Educators (ANDES), a union organized in 1965 for teachers who work for social change by organizing in the slums and the poorest villages for people's right to food, housing, and education. The group argued that they could not teach starving children about good nutrition. Doing so would have been a cruel farce. They could not teach children who had no pencils to write with rifles. By 1978, 264 ANDES members had been assassinated by government forces backed with United States money and by right-wing death squads. Hundreds of other teachers were tortured—as Rivera was.

> They stripped me naked and began to interrogate me. They kept hitting me with their rifles until my face opened up and my jaw broke. They made cuts all over my body with a razor blade. They cut off all my hair, shaved my eyebrows and even tried to cut out my tongue, but my broken jaw got in their way.

Finally, the National Guardsmen threw Rivera into a garbage dump, where she was found and brought back to the university. Rivera recovered and continued to fight for the poor of El Salvador and for the children.

What is the shape of courage?

POLAND'S SECRET EXTERMINATION CAMP, SOBIBOR, was a small but efficient Nazi death machine, where most of the imprisoned were killed within twenty-four hours of their arrival. In only eighteen months of operation 250,000 Jews died there.

At approximately five p.m. on a clear October day in 1943, the first day of Succoth—the holy days commemorating God's protection of the Jews who had escaped from Egypt—six hundred Jewish death camp prisoners, left alive only to maintain the camp, rose up against their Nazi guards. A small team of prisoners had already cut the camp's telephone lines, killed several of the guards, and captured some weapons; when the signal was given, all but the frailest of the camp's prisoners made an attempt to escape.

Amid gunfire and jubilant shouts of "Hurrah! Long live freedom!" and urgent cries of "Forward! Forward!" almost three hundred made it past the barbed wire fences into the mine fields surrounding the camp. Roughly half of this number managed to escape to the woods, into "the forest of the owls."

Sergeant Karl Frenzel, one of the bewildered SS officers back at the camp, soon discovered that the phones were dead. He raced through the main gates, across the railroad tracks to the little station where he sent a telegram: "JEWS REVOLTED. SOME ESCAPED....SOME SS OFFICERS, NON-COMS, FOREIGN GUARDS DEAD....SOME JEWS STILL INSIDE THE CAMP....SEND HELP!"

Twenty-five miles away, the young woman telegrapher on duty at the Chelm station received the urgent message. It was her job to transmit the message immediately to the Security Police headquarters. But she understood the message and knew what was most important for the success of the escaped prisoners—time.

In all probability, she didn't know the extent of the atrocities taking place daily in the nearby camp, especially on special occasions, such as the visit of SS chief Heinrich Himmler on February 12, 1943. The SS had worn their very best uniforms and polished their boots that day and had selected two hundred of the most attractive young Jewish women and girls to demonstrate the extraordinarily efficient gas chambers. While she would not have known about the gas chambers, she must have seen the trainloads of people and heard their cries, and perhaps she had noticed the strange and constant smoke that had begun rising from the woods during the previous winter. The young telegrapher would not have known about the many attempted escapes and the high spirit of resistance at the camp.

Rereading the words of the telegram, "JEWS REVOLTED....SOME ESCAPED....SEND HELP," the young woman imagined trembling people, desperate for sanctuary, hiding now "in the forest of the owls" and she knew where her sympathies lay. It was her duty to send the message. And she would—later.

Every minute of her shift was agony. If she were found out, she would lose her life. Nevertheless, she withheld the message for over four hours. With this small but courageous gesture of slow compliance, this woman (whose name is not known) played her part in the biggest prison escape of World War II. Hers was just one of the many small acts of sabotage vital to the undermining of the Nazis and the strengthening of the resistance.

The next day, the Security Police sent a report to Berlin stating that the revolt of the Sobibor Jews had started about five p.m., that military police and armed forces had been notified "immediately" and that they had taken over security of the camp at "about 1:00 a.m."—hours after the camp officials called for help.

Five days after the revolt, the enraged Himmler ordered all evidence of the Sobibor camp erased: the gas chambers and barracks were dynamited; documents pertaining to the camp were destroyed; all the remaining prisoners were murdered; and the ground was plowed and a forest of pine trees was planted there. But even the Nazis couldn't kill the truth. Thirty of the Jews who escaped from Sobibor survived being hunted in the woods. The story of their courage is told in history books. The story of their unknown, unseen, solitary young friend and her act of sabotage was passed down to her children and her children's children.

COLD WAR POLITICIANS WHIPPED THEMSELVES into a frenzy over civil defense in the mid-1950s. In school, young students were required to crouch on demand under their desks in "Duck and Cover" air raid drills, while older students practiced standing in the hallways with their arms over their heads for protection from atomic bombs. It was a period when questioning even such ludicrous notions might be construed as "un-American," a time when being labeled un-American could cost you your career, your place in the community, your dreams.

On June 15, 1955, New York City set off 679 sirens in a massive air-raid drill. All people in the city were required to get off the streets for a minimum of ten minutes as required by the Civil Defense Act. According to the drill's engineers, an imaginary H-bomb had detonated at the corner of North 7th Street and Kent Avenue in Brooklyn, incinerating 2,991,185 citizens with another 1,776,899 New Yorkers listed as injured in the imaginary flames that roared through the city. The next day, the *New York Mirror* reported that the drill had been a major success—almost. "Millions of New Yorkers took shelter in the city's greatest air raid drill—an exercise marred only by 29 arrests."

And who had marred the grim exercise? Dorothy Day, radical pacifist and founder of the Catholic Workers, with twenty-eight others, had refused to participate in the drill and had deliberately stood on the street awaiting arrest.

"We wanted to act against war and the preparation for war," explained Day, listing the elements of the modern military state being protested: nerve gas, guided missiles, the testing and stockpiling of nuclear bombs, conscription, and the collection of income tax for war-related expenses. " the testing and stockpiling of nuclear bombs, conscription, and the collection of income tax for war-related expenses. "We made our gesture," she said. "We disobeyed the law."

The judge who heard their arguments was not moved. These protesters, after all, had disrupted the imaginary holocaust. Bail was set at $1,500, and the judge denounced the protesters as "murderers" who "by their conduct and behavior contributed to the utter destruction of these three million theoretically killed in our city." That year the sentences were suspended. The next year, the action resulted in thirty-day jail sentences. But every year the protest grew, despite the threat of jail, until 1961 when thousands stood in City Hall Park, defying the shrieking sirens.

While the judges who sentenced the New York City protesters were not moved by their action, others were, including a shy, thirty-six-year-old woman in upstate New York whose name was Ruth Best. (Many years later she changed her name to Ruth Dreamdigger.)

On the day of the drill in 1957, Ruth was driving a station wagon filled with four lively children on their way to shop in Spring Valley. Suddenly a policeman pulled her over to the curb and explained that the siren blaring in the background meant all traffic must stop in observance of the annual air raid drill. Ruth did as she was told.

But as Ruth sat there, the enormity of the situation swept over her. "I was supposed to sit there passively in the station wagon with my four little kids," she said later, "while an atomic bomb dropped on us!" She vowed that day that she would never again participate in the drill.

But the moment passed and, in the immediacy of daily life with children, Ruth forgot about the yearly air raid drill until one morning the following spring. That day she awoke with a tremendous headache and felt shaky and tearful. All day there seemed to be something as tiny and mean as a killer bee waiting in a corner of her mind. It was not until that evening when she climbed, exhausted, into bed that she remembered seeing a notice about the annual air raid drill. It would be the next day. Ruth began to sob and immediately her headache stopped. She turned to her husband and announced that the next day she would make a trip to the office of the Fellowship of Reconciliation (FOR) twenty minutes away to pick up antiwar leaflets and return to distribute them during and in defiance of the drill in Spring Valley.

The next day, after arranging for child care for her son, Jonathan, who was still too young for school, Ruth picked up the leaflets and drove back to the outskirts of Spring Valley. She was trembling at the thought of breaking the law. Leafletting would be hard enough for the shy woman. She decided to begin passing out the flyers at the far end of town.

And there she stood, as her knees almost gave out, in the middle of the lonely sidewalk when the siren went off. And there she stood and stood and stood, unnoticed by anyone, but very brave, nevertheless, breaking all kinds of barriers in her own mind and heart, making a new record in courage in the context of her own life. She thought she could see a police officer far off up the street, but he evidently didn't see her, and soon the all-clear siren was sounded. "I raced for the car and headed home," she remembered of her triumph that day, "grateful to have had it both ways."

Courage has an odd way of gaining weight and muscle and shape as it is exercised. Ruth had had a taste of breaking the law in the service of her conscience, albeit breaking the law when no one else happened to notice, and she was ready to do it again, with gusto.

In the spring of 1959 she was ready. By then she had heard about a woman in the next town, Vera Williams, who also wanted to protest the drill. They went to Haverstraw, another small town in Rockland County, New York, on the day of the drill. When the drill sounded, the two women were in the middle of town distributing leaflets. Vera went in and out of stores with her leaflets. Ruth stood in the middle of the sidewalk with hers and was arrested immediately.

Ruth remembered later, "The policeman and I had a pleasant and reasonable talk while we walked together to the police station. But reasonableness and pleasantness ended there. The police chief was very angry that his air raid drill had been spoiled." The chief shook his fist in Ruth's face and roared, "If you were a man I'd bash your brains in!" And Ruth roared right back, "Don't you dare hurt me or all of Rockland County will hear about it!" Was this the same Ruth who, just one year earlier, had all but fainted as she stood meekly on the lonely sidewalk in defiance of the siren?

They put her in the courtroom to cool off while Vera was brought into the station. The courtroom reminded Ruth of a Quaker meetinghouse with its wooden benches and austere design. Ruth began to meditate in the stillness and was calm by the time Vera paid bail for both of them.

When she got home her phone was ringing; it was a local radio announcer. Civil disobedience was the big news in Rockland County that day and the station wanted an interview. Ruth told the reporter, "I'm nervous about talking on the radio. Could you wait a couple of days?" The announcer laughed and explained that in a couple of days the action would not be news at all and said he'd call back in five minutes.

On the day of the hearing, the FOR National Council took a break from its long meeting and showed up in the courtroom to give moral support. Ruth spoke briefly about personal responsibility, civil disobedience, and the foolishness of the civil defense law.

Later, she and Vera received a supportive letter from pacifist leader A.J. Muste and another from Catholic Worker activist, Ammon Hennacy, who urged the women to join the protest in New York City the next year. "But I always knew," said Ruth, "that there was more mileage in doing civil disobedience in my own home town. There was lot of newspaper coverage because we were locally known—with the original story and editorials and letters to the editor going on for quite a while."

By the spring of 1960, the two had grown to six, and Ruth had decided not to post bail or pay a fine after the arrest. She knew that this time she would go to jail. Again, Ruth was pushing the limits of her courage. What if there were drug addicts in the jail? she wondered. What would they do to her, "an inexperienced, unworldly housewife who knew nothing about such a life"? The night before the air raid drill, Ruth locked herself in her bedroom. She wept and wailed, shook and raged. She pleaded with God to let her off the hook. When she opened her door and saw the faces of her children, Ruth was again calm. But still, that night Ruth didn't go to bed. Instead, she cleaned the house from top to bottom, did the laundry, fixed food to be frozen and heated for suppers, wrote letters to her relatives and wrote detailed instructions to the children—reminders to wash their hands, keep their noses clean, feed the cat and dog, clear the table, and go to school together so that "you can help each other if necessary."

The next day, when she was arrested with the other five protesters in Spring Valley, Ruth refused to sign the arrest form until the words "maliciously and corruptly" were stricken from the text. She eventually had her way and was sent off to jail for five days. Just as she had feared, there were two drug addicts doing time in the women's section, but they were not what she had expected. "Two more gentle and likeable people could not be found. My fears had been totally inappropriate." From her jail cell she wrote to her husband, "In heart and conscience I feel free as a bird."

Every year Ruth grew bolder, and every year the number of protesters grew. When she was arrested in 1961, with more than fifty supporters standing in solidarity under a nearby awning, Ruth was ready for Police Justice Arnold Becker's decision to "get tough." He gave those arrested a choice: either pay a $25 fine or go to jail for twenty-five days. The others chose to pay the fine, but Ruth found it impossible to fit her rage and her grief for the planet into a $25 penalty. She chose jail.

As she stood alone before the courtroom, Ruth thought of being away from her children for almost a month. Through tears she began to speak, slowly at first, about the many friends who would willingly pay the fine for her and about the pain it caused her to leave her children. And then she really got going. She made the newspaper headlines with her stand.

> Mrs. Best made a lengthy impassioned address to the court after entering a guilty plea. The mother of four young children wept as she related her beliefs in loving her enemies and not wishing to save herself at the expense of other people. "It is time for the people of Rockland County to wake up and protect their children," Mrs. Best, a small bespectacled woman, said. "Humanity is working at hatred, all the time devising new means of killing people. An H-Bomb will kill all within a 20 mile area. The government is developing a chemical warfare weapon called Q-fever," she said. "One ounce of Q-fever will kill 11 times the population of the world."

Ruth went on to quote Henry David Thoreau's essay, "On Civil Disobedience," as well as several religious authors she had been reading. "Without a doubt," she said later, "it was the best talk I ever gave. When I stopped, the courtroom was deathly quiet. Judge Becker began to shuffle some papers. Then he sentenced me to five days in jail, the same sentence that I had received before. What a relief!"

This time there was no one else imprisoned in the women's section of the jail; Ruth remembers it as a peaceful time of rest and reflection. She remembers, too, that her husband brought the children to look up at her through the bars and that she waved from the window. She remembers that they looked so innocent and lovely in the sunlight and that the matron, seeing them, asked, "Aren't you ashamed for them to see you in jail?" But Ruth just beamed. She was a courageous woman, far more courageous than she had ever dreamed she could become. Years later one of her daughters remembered looking up at the jailhouse windows. "It seemed kind of exotic to have a mother who went to jail," she grinned.

1961 was the last year for the New York State compulsory air raid drill. "Hundreds of laughing and singing people had been arrested in New York City," said Ruth. "Not many people believed any longer that there could be safety in a nuclear war."

COURAGE IS SOMETIMES REQUIRED IN LIFE'S CRACKS and crevices. When the reporters and historians are at lunch, and no one will notice, the courage required to do the right thing becomes the measure of a life. Facing a lonely stand, we stare down the questions: "Am I just making a big deal out of nothing? Who will know if I just compromise a little bit today? After all, how will this little stand effect anything in the world? No one's looking. And the costs are so great. For what? For what?" The temptations are great when the gesture might so easily be overlooked. But it is precisely at such moments that the heart beats the hardest and the breath catches at the throat, because, after all, these are the moments in a lifetime that really do matter, and we know it. Holly Near sings, "Linger on the details, the parts that reflect the change. There lies revolution."

Marie Bloom faced such a moment on her very first job through a temporary employment agency. She had just left the staff of the War Resisters League, where she had worked hard on a range of issues, including a campaign against war toys. She looked her secretarial best the day she was sent to a big Madison Avenue advertising firm. And she was making a pretty good impression answering phones—until they handed her something to type. It was the audio voice-over script for a television advertisement promoting the newest war toy to hit the already booming market. Irony of ironies.

Marie sat with the ironies for a while before she took the script, untyped, back to the man who had asked her to type it. She explained that her life's work was about challenging militarism in all its guises, including its manifestation in toy form, and that she couldn't type the script for a war toy ad. At first, the man laughed. He said that this particular toy was really innocuous. "There are some other toys you really wouldn't like," he chuckled. But when Marie didn't laugh he sputtered, "But these are the rules!" "Yes," replied Marie quietly, "but they are your rules, not mine."

She returned to her desk, silently calculating what she feared might be the lost income for the day, income she so desperately needed at the time. The afternoon was awkward. With nothing to do, she found a novel in the desk and began to skim it, delighted to find in the story a pacifist character. Another secretary was assigned the work of typing the war toy ad, but throughout the afternoon Marie overheard the other office workers talking about what she had done. Everywhere she walked she heard the word "nonviolence" whispered after her. The word was repeated in expanding circles throughout the office, carried and repeated like the most subtle of ripples in a pond, ripples carrying the amazing news of a nonviolent activist who had questioned authority in the very heart of corporate America.

Linger on the details. There lies revolution.

SOURCES

Julia Emory and the Night of Terror

Day, Dorothy. *The Long Loneliness: An Autobiography.* Garden City, NY: Doubleday, 1959.

Irwin, Inez Haynes. *The Story of Alice Paul and The National Women's Party.* Fairfax, VA: Denlinger's Publishers, Ltd., 1964/1977.

Papachristou, Judith. *Women Together: A History in Documents of the Women's Movement in the United States.* New York: Alfred A. Knopf, 1976.

Sobibor and the Lone Woman Telegrapher

Novitch, Miriam. *Sobibor: Martyrdom and Revolt—Documents and Testimonies.* New York: Waldon Press, Inc., 1980.

Rashke, Richard. *Escape from Sobibor: The Heroic Story of the Jews Who Escaped from a Nazi Death Camp.* Boston: Houghton Mifflin Co., 1982.

Sharp, Gene. *The Politics of Nonviolent Action: Part Two—The Methods of Nonviolent Action.* Boston: Porter Sargent Publishers, 1973.

Other Stories

al-Hamdani, Laila. "A Palestinian Woman in Prison." In *Women In the Middle East.* London: Zed Books, 1987.

Allport, Catherine. "Voices of South Africa." *Fellowship* (Oct./Nov. 1985).

"ANDES: Teachers Organizing for a New Society." Pamphlet, 1984.

Bloom, Marie. Personal interview, July, 1988.

Dreamdigger, Ruth. Personal interview and correspondence, 1988.

Hentoff, Nat. *American Heroes: In and Out of School.* New York: Delacorte Press, 1987.

Sterling, Dorothy and Donald Gross. *Tender Warriors.* New York: Hill and Wang, 1958.

"Teachers as 'Troublemakers'." *NEA Today* (Oct. 1983).

To Honour Women's Day: Profiles of Leading Women In the South African and Namibian Liberation Struggles. International Defence and Aid Fund for Southern Africa in co-operation with United Nations Centre Against Apartheid. London: 1981.

Williams, Juan. *Eyes on the Prize: America's Civil Rights Years, 1954-1965.* New York: Penguin Books, 1987.

AFTERWORD
How One Life Brushed Against Mine And Why It Still Matters

In the days following the outrage over the U.S. invasion of Cambodia, Allison Beth Krause was a leggy, bright-eyed woman-child stomping at the bit, eager to take in all that life had to offer. She was a college freshman at Kent State University, immersed in everything from African-American history to art and psychology. She loved a boy named Barry and a kitten named Yossarian (named after the anti-hero of *Catch-22*) and a recording artist named Melanie. She was an honor student, a bossy roommate, a naive good-girl photographed offering a flower to a sweet-faced national guardsman. By all accounts Allison was a mess of untamed contradictions with a generous heart and a passionate soul.

Monday, May 4, 1970 was a stunningly beautiful, sunny day in Ohio. That day Allison was distraught about the threatening nature of the national guardsmen on campus. Distraught is perhaps too tame a word. She was enraged. As the guardsmen advanced on the students who were gathering for a noon rally, she was one of the last to move—holding fiercely to her right to dissent, her right to free speech, her right to protest the war policies of her elected government. For a few moments she stood boldly on the commons in her jeans, sneakers, gray "Kennedy" t-shirt, and army-surplus jacket shouting at everyone with perhaps some of the clear-eyed madness of my great Uncle Harry. But she did run. She and her friend Barry ran with the others away from the soldiers. They ran toward the parking lot and hid behind a car. When the national guard knelt and aimed their bayonnetted rifles at the students, she and Barry somehow reasoned that it was all show, a bluff. There had been no warning shot. And anyway, who could imagine the national guard shooting into a rally of unarmed, *white*, middle-class college students? After the shots rang out she whispered to Barry, "I'm hit."

197

No one in the college administration thought to inform her parents of her death until the next afternoon. By then, they had heard about it on the evening television news.

I remember as if in a dream how word of the Kent State killings spread across the little college campus in mid-Pennsylvania where I too was a politically-involved, bright-eyed freshman. In my memory of that soft dusk we all seemed to be running and whispering, whispering, whispering the news. I remember the shock. I remember thinking, "This is real! This is real!... It could have been me. It could have been me."

I do not know what prompted my parents to write to Allison's parents, how they got the address, or why they didn't write to the other parents. But my parents wrote to the Krauses. They wrote that they too had a daughter—Pamela Marie—the same age as Allison, who also participated in campus peace rallies. Allison's parents wrote back to mine with the message that they hoped I would carry on the legacy of the passion for justice, the enthusiasm and the love which had characterized Allison's brief life.

I am glad I lived through those college years.

I am glad I lived and had the opportunity to grow up—to learn from my mistakes and gain new skills. Through the years—the ones taken from Allison—I've been blessed with a widening circle of friends and a range of precious experiences I could never have dreamed of back in college.

I am glad I lived and that I had the opportunity to meet Barbara Deming and learn about feminism and nonviolence. I am grateful that I had the chance to grow to adulthood and follow my passion for chronicling generations of women's resistance and action. I like to think of myself as the witness, the one who remembers, the troubadour who tells the tale as I wander so that our stories will live on. My journey through the wilderness has led me to a river of courage. It is this river that sustains me. I am in awe of it and honor it by remembering, remembering.

Sometimes now, when lists of martyrs are read and each name is affirmed by the crowd with the cry "¡Presènte!", I whisper the woman-child's name in my heart.

"Allison Krause. ¡Presènte!"

CHRONOLOGY OF WOMEN'S NONVIOLENT ACTIONS

The following is a chronology of events mentioned in this book. It is not intended to be a general or comprehensive list of women's nonviolent action, but to summarize only the contents of this book.

1300 B.C.E. Egypt   Hebrew midwives disobey pharoah.

  Egypt   Jewish slave-mother joins Egyptian princess in conspiracy to rescue baby Moses from Pharoah's genocidal policy.

1500 C.E. Nicaragua   "Strike of the Uterus."

1536   **Europe**   Gracia Nasi assists in directing covert operation to rescue Jews trying to escape persecution by the Catholic Church.

1600   **Iroquois Indian Nation**   Women initiate Lysistrata action to protest men's control of wartime decisions.

1622   **France**   Marie de Gournay writes about the equality of men and women.

1730   **India**   Amrita Devi leads 360 villagers in hugging the trees to prevent their felling.

1776   **United States**   Abigail Adams writes to her husband John urging male revolutionaries to "remember the ladies."

1789   **France**   800 women march to Versailles to demand bread.

1791   **France**   Publication of France's first feminist magazine.

  France   Olympe de Gouges writes "Declaration of the Rights of Woman and of the Citizen."

1800s   **India**   Tarigonda Venkamma, a Hindu holy woman, refuses to shave her head, the custom for new widows.

1839   **South Carolina**   Harriet Jacobs seeks sanctuary in African-American population to escape slavery.

1848   **Seneca Falls, NY**   Woman's Rights Convention passes a Declaration of Sentiments calling for an end to the oppression of women.

1849   **United States**   Fanny Kemble wears baggy trousers under a shortened skirt and Lydia Sayer designs a kneelength skirt to be worn over pantaloons and is refused admission to Seward Seminary because of her clothes.

1851 **Seneca Falls, NY** Libby Smith Miller wears her Turkish trousers while visiting Elizabeth Cady Stanton. Amelia Bloomer publisizes the new dress in her newsletter and the outfit becomes known as "bloomers."

Ohio 60 women in Akron and 200 in Cleveland wear "bloomers" to July 4th balls.

Lowell, MA Factory girls organize a Bloomer Institute.

England Association of Bloomers is formed.

1856 **New York State** Lydia Sayer Hasbrouck edits feminist newspaper *Sibyl: A Review of the Tastes, Errors, and Fashions of Society* and promotes dress reform.

1861 **United States** Harriet Jacobs writes her autobiography, *Incidents In the Life of a Slave Girl: Written By Herself.*

Albany, NY Lydia Mott and Susan B. Anthony provide sanctuary for abused woman and child.

1863 **United States** Lydia Sayer Hasbrouck serves as president of the National Dress Reform Association.

1870 **United States** Julia Ward Howe issues "An Appeal to Womanhood Throughout the World" proposing a women's global peace gathering.

1871 **Japan** Women form organization to encourage short hairstyles. A year later, short hair is banned for women.

1873 **Global** Women celebrate the first "Mother's Day" as the peace holiday proposed by Julia Ward Howe.

1876 **Philadelphia** Feminists invade the men's centennial celebration and present a "Women's Declaration of Independence."

1880s **England** Lady Harberton founds the Rational Dress Society.

1892 **China** Unbound Feet Society founded.

1898 **France** Caroline Kauffmann becomes secretary-general of Solidarite des Femmes, a socialist suffrage group.

1900s **France** Arria Ly preaches "virginal feminism."

1900 **Pennsylvania** Mary "Mother" Jones leads women through the mountains to encourage strike by miners.

1904 **France** Women protest 100th anniversary of Napoleon's Civil Code by releasing balloons with words "THE CODE CRUSHES WOMEN."

1905 **England** Annie Kenney and Christabel Pankhurst disrupt public meetings by calling for "votes for women."

Bengal (Bangladesh) Rokeya Sakhawat Hossain writes utopian story, *Sultana's Dream*, describing Ladyland where reverse *purdah* is observed.

Iran Women of the royal harem launch a nationwide boycott of British tobacco to protest foreign economic donimation.

1906 **London** Suffragists pack the "Ladies' Gallery" in Parliament and laugh as they are ousted by police.
Paris Feminists sponsor suffrage rallies.
Paris Madeleine Pelletier and Caroline Kauffmann disrupt legislative proceedings by flinging suffrage leaflets from balcony.
Paris Madeleine Pelletier leads 100 women to disrupt the French legislature in pro-suffrage protest.
Iran Veiled women protest in the streets to demand a written constitution. Later, women surround the Shah's carriage and hand him a petition.

1907 **Philadelphia** Anna Jarvis proposes "Mother's Day."
Paris Madeleine Pelletier leads French women and British suffragettes in march to the parliament.

1908 **London** Suffragettes chain themselves to railing at 10 Downing Street.
London Muriel Matters chains herself to the grille in the gallery at the House of Commons and makes suffrage speech.
New York City Socialist women sponsor mass meeting on women's rights.
Iran Women launch a literacy campaign.

1909 **New York City** Socialists designate the last Sunday in February as "National Woman's Day."
London Muriel Matters sails over the House of Commons in a dirigible balloon painted with the words "VOTES FOR WOMEN."

1910 **Copenhagen** The Conference of Socialist Women proposes International Women's Day.
Iran A secret women's society publishes a weekly newspaper, *Knowledge*.

1911 **Global** Socialists and suffragists celebrate International Women's Day.
China Tang Junying leads suffragists in storming the Assembly.
Calcutta Rokeya Sakhawat Hossain opens the Sakhawat Memorial Girls' School and urges moderate system of *purdah*.
Iran 300 veiled women invade the National Assembly.

1913 **England** Suffrage Pilgrimage.
Germany Rosa Luxemburg proposes a "birth strike."

1915 **Europe** Marion Graig Wentworth writes *War Brides*.
Switzerland Women use International Women's Day for anti-war demonstrations.

1916 **Washington D.C.** Suffragists disrupt address by President Woodrow Wilson in House of Representatives.
Calcutta Rokeya Sakhawat Hossain organizes the Muslim Women's Association which assists widows, battered women and poor, illiterate women.

1917   **Europe**   International Women's Day is a day of protest against war and hunger in hundreds of demonstrations.
Russia   Thousands of women take to the streets to celebrate International Women's Day and demand bread and inspire the last push of the Russian Revolution.
Virginia   Suffragists imprisoned in the Occoquan Workhouse endure the "Night of Terror."

1918   **Austria**   3,000 women demonstrate for peace on International Women's Day despite ban on all protests.

1919   **France**   Nelly Roussel calls for a "strike of the wombs."
Iran   Sediqeh Dovlatabady founds a newspaper, *Women's Voice.*

1920s   **Soviet Union**   Women in the Bryansk province go on a sex strike.
Soviet Central Asia   Women's centers are set up to provide sanctuary to battered women. Also, dress reform is instituted throughout the region.
China   Refuge for battered women is provided by women's unions.
Iran   Women publish magazines with anti-veil editorials and urge women's rights.
China   Women propogandists form unions to reshape ancient traditions such as footbinding.

1920   **United States**   Angelina Weld Grimke writes *Rachel.*

1921   **Global**   Women attending the International Women's Secretariat of the Communist International vote to make March 8th the official date of International Women's Day.

1922   **United States**   Children's Crusade for Amnesty.

1923   **Egypt**   Huda Sharawi throws her veil into the Mediterranean.

1927   **Soviet Central Asia**   Thousands of Islamic women in Bukhara celebrate International Women's Day by removing and destroying their veils.

1936   **Spain**   La Pasionaria (Dolores Ibaurri) leads thousands of women in a demonstration on International Women's Day.

1940s   **China**   Women participate in a Lysistrata action.

1943   **Denmark**   Ellen Nielsen and Elise Petersen join the underground Anti-Nazi resistance efforts.
Poland   Telegraph operator delays sending Nazi call for help after uprising at Sobibor death camp.

1944   **Venezuela**   On International Women's Day a suffrage petition with 11,000 names is presented to congress.

1950s   **Canada**   Mary Two Axe Early protests Section 12(1)b of the Indian Act.
South Africa   Frances Baard endures long periods of imprisonment for her union organizing and anti-apartheid work.

1952   **China**   China's first squadron of women fliers performs for crowds on International Women's Day.

Iran   Women secure 100,000 signatures on a petition demanding equal rights with men.

1953   **France**   Simone de Beauvoir writes *The Second Sex.*

1955   **China**   Women organize a "March 8th Tree-Planting Team."

Indonesia   500,000 women demonstrate for women's rights on International Women's Day.

New York City   Dorothy Day refuses to participate in civil defense drills.

1957   **Little Rock, AR**   15-year-old Elizabeth Eckford attempts to enter a segregated high school.

1958   **Europe-Soviet Union**   Women's Caravan of Peace.

China   Women form the March 8th unit of fishing boats.

New York State   Ruth Best refuses to participate in civil defense drill and actively distributes anti-war leaflets.

1959   **New York State**   Ruth Best and Vera Williams protest the annual civil defense drill.

1960s   **Mississippi**   Civil Rights Activist Fanny Lou Hamer fights for voter registration for African-Americans.

1960   **New York State**   Ruth Best commits civil disobedience and is incarcerated in protest of the annual civil defense drill.

1961   **United States**   Women's Strike for Peace.

New York State   Ruth Best is again incarcerated for her protest of the annual civil defense drill.

1962   **Washington DC**   Women's Strike for Peace disrupts proceedings of the House Un-American Activities Committee.

1963   **Jackson, MS**   Students "sit-in" at segregated lunch counter.

1967   **Washington DC**   2,500 women storm the Pentagon.

1970s   **Iran**   Women return to wearing the veil (*chador*) as a sign of protest against the Shah and Western cultural domination.

El Salvador   Marta Alicia Rivera risks torture and death as member of a teachers union.

1970   **Ireland**   Feminists ride "Pill Train" with smuggled contraceptives.

Copenhagen   Members of "Thilde's Children" block parking lot with baby carriages.

United States   Women's Strike for Equality.

China   Women electricians form a "March 8th team."

1971   **London**   Erin Pizzey organizes the Chiswick Women's Aid for battered women.

1973   **Boston, MA**   Flo Kennedy leads "pee-in" on the Harvard Yard.

1974   **India**   Gaura Devi leads villagers in protecting trees.

St. Paul, MN   Women's Advocates Collective opens a shelter for battered women.

Amsterdam   Women provide sanctuary for battered women in a shelter named "Hands Off My Body."

Sydney, Australia   Feminists open "Elsie," a shelter for battered women.

Glasgow   Feminists open "Interval House" as shelter for women escaping violent homes.

Vancouver   Canadian feminists open "Transition House" for battered women.

1975   **Portland, OR**   Two 65-year-old women "sleep-in" at electric company offices to protest high rates.

Lyon, France   150 prostitutes occupy the Church of St. Nizier to call attention to grievances.

1976   **Canada**   Native American Juanita Perley and her ten children occupy tribal office.

1977   **Canada**   Native American Sandra Lovelace files complaint against Canadian government with the United Nations Human Rights Committee.

Canada   Native American women from the Tobique Reserve petition, lobby, demonstrate, picket and occupy tribal office to protest housing discrimination.

India   Women in Chipko Movement save trees in the Advani Forest.

Italy   Feminists circulate a "Lysistrata Petition."

Crossroads, South Africa   Women defend homes and protest apartheid policies.

1978   **Seattle**   Lesbians protest custody battles on Mother's Day.

Seattle   The Mother's Day Brigade glues shut the doors of a pornographic movie theater.

United States   Audre Lorde, the Mother of Black Feminism, refuses to wear a prosthesis after a mastectomy.

Lima, Peru   300 women factory workers occupy building to claim cooperative ownership.

Crossroads, South Africa   Women obstruct demolition of their homes by sitting in front of bulldozers.

Love Canal, NY   Lois Gibbs initiates the inquiry of the area contaminated by dangerous chemicals.

1979   **Canada**   Native women from the Tobique Reserve participate in 100-mile walk.

Germany   On Mother's Day, over 1,000 women pledge not to bear children in anti-nuclear campaign.

Chile   The Union of Housemaids sponsors a March 8th celebration to which thousands of people come shouting for "Freedom."

Iran   Thousands of women take to the streets in a March 8th demonstration chanting, "In the dawn of freedom, there is no freedom."

Iran   The Conference of the Unity of Women convenes in candlelight.

Copenhagen   Danish feminists claim Danner House as a shelter for battered women.

Peru   Women factory workers begin a two-year occupation for the legal right to assume control of production.

Big Mountain   Katherine Smith, a Navajo elder, leads resistance to U.S. government forced relocation.

1980   **Canada**   Women protest annual Seal Hunt.

Peru   Women protest sexism on Mother's Day.

Nicaragua   Women celebrate the Sandinista victory on International Women's Day.

Big Mountain   Navajo women obstruct relocation efforts.

1981   **Canada**   Breastfeed-in at Toronto mall.

Germany   "Die-in" at a NATO airbase by Women for Peace.

Washington DC   Members of the Congressional Union chain themselves to White House fence to urge passage of the Equal Rights Amendment.

Sicily   Women issue anti-war statement threatening to stop motherhood.

Washington DC   Mother's Day Coalition for Nuclear Disarmament sponsors protest of militarism and economic injustices in front of Reagan White House.

Thailand   Kanitha Wichiencharoen founds a shelter for battered women in her home.

San Francisco   Dorothy Reed, an African-American, refuses to give up her right to wear the cornrow hairstyle.

Virginia   Librarian Kathy Russell defends the First Amendment from would-be censors.

1982   **United States**   Helene Aylon's Earth Ambulance carries injured earth to the United Nations.

London   "Die-in" at stock exchange.

London   Prostitutes occupy Holy Cross Church for 12 days. Women in the U.S. stage solidarity demonstrations, and prostitutes in Italy picket the English Consulate in Venice.

1983   **New York City/ Seneca Women's Peace Encampment**   Women sleep beneath pillowcase art illustrating women's dreams and nightmares in the nuclear age.

Greenham Common   Women dance on top of missile silo at dawn on New Year's Day.

Seneca, NY   Barbara Deming participates in the Women's Peace Walk, NYC to Seneca Army Depot.

Seneca, NY   Civil disobedience at the army base involves a range of women, including some with disabilities.

Honduras   150 North American religious women make peace pilgrimage to Honduras.

Ireland   Women from England join Irish women to picket outside the Armagh women's jail on International Women's Day.

Sicily   Women from around the world celebrate International Women's Day with protests against deployment of Cruise missiles.

Angola   A peace march on International Women's Day steps off at the Square of the Heroines.

1984   **Burkina Faso**   "Market Day for Men"

Peru   Women of Telitha Cumi publish "Reflections on Mother's Day."

California   150 women gather on March 8th to picket, protest and commit civil disobedience at an army base.

1985   **Iceland**   "Day Off for Women."

India   College women break off relations with male students to protest sexual harassment.

Germany   Serife Sahin, a Turkish woman, refuses to give up her right to wear the veil.

United States   Four Navajo grandmothers tour the West Coast to educate people about the struggle at Big Mountain.

1986   **South Africa**   The Port Alfred Women's Organization initiates women's "stayaway strike" to protest rape and racial violence.

Finland   4,000 women sign Lysistrata petition protesting pro-nuclear policies.

India   Women deface pornographic posters and petition for land in March 8th demonstrations.

New York City   Conference: The Politics of Child Custody.

Phoenix, AZ   Sister Darlene Nicgorski, active in the Sanctuary Movement, is found guilty of transporting, aiding and abetting the harboring of illegal aliens from Central America.

1987   **South Africa**   Women initiate "sleep-in" action at barracks of coal mining husbands.

United States   Clergy and Laity Concerned calls for Mother's Day protest of U.S. aggression against Nicaragua.

Nevada   3,000 people gather on Mother's Day at Nevada Test Site to protest preparations for nuclear war.

Mauritius   International Women's Day is used to present women's list of demands for workers' rights.

Toronto   Homeless woman occupies a doll house in a city square to protest lack of housing.

Toronto   Amber Cooke pitches a tent in front of City Hall to publicize her hardships as a homeless mother.

New York City   Marie Bloom refuses to type the script for a television ad for war toys at a Madison Avenue advertising firm.

1989   **Canada**   International Women's Day is celebrated with a variety of actions in cities across the country including Vancouver, Montreal,

Prince Albert, Edmonton and Halifax. Toronto's March 8th theme is "Women Against Poverty." "Broads of Bay Street" members are arrested for disrupting traffic in the business district.

Israel   Tandi (the Movement of Democratic Women) organizes a Peace Tent in Tel Aviv on March 8th. Israeli and Palestinian women meet.

Harare, Zimbabwe   Women open a counseling service for survivors of rape and battery.

WOMEN AND WOMEN'S ORGANIZATIONS FOR PEACE AND JUSTICE

The following is a list of the women and women's organizations for peace and justice whose actions are described in this book. It is not intended to be a comprehensive list of individuals or groups, but a listing pertaining only to this book.

Abigail Adams
writes to her husband John urging male revolutionaries to "remember the ladies," 1776

Susan B. Anthony
provides sanctuary for an abused woman and child, 1861. Distributes "Women's Declaration of Rights" at centennial celebration, 1876

Louise Armstrong
addresses conference on The Politics of Child Custody, NYC, 1986

Association of Bloomers
organizes in Britain to promote dress reform, 1851

Helene Aylon
promotes Earth Ambulance and pillowcase art, 1982

Frances Baard
South African anti-apartheid activist endures long periods of imprisonment for her union organizing

Mira Behn
Gandhian disciple moves to Himalayan region and writes about deforestation there, 1940s

Ruth Best (Ruth Dreamdigger)
refuses to participate in annual civil defense drills of the cold war era, 1958-61

Lille Blake	distributes "Women's Declaration of Rights" at centennial celebration, 1876
Marie Bloom	refuses to type script for war toy ad at Madison Avenue advertising firm, 1987
Amelia Bloomer	advocates trousers for women, 1850's
Bloomer Institute	dress reform group organized by "factory girls" at Lowell, Mass., 1851
Gillian Booth	lesbian mother participates in "die-in" at London Stock Exchange, 1982
E.M. Broner	addresses conference on The Politics of Child Custody, NYC, 1986
Charlotte Bunch	reads aloud the National Plan for Women's Equality, Union and Justice at White House protest, 1981
Bee Burgess	dances with 43 other feminist peace activists on top of missile silo at Greenham Commons, dawn, Jan. 1, 1983
Lucy Burns	U.S. suffrage activist is imprisoned during the "Night of Terror," 1917
Helen Caldicott	tells people to "use where you are in your life to stop the Arms Race" and inspires artist Helen Aylon, 1980
Gloria Carrion	General Secretary of the Association of Nicaraguan Women speaks about women's new role at celebration of International Women's Day, 1980
Lydia Maria Child	edits work by escaped slave Harriet Jacobs, 1861
Chinese Suffragette Society	founded by Tang Junying, 1911
Congressional Union	U.S. suffrage direct action organization, members disrupt speech by President Wilson by hanging suffrage banner from balcony, 1916. Members chain themselves to the White House railing, 1981
Susan Constantine	organizes Mother's Day protest at Nevada Test Site, 1987

Amber Cooke	pitches a tent in front of City Hall, Toronto, to publicize her homelessness, 1987
Selina Cooper	working class suffrage activist participates in nationwide "Suffrage Pilgrimage," 1913
Alice Cosu	U.S. suffrage activist is imprisoned during the "Night of Terror," 1917
Phoebe Couzins	distributes "Women's Declaration of Rights" at centennial celebration, 1876
Crossroads Women's Committee	organizes defense of homes and protests apartheid in South Africa
Dorothy Day	is imprisoned during the "Night of Terror," 1917. Refuses to participate in annual civil defense drill in New York City in the late 1950s
Simone de Beauvoir	writes *The Second Sex* (1953). Supports action by prostitutes, 1975
Olympe de Gouges	writes "Declaration of the Rights of Woman and of the Citizen," France, 1791
Marie de Gournay	French feminist writes about equality of men and women, 1622
Barbara Deming	Lesbian feminist pacifist writer witnesses women's courage at Seneca Women's Peace Encampment, 1983
Amrita Devi	leads villages in hugging the trees to prevent their felling, India, 1730
Gaura Devi	leads others in protecting trees, 1974
Sediqeh Dovlatabady	founds newspaper, *Women's Voice*, Iran, 1919
Flora Drummond	arrested at 10 Downing Street for suffrage action, 1908
Mary Two Axe Early	protests Canada's Indian Act in the 1950s
Elizabeth Eckford	at 15 years of age attempts to enter a segregated high school in Little Rock, Arkansas, 1957

Julia Emory	suffrage activist imprisoned during "Night of Terror," 1917
English Collective of Prostitutes	occupies London's Holy Cross church for 12 days to air grievances, 1982
Caroline Ennis	participates in Native women's 100-mile walk to Ottawa, 1979
Mathilde Fibiger	19th-century pioneer of the Danish feminist movement
Vigdis Finnbogadottir	Iceland's president, supports "Day Off for Women" strike action, 1985
Elizabeth Gurley Flynn	U.S. labor organizer supports women's amnesty action, 1922
Bertha Fraser	gives anti-war speech at NYC's celebration of International Women's Day, 1911
Iris Freed	testifies before House Un-American Activities Committee, 1962
Betty Friedan	author of *The Feminine Mystique* (1963) calls for "Women's Strike for Equality," 1970
Matilda Joslyn Gage	writes and distributes "Women's Declaration of Independence" at centennial celebration, 1876
Lois Gibbs	initiates inquiry into chemical contamination in Love Canal, NY, 1978
Charlotte Perkins Gilman	feminist economist, author of *Herland*, participates in early celebrations of International Women's Day, 1909, 1910
Mavis Goeres	protests lack of Indian status and housing for women in Tobique reserve, 1970s
Greenham Common Women's Peace Camp	women dance on missile silo at dawn, January 1, 1983
Angelina Weld Grimke	African-American playwright authors *Rachel*, 1920

Sarah Grimke	writes letter to her sister Angelina articulating political significance of women's fashion, 1838
Fanny Lou Hamer	African-American civil rights activist fights for voter registration, 1960s
Lorraine Hansberry	author of *Raisin in the Sun* supports Women's Strike for Peace, 1962
Lady Harberton	founds the Rational Dress Society in England in the 1880s
Lilly Harris	participates in Native women's 100 mile walk to Ottawa, 1979
Lydia Sayer Hasbrouck	edits feminist dress reform newspaper *Sibyl: A Review of the Tastes, Errors, and Fashions of Society*, 1856
Rokeya Sakhawat Hossain	Bengali author of *Sultana's Dream* (1905) organizes the Muslim Women's Association to assist Calcutta's battered women, poor and widows, 1916
Julia Ward Howe	issues "An Appeal to Womanhood Throughout the World" (1870) and promotes Mother's Day as peace holiday (1873)
Dolores Ibaurri	"La Pasionara," leader of the Spanish Communist Party, leads demonstration of women opposed to fascist threat on International Women's Day, 1936
Harriet Jacobs	after hiding for 7 years, writes her autobiography, *Incidents in the Life of a Slave Girl*, 1861
Sonya Johnson	commits civil disobedience for the Equal Rights Amendment at White House protest, 1981
Mary "Mother" Jones	leads women through Pennsylvania mountains to encourage strike by miners, 1900
Tang Junying	founds Chinese Suffragette Society and leads activists in storming the Chinese Assembly, 1911

Caroline Kauffmann	Secretary-General of socialist/suffrage Solidarité des Femmes, 1898. Disrupts French legislature in suffrage protest, 1906
Fanny Kemble	wears trousers to climb mountains, 1849
Florynce Kennedy	African-American lawyer leads women's protest "pee-in" on Harvard Yard, 1973
Annie Kenney	disrupts public meetings by calling for "votes for women," 1905
Alexandra Kollontai	Russian delegate to International Socialist Congress where International Women's Day was born, 1910
Lisa Larges	challenges assumptions and privileges of sighted people
Audre Lorde	refuses to wear a prosthesis after a mastectomy, 1978
Sandra Lovelace	files complaint as Native American against Canadian government with the United Nations, 1977
Alexandre Luke	member of the Crossroads Women's Committee helps blockade demolition of homes in resistance to apartheid policies, 1977/78
Barbara Lupo	Coordinator of Clergy and Laity Concerned issues statement for Mother's Day protest, 1987
Rosa Luxemburg	proposes a "birth strike" in Germany, 1913
Arria Ly	preaches "virginal feminism" in France, 1900s
Muriel Matters	chains herself to the grille in the gallery at the House of Commons to make a suffrage speech (1908) and sails over London in a dirigible balloon painted with the words "VOTES FOR WOMEN" (1909)
Nell McCafferty	rides "Pill Train" in action for reproductive rights, Ireland, 1970

Libby Smith Miller	wears her Turkish trousers while visiting in Seneca Falls, NY and inspires "Bloomer" dress reform, 1851
Kate Millett	author of *Sexual Politics* visits Iran, 1979
Elizabeth Morgan	chooses to be incarcerated rather than disclose location of her abused child and risk loss of custody to accused abuser
Moses' mother	conspires with Pharoah's daughter to rescue baby Moses (1300 BC)
Mother's Day Brigade	glues shut the doors of a pornographic movie theater, Seattle, 1978
Mother's Day Coalition for Nuclear Disarmament	sponsors Washington DC march/protest, 1981
Mothers of the Plaza (Madres de la Plaza de Mayo)	keep vigil for the "disappeared in Argentina"
Lucretia Mott	provides leadership at Women's Rights Convention, 1848. Wears Bloomer outfit, 1850s. Attends "World Congress of Women in Behalf of International Peace, 1870. Supports women's "centennial" action, 1876
Lydia Mott	provides sanctuary for an abused woman and child, 1861
Muslim Women's Association	founded to provide assistance to Calcutta's widows, battered and illiterate women, 1916
Diane Nash	participates in civil rights sit-ins of the 1960s
Gracia Nasi	directs covert rescue of other Jews trying to escape the Inquisition, 1536
National Association of Action for the Defense of Prostitute Women	publishes newspaper, "Echo from the Pavement," France, 1970s
National Dress Reform Association (U.S.)	under leadership of Lydia Sayer Hasbrouck, 1863
National Organization for Women (NOW)	chapters throughout U.S. celebrate Women's Strike for Equality, 1970

National Woman Suffrage Association	sponsors Women's Declaration at centennial protest, Philadelphia, 1876
Native Women's Association of Canada	received increased funding after 100-mile walk of Tobique women to Ottawa
Matilda Neruda	addresses March 8th celebration in face of political repression in Chile, 1979
Edith New	chains herself to the railing at 10 Downing Street, 1908
Karen Newsom	chooses to be incarcerated rather than disclose location of her abused child and risk loss of custody to accused abuser
Darlene Nicgorski	Sanctuary Movement activist is found guilty of transporting, aiding and abetting the harboring of illegal aliens from Central America, 1986
Ellen Nielsen	joins underground anti-Nazi resistance efforts in Denmark, 1943
Koleka Nkwinti	leader in Port Alfred Women's Organization is imprisoned after anti-rape, anti-racism women's strike, South Africa, 1986
Mary Nolan	arrested during "Night of Terror," 1917
Regina Ntongana	member of the Crossroads Women's Committee helps blockade demolition of homes in resistance to apartheid, 1977/78
Kate Richards O'Hare	arrested for giving anti-war speech in North Dakota, 1917. Agitates for amnesty for political prisoners, 1922
Leonora O'Reilly	speaks at socialist/suffragist celebration of National Women's Day, NYC, 1909
Organization of Angolan Women (OMA)	concludes its first congress with peace march on International Women's Day, 1983
Josephine Ouedaogo	organizes "Market Day for Men," Burkina Faso, 1984
Christabel Pankhurst	disrupts London political meetings by calling for votes for women, 1905

Emmeline Pankhurst	defends the heckling of British legislators, 1905
Sylvia Pankhurst	pacifist, socialist daughter of Emmeline Pankhurst laughs at police, 1906
Farrokhrou Parsa	is charged with "warring against God" by Iran's Islamic fundamentalist government and is executed, 1979
Alice Paul	is incarcerated for picketing the White House in suffrage protests, 1917
Bet-te Paul	participates in Native women's 100-mile walk to Ottawa, 1979
Peace Pilgrim	walks bearing messages of change and hope
Madeleine Pelletier	leads French women and British suffragettes in march to French parliament, 1907
Glenna Perley	participates in Native women's 100-mile walk to Ottawa, 1979
Juanita Perley	Native American mother occupies tribal office with her ten children, 1976
Karen Perley	participates in Native women's 100-mile walk to Ottawa, 1979
Elise Petersen	joins underground anti-Nazi resistance efforts in Denmark, 1943
Pharoah's daughter	assists a Jewish slave in rescuing her baby (Moses), 1300 B.C.
Marge Piercy	writes poem "The Pay Toilet" for Harvard Yard "pee-in" protest, 1973
Erin Pizzey	organizes the Chiswick Women's Aid for battered women in London, 1971
Port Alfred Women's Organization	initiates women's "stayaway" strike to protest rape and racial violence, South Africa, 1986
Margaret Randall	commends Cuba's Family Code made official on International Women's Day, 1975

Louise Rasmussen	builds palace in Copenhagen for homeless and poor women, 1800s
Rational Dress Society (England)	founded by Lady Harberton, 1880s
Dorothy Reed	African-American TV news reporter refuses to give up her right to wear the cornrow hairstyle, California, 1981
Marta Alicia Rivera	teacher risks torture and death in El Salvador to join union, 1970s
Nelly Roussel	French feminist calls for "a strike of the wombs," 1919
Dora Russell	inspires and leads Women's Caravan of Peace from Great Britain to Soviet Union, 1958
Kathy Russell	librarian defends the First Amendment from enemies of free speech in Virginia, 1981
Julia Ruutila	attempts a "sleep-in" to protest electric company rate hike, 1975
Serife Sahin	as a Turkish immigrant to West Germany, refuses to give up her right to wear the veil, 1985
Beulah Sanders	speaks to Mother's Day protest at White House, 1981
Margaret Sanger	advocates birth control for working class as a tactic to pressure capitalist class, 1913
Eva "Gookum" Saulis	protests lack of Indian status and housing for women in Tobique reserve, 1970s
Harriet Schleifer	chains herself to furniture in Toronto's Department of Fisheries office to protest annual seal hunt, 1980
Marj Schneider	edits Womyn's Braille Press newsletter
Fay Sellin	assists Helen Aylon in planning route for Earth Ambulance, 1982

Seneca Women's Encampment for a Future of Peace with Justice	women protest at army depot, 1983
Shani (Israeli Women's Alliance to End the Occupation)	participates in Peace Tent action on March 8, 1989, bringing together Israeli and Palistinian women
Huda Sharawi	Egyptian feminist activist throws her veil in the Mediterranean, 1923
Katherine Smith	Navajo elder leads resistance to U.S. government forced relocation from Big Mountain, 1979
Olivia Smith	chains herself to railing of 10 Downing Street, London, 1908
Solidarite des Femmes	socialist/ suffrage organization under leadership of Caroline Kauffmann, 1898
Sara Andrews Spencer	distributes "Women's Declaration of Rights" at centennial celebration, 1876
Elizabeth Cady Stanton	provides leadership at Women's Rights Convention, 1848. Wears Bloomer outfit, 1850s. Supports women's "centennial" action, 1876
Metta Stern	calls for women's rights at socialist celebration of National Woman's Day, 1909
Lucy Stone	wears Bloomer outfit, 1850s
Harriet Beecher Stowe	attends World Congress of Women in behalf of International Peace, 1870
Anna Louise Strong	as journalist, solicits stories from women struggling for justice in China, 1927
Amy Swerdlow	founder of New York Women's Strike for Peace
Tandi (The Movement of Democratic Women)	organizes Peace Tent action on March 8, 1989 bringing together Israeli and Palestinian women
Telitha Cumi (Woman, Arise!)	Peruvian feminist study group to address issues of faith and feminism, 1980s

Thilde's Children	Danish feminist group barricades entrace of parking lot with baby carriages, 1970
Sojourner Truth	19th century ex-slave travels country to address issues of justice, racism, and sexism
Harriet Tubman	escaped slave, conductor of underground railroad, leads many to freedom
Unbound Feet Society	founded in China, 1892
Union of Housemaids (Chile)	sponsors March 8th celebration despite political repression in Chile, 1979
Tarigonda Venkamma	Hindu holy woman refuses to shave her head in the tradition of new widows, 1800s
Mabel Vernon	as member of the Congressional Union, helps disrupt annual address by President Wilson by hanging suffrage banner from balcony, 1916
Mary Heaton Vorse	labor journalist/feminist writes about women's amnesty action, 1922
Ilona Wagner	participates in West Germany Mother's Day anti-nuclear "Lysistrata" action, 1979
Wang Suzhen	becomes president of local women's union and expands its membership to the hundreds promoting women's rights, short hair, and unbound feet, 1920s. Tortured and killed by Chiang Kai Shek's soldiers, 1927
Wei Yu-hsiu	born 1886, later writes autobiography, *My Revolutionary Years*
Angelina Grimke Weld	white feminist abolitionist orator, 1800s
Marion Graig Wentworth	writes *War Brides*, 1915
Yu Whei	as 10-year-old, escapes slavery and finds refuge in women's shelter in Hupeh province, 1920s
Kanitha Wichiencharoen	lawyer founds shelter for battered women in her home in Thailand, 1981

Vera Williams	joins with Ruth Best to resist annual civil defense drill in upstate New York, 1950s
Dagmar Wilson	inspires Women's Strike for Peace, 1961
Woman's International Peace Association	Julia Ward Howe becomes first president of the American branch, 1871
Women For Peace	participate in "die-in" at NATO airbase in West Germany and release balloons carrying anti-nuclear message, March 8, 1981
Women In Black (Israel)	holds weekly peace vigils throughout Israel, 1980s. Participates in Peace Tent action on March 8, 1989 bringing together Israeli and Palestinian women
Women's National Salvation Association of the Chinese Red Army	members bang on pots and pans to celebrate March 8th despite Japanese occupation of China, 1938
Women's Strike for Peace	initiated by Dagmar Wilson as a one-day strike by women protesting war preparedness, 1961. Participants called to testify before House Un-American Activiites Committee, 1962
Faye Yager	establishes Atlanta-based underground railroad to provide sanctuary for women and children running from custody-seeking abusive fathers, 1987
Clara Zetkin	German socialist feminist seconds motion to initiate International Women's Day at Conference of Socialist Women in Copenhagen, 1910
Karen Ziegler	lesbian/feminist pastor of Metropolitan Community Church of NYC participates in peace pilgrimage to Central America with 150 other North American religious women, 1983
Luise Zietz	makes motion to initiate International Women's Day at Conference of Socialist Women in Copenhagen, 1910

PLACES WHERE WOMEN HAVE ACTED NONVIOLENTLY

The following is a listing of the places where women have acted nonviolently that are mentioned in this book. (It is not intended to be a general or comprehensive list, but to summarize only the contents of this book.)

AFRICA:

Angola
1983, A peace march on International Women's Day steps off at the Square of the Heroines.

Burkina Faso
1984, "Market Day for Men"

Mauritius
1987, International Women's Day is used to present women's list of demands for workers' rights.

South Africa
1950s, Frances Baard endures long periods of imprisonment for her union organizing and anti-apartheid work.

1977, Crossroads: Women defend homes and protest apartheid policies.

1978, Crossroads: Women obstruct demolition of their homes by sitting in front of bulldozers.

1986, The Port Alfred Women's Organization initiates women's "stayaway strike" to protest rape and racial violence.

1987, Women initiate "sleep-in" action at barracks of coal-mining husbands.

Zimbabwe
1989, Women in Harare open a counseling service for survivors of rape and battery.

ASIA:

Bengal (Bangladesh)

1905, Rokeya Sakhawat Hossain writes utopian story, *Sultana's Dream,* describing Ladyland where reverse *purdah* is observed.

China

1892, Unbound Feet Society founded.

1911, Tang Junying leads suffragists in storming the Assembly.

1920s:
— Refuge for battered women is provided by women's unions.
— Women propagandists form unions to reshape ancient traditions such as footbinding.

1940s, Women participate in a Lysistrata action.

1952, China's first squadron of women fliers performs for crowds on International Women's Day.

1955, Women organize a "March 8th Tree-Planting Team."

1958, Women form the March 8th unit of fishing boats.

1970, Women electricians form a "March 8th team."

India

1730, Amrita Devi leads 360 villagers in hugging the trees to prevent their felling.

1800s, Tarigonda Venkamma, a Hindu holy woman, refuses to shave her head, the custom for new widows.

1911:
— Rokeya Sakhawat Hossain opens the Sakhawat Memorial Girls' School and urges moderate system of *purdah.*
— Rokeya Sakhawat Hossain organizes the Muslim Women's Association which assists widows, battered women and poor, illiterate women.

1974, Gaura Devi leads villagers in protecting trees.

1977, Women in Chipko Movement save trees in the Advani Forest.

1985, College women break off relations with male students to protest sexual harassment.

1986, Women deface pornographic posters and petition for land in March 8th demonstrations.

Indonesia

1955, 500,000 women demonstrate for women's rights on International Women's Day.

Japan

1871, Women form organization to encourage short hairstyles. A year later, short hair is banned for women.

Soviet Central Asia

1920s, Women's centers are set up to provide sanctuary to battered women. Also, dress reform is instituted throughout the region.

1927, Thousands of Islamic women in Bukhara celebrate International Women's Day by removing and destroying their veils.

Thailand

1981, Kanitha Wichiencharoen founds a shelter for battered women in her home.

CENTRAL AND SOUTH AMERICA:

Chile

1979, The Union of Housemaids sponsors a March 8th celebration to which thousands of people come shouting for "Freedom."

El Salvador

1970s, Marta Alicia Rivera risks torture and death as member of a teachers union.

Honduras

1983, 150 North American religious women make peace pilgrimage to Honduras.

Nicaragua

1500, "Strike of the Uterus."

1800, Women celebrate the Sandinista victory on International Women's Day.

Peru

1978, 300 women factory workers occupy building to claim cooperative ownership.

1979, Women factory workers begin a two-year occupation for the legal right to assume control of production.

1980, Women protest sexism on Mother's Day.

1984, Women of Telitha Cumi publish "Reflections on Mother's Day."

Venezuela

1944, On International Women's Day a suffrage petition with 11,000 names is presented to congress.

EUROPE:

Europe

1536, Gracia Nasi assists in directing covert operation to rescue Jews trying to escape persecution by the Catholic Church.

1915, Marion Graig Wentworth writes *War Brides*.

1917, International Women's Day is a day of protest against war and hunger in hundreds of demonstrations.

1958, Women's Caravan of Peace.

Austria

1918, 3,000 women demonstrate for peace on International Women's Day despite ban on all protests.

Denmark

1910, In Copenhagen the Conference of Socialist Women proposes International Women's Day.

1943, Ellen Nielsen and Elise Petersen join the underground Anti-Nazi resistance efforts.

1970, In Copenhagen, members of "Thilde's Children" block a parking lot with baby carriages.

1979, Danish feminists in Copenhagen claim Danner House as a shelter for battered women.

England

1851, Association of Bloomers is formed.

1880s, Lady Harberton founds the Rational Dress Society.

1905, Annie Kenney and Christabel Pankhurst disrupt public meetings by calling for "votes for women."

1906, London suffragettes pack the "Ladies' Gallery" in Parliament and laugh as they are ousted by police.

1908:
— Suffragettes chain themselves to railing at 10 Downing Street.
— Muriel Matters chains herself to the grille in the gallery at the House of Commons and makes suffrage speech.

1909, Muriel Matters sails over the House of Commons in a dirigible balloon painted with the words "VOTES FOR WOMEN."

1913, Nationwide Suffrage Pilgrimage.

1971, London's Erin Pizzey organizes the Chiswick Women's Aid for battered women.

1982:
— Women stage "die-in" at London stock exchange.
— Prostitutes occupy Holy Cross Church for 12 days. Women in the U.S. stage solidarity demonstrations and prostitutes in Italy picket the English Consulate in Venice.

1983, Women at the Greenham Common Peace Camp dance on top of missile silo at dawn on New Year's Day.

Finland

1986, 4,000 women sign Lysistrata petition protesting pro-nuclear policies.

France

1622, Marie de Gournay writes about the equality of men and women.

1789, 800 women march to Versailles to demand bread.

1791:

— Publication of France's first feminist magazine.

— Olympe de Gouges writes "Declaration of the Rights of Woman and of the Citizen."

1898, Caroline Kauffmann becomes secretary-general of Solidarite des Femmes, a socialist suffrage group.

1900s, Arria Ly preaches "virginal feminism."

1904, Women protest 100th anniversary of Napoleon's Civil Code by releasing balloons with words "THE CODE CRUSHES WOMEN."

1906:

— Paris: Feminists sponsor suffrage rallies.

— Paris: Madeleine Pelletier and Caroline Kauffmann disrupt legislative proceedings by flinging suffrage leaflets from balcony.

— Paris: Madeleine Pelletier leads 100 women to disrupt the French legislature in pro-suffrage protest.

1907, In Paris, Madeleine Pelletier leads French women and British suffragettes in march to the parliament.

1919, Nelly Roussel calls for a "strike of the wombs."

1953, Simone de Beauvoir writes *The Second Sex.*

1975, Lyon: 150 prostitutes occupy the Church of St. Nizier to call attention to grievances.

Germany

1913, Rosa Luxemburg proposes a "birth strike."

1979, On Mother's Day, over 1,000 women pledge not to bear children in antinuclear campaign.

1981, "Die-in" at a NATO airbase by Women for Peace.

1985, Serife Sahin, a Turkish woman, refuses to give up her right to wear the veil.

Iceland

1985, "Day Off for Women."

Ireland

1970, Feminists ride "Pill Train" with smuggled contraceptives.

1983, Women from England join Irish women to picket outside the Armagh women's jail on International Women's Day.

Italy

1977, Feminists circulate a "Lysistrata Petition."

Netherlands

1974, Amsterdam: Women provide sanctuary for battered women in a shelter named "Hands Off My Body."

Poland

1943, Telegraph operator delays sending Nazi call for help after uprising at Sobibor death camp.

Scotland

1974, Glasgow feminists open "Interval House" as shelter for women escaping violent homes.

Sicily

1981, Women issue antiwar statement threatening to stop motherhood.

1983, Women from around the world celebrate International Women's Day with protests against deployment of Cruise missiles.

Spain

1936, La Pasionaria (Dolores Ibaurri) leads thousands of women in a demonstration on International Women's Day.

Switzerland

1915, Women use International Women's Day for antiwar demonstrations.

Union of Soviet Socialist Republics

1917, Petrograd (St. Petersburg): Thousands of women take to the streets to celebrate International Women's Day and demand bread and inspire the last push of the Russian Revolution.

1920s, Women in the Bryansk province go on a sex strike.

MIDDLE EAST:

Egypt

1300 B.C.E.:

— Hebrew midwives disobey pharoah.

— Jewish slave-mother joins Egyptian princess in conspiracy to rescue baby Moses from Pharoah's genocidal policy.

1923, Huda Sharawi throws her veil into the Mediterranean.

Iran

1905, Women of the royal harem launch a nationwide boycott of British tobacco to protest foreign economic domination.

1906, Veiled women protest in the streets to demand a written constitution. Later, women surround the Shah's carriage and hand him a petition.

1908, Women launch a literacy campaign.

1910, A secret women's society publishes a weekly newspaper, *Knowledge*.

1911, 300 veiled women invade the National Assembly.

1919, Sediqeh Dovlatabady founds a newspaper, *Women's Voice*.

1920s, Women publish magazines with anti-veil editorials and urge women's rights.

1952, Women secure 100,000 signatures on a petition demanding equal rights with men.

1970s, Women return to wearing the veil (*chador*) as a sign of protest against the Shah and Western cultural domination.

1979:

— Thousands of women take to the streets in a March 8th demonstration chanting, "In the dawn of freedom, there is no freedom."

— The Conference of the Unity of Women convenes in candlelight.

Israel

1989, Tandi (the Movement of Democratic Women) organizes a Peace Tent in Tel Aviv on March 8th. Israeli and Palestinian women meet.

NORTH AMERICA:

Native Peoples of the Americas

1600, Iroquois Indian Nation: Women initiate Lysistrata action to protest men's control of wartime decisions.

1950s, Mary Two Axe Early protests Canada's Section 12(1)b of the Indian Act.

1976, Juanita Perley and her ten children occupy tribal office on the Tobique Reserve in Canada.

1977:

— Sandra Lovelace files complaint against Canadian government with the United Nations Human Rights Committee.

— Women from the Tobique Reserve petition, lobby, demonstrate, picket and occupy tribal office to protest housing discrimination.

1979:

— Native women from the Tobique Reserve participate in 100-mile walk to Ottawa.

— Big Mountain: Katherine Smith, a Navajo elder, leads resistance to U.S. government forced relocation.

1980, Big Mountain: Navajo women obstruct relocation efforts.

1985, Four Navajo grandmothers tour the West Coast of the U.S. to educate people about the struggle at Big Mountain.

Canada (see also Native Peoples of the Americas)

1974, Vancouver feminists open "Transition House" for battered women.

1980, Women protest annual Seal Hunt.

1981, Nursing mothers stage breastfeed-in at Toronto mall.

1987:

— Homeless woman occupies a doll house in a Toronto city square to protest lack of housing.

— Amber Cooke pitches a tent in front of Toronto's City Hall to publicize her hardships as a homeless mother.

1989, International Women's Day is celebrated with a variety of actions in cities across the country including Vancouver, Montreal, Prince Albert, Edmonton and Halifax. Toronto's March 8th theme is "Women Against Poverty." "Broads of Bay Street" members are arrested for disrupting traffic in the business district.

United States (see also Native Peoples of the Americas)

Arkansas

1957, Little Rock: 15-year-old Elizabeth Eckford attempts to enter a segregated high school.

Arizona

1986, Phoenix: Sister Darlene Nicgorski, active in the Sanctuary Movement, is found guilty of transporting, aiding and abetting the harboring of illegal aliens from Central America.

California

1981, San Francisco: Dorothy Reed, an African-American, refuses to give up her right to wear the cornrow hairstyle.

1984, 150 women gather on March 8th to picket, protest and commit civil disobedience at an army base.

District of Columbia

1916, Suffragists disrupt address by President Woodrow Wilson in House of Representatives.

1962, Women's Strike for Peace disrupts proceedings of the House Un-American Activities Committee.

1967, 2,500 women storm the Pentagon.

1981:

— Members of the Congressional Union chain themselves to White House fence to urge passage of the Equal Rights Amendment.

— Mother's Day Coalition for Nuclear Disarmament sponsors protest of militarism and economic injustices in front of Reagan White House.

Massachusetts

1851, Lowell: Factory girls organize a Bloomer Institute.

1973, Boston: Flo Kennedy leads "pee-in" on the Harvard Yard.

Minnesota

1974, St. Paul: Women's Advocates Collective opens a shelter for battered women.

Mississippi

1960s, Civil Rights Activist Fanny Lou Hamer fights for voter registration for African-Americans.

1963, Jackson: Students "sit-in" at segregated lunch counter.

Nevada

1987, 3,000 people gather on Mother's Day at Nevada Test Site to protest preparations for nuclear war.

New York

1848, Seneca Falls: Woman's Rights Convention passes a Declaration of Sentiments calling for an end to the oppression of women.

1851, Seneca Falls: Libby Smith Miller wears her Turkish trousers while visiting Elizabeth Cady Stanton. Amelia Bloomer publicizes the new dress in her newsletter and the outfit becomes known as "bloomers."

1856, Lydia Sayer Hasbrouck edits feminist newspaper, *Sibyl: A Review of the Tastes, Errors, and Fashions of Society,* and promotes dress reform.

1861, Albany: Lydia Mott and Susan B. Anthony provide sanctuary for abused woman and child.

1908, New York City: Socialist women sponsor mass meeting on women's rights.

1909, New York City: Socialists designate the last Sunday in February as "National Woman's Day."

1955, New York City: Dorothy Day refuses to participate in civil defense drills.

1958, Rockland County: Ruth Best refuses to participate in civil defense drill and actively distributes antiwar leaflets.

1959, Ruth Best and Vera Williams protest the annual civil defense drill.

1960, Ruth Best commits civil disobedience and is incarcerated in protest of the annual civil defense drill.

1961, Ruth Best is again incarcerated for her protest of the annual civil defense drill.

1978, Love Canal, NY: Lois Gibbs initiates the inquiry of the area contaminated by dangerous chemicals.

1983:

— New York City/ Seneca Women's Peace Encampment: Women sleep beneath pillowcase art illustrating women's dreams and nightmares in the nuclear age.

— Seneca: Barbara Deming participates in the Women's Peace Walk, NYC to Seneca Army Depot.

— Seneca: Civil disobedience at the army base involves a range of women, including some with disabilities.

1986, New York City Conference: The Politics of Child Custody.

1987, New York City: Marie Bloom refuses to type the script for a television ad for war toys at a Madison Avenue advertising firm.

Ohio

1851, 60 women in Akron and 200 in Cleveland wear "bloomers" to July 4th balls.

Oregon

1975, Portland: Two 65-year-old women "sleep-in" at electric company offices to protest high rates.

Pennsylvania

1876, Philadelphia: Feminists invade the men's centennial celebration and present a "Women's Declaration of Independence."

1900, Mary "Mother" Jones leads women through the mountains to encourage strike by miners.

1907, Philadelphia: Anna Jarvis proposes "Mother's Day."

South Carolina

1839, Harriet Jacobs seeks sanctuary in African-American population to escape slavery.

Virginia

1917, Suffragists imprisoned in the Occoquan Workhouse endure the "Night of Terror."

1981, Librarian Kathy Russell defends the First Amendment from would-be censors.

Washington

1978:

— Seattle: Lesbians protest custody battles on Mother's Day.

— Seattle: The Mother's Day Brigade glues shut the doors of a pornographic movie theater.

Other (United States: nationwide or unspecified location.)

1776, Abigail Adams writes to her husband John urging male revolutionaries to "remember the ladies."

1849, Fanny Kemble wears baggy trousers under a shortened skirt and Lydia Sayer designs a kneelength skirt to be worn over pantaloons and is refused admission to Seward Seminary because of her clothes.

1861, Harriet Jacobs writes her autobiography, *Incidents In the Life of a Slave Girl: Written By Herself.*

1863, Lydia Sayer Hasbrouck serves as president of the National Dress Reform Association.

1870, Julia Ward Howe issues "An Appeal to Womanhood Throughout the World," proposing a women's global peace gathering.

1920, Angelina Weld Grimke writes *Rachel.*

1922, Children's Crusade for Amnesty.

1961, Women's Strike for Peace.

1970, Women's Strike for Equality.

1978, Audre Lorde, the Mother of Black Feminism, refuses to wear a prosthesis after a mastectomy.

1982, Helene Aylon's Earth Ambulance carries injured earth to the United Nations.

1987, Clergy and Laity Concerned calls for Mother's Day protest of U.S. aggression against Nicaragua.

SOUTH PACIFIC:

Australia

1974, Sydney: Feminists open "Elsie," a shelter for battered women.

WORLDWIDE:

1873, Women celebrate the first "Mother's Day" as the peace holiday proposed by Julia Ward Howe.

1911, Socialists and suffragists celebrate International Women's Day.

1921, Women attending the International Women's Secretariat of the Communist International vote to make March 8th the official date of International Women's Day.

INDEX